Unearthing the Unknown Whitehead

Contemporary Whitehead Studies

Edited by Roland Faber, Claremont School of Theology,
and Brian G. Henning, Gonzaga University

Contemporary Whitehead Studies, co-sponsored by the Whitehead Research Project, is an interdisciplinary book series that publishes manuscripts from scholars with contemporary and innovative approaches to Whitehead studies by giving special focus to projects that: explore the connections between Whitehead and contemporary Continental philosophy, especially sources like Heidegger, or contemporary streams like poststructuralism; reconnect Whitehead to pragmatism, analytical philosophy and philosophy of language; explore creative East/West dialogues facilitated by Whitehead's work; explore the interconnections of the mathematician with the philosopher and the contemporary importance of these parts of Whitehead's work for the dialogue between sciences and humanities; reconnect Whitehead to the wider field of philosophy, the humanities, the sciences and academic research with Whitehead's pluralistic impulses in the context of a pluralistic world; address Whitehead's philosophy in the midst of contemporary problems facing humanity, such as climate change, war and peace, race, and the future development of civilization.

Recent Titles in this Series
Unearthing the Unknown Whitehead, by Joseph Petek
Whitehead and the Pittsburgh School: Preempting the Problem of Intentionality, by Lisa Landoe Hedrick
On Philosophy, Intelligibility, and the Ordinary: Going the Bloody Hard Way, by Randy Ramal
Untying the Gordian Knot: Process, Reality and Context, by Timothy E. Eastman
Mind, Value, and the Cosmos: On the Relational Nature of Ultimacy, by Andrew M. Davis
Whitehead's Radically Temporalist Metaphysics: Recovering the Seriousness of Time, by George Allan
Propositions in the Making: Experiments in a Whiteheadian Laboratory, edited by Roland Faber, Michael Halewood, and Andrew M. Davis
Whitehead and Continental Philosophy in the Twenty-First Century: Dislocations, edited by Jeremy D. Fackenthal
Beyond Whitehead: Recent Advances in Process Thought, edited by Jakub Dziadkowiec and Lukasz Lamza
Tragic Beauty in Whitehead and Japanese Aesthetics, by Steve Odin

Unearthing the Unknown Whitehead

Joseph Petek

LEXINGTON BOOKS
Lanham • Boulder • New York • London

Published by Lexington Books
An imprint of The Rowman & Littlefield Publishing Group, Inc.
4501 Forbes Boulevard, Suite 200, Lanham, Maryland 20706
www.rowman.com

86-90 Paul Street, London EC2A 4NE

Copyright © 2022 by The Rowman & Littlefield Publishing Group, Inc.

All rights reserved. No part of this book may be reproduced in any form or by any electronic or mechanical means, including information storage and retrieval systems, without written permission from the publisher, except by a reviewer who may quote passages in a review.

British Library Cataloguing in Publication Information Available

Library of Congress Cataloging-in-Publication Data on File

ISBN 978-1-66692-011-6 (cloth)
ISBN 978-1-66692-013-0 (pbk.)
ISBN 978-1-66692-012-3 (electronic)

Contents

Acknowledgments		vii
Abbreviations		ix
Introduction		1
1	The Gospels according to Whitehead's Students	5
2	Whitehead's Lectures as Book Drafts	27
3	Muddle-Headedness versus Simple-Mindedness, Round 2	43
4	Conciliating Privacy and Socialism	67
5	Religion and Hatred	83
6	Redefining Wit and Humour	101
7	Whitehead's Other Dialogues	115
8	Conclusion: Footnotes to Whitehead	131
References		155
Index		163
About the Author		169

Acknowledgments

Chapter 5 of this book was originally published in *Process Studies* 51.1 as "Religion and Hatred: Examining an Unpublished Whitehead Essay." My thanks to the University of Illinois Press for allowing its republication.

I am grateful to Edinburgh University Press for allowing me to quote extensively from the first two volumes of the Edinburgh Critical Edition of the Complete Works of Alfred North Whitehead:

HL1—Bogaard, Paul A., and Jason Bell (eds), *The Harvard Lectures of Alfred North Whitehead, 1924-1925: Philosophical Presuppositions of Science* (Edinburgh University Press, 2017).

HL2—Henning, Brian G., Joseph Petek, and George Lucas (eds), *The Harvard Lectures of Alfred North Whitehead, 1925-1927: General Metaphysical Problems of Science* (Edinburgh University Press, 2021).

I am pleased that Sherborne School in Dorset has allowed me to use their scan of an old Whitehead photo for the cover. It shows a sixteen-year-old Whitehead with his sixth form class on Christmas 1877, nearly a century and a half ago.

Finally, I would like to thank Brian G. Henning for reading a draft of the book and making many helpful suggestions for its improvement.

Abbreviations

This book uses the following well-established abbreviations to refer to Whitehead's books.

AE	*The Aims of Education and Other Essays* (1929)
AI	*Adventures of Ideas* (1933)
CN	*The Concept of Nature* (1920)
FR	*The Function of Reason* (1929)
HL1	*The Harvard Lectures of Alfred North Whitehead, 1924–1925*, ed. Paul A. Bogaard and Jason Bell (2017)
HL2	*The Harvard Lectures of Alfred North Whitehead, 1925–1927*, ed. Brian G. Henning, Joseph Petek, and George Lucas (2021)
MT	*Modes of Thought* (1938)
OT	*The Organisation of Thought, Educational and Scientific* (1917)
PNK	*An Enquiry Concerning the Principles of Natural Knowledge* (1919)
PR	*Process and Reality: An Essay in Cosmology* (1929)
R	*The Principle of Relativity: With Applications to Physical Science* (1922)
RM	*Religion in the Making* (1926)
S	*Symbolism* (1927)
SMW	*Science and the Modern World* (1925)

The following abbreviations are used for newly discovered Whitehead essays.

FO	"Freedom and Order"
RPWP	"Religious Psychology of the Western Peoples"

Introduction

Since the Critical Edition of Whitehead Project began in 2005, it has collected thousands of pages of archival Whitehead material, including much that is either little studied, nearly forgotten, or that has never been seen by any Whitehead scholar at all. The collection process began with Whitehead's known bibliography and the materials gathered by Whitehead's biographer, Victor Lowe—which now reside at the Johns Hopkins University archives—and expanded into other university archives and personal collections across the United Kingdom, United States, and Canada. In early 2019, it even came to include a cache of more than six hundred items donated by Whitehead's grandson and heir that were falsely believed to have been destroyed upon Whitehead's death.

This latter material was made available online in April 2020, following the publication in 2017 of the first volume of student lecture notes (*HL1*) covering Whitehead's first year (1924–1925) at Harvard. The second volume of student notes (*HL2*) covering Whitehead's second and third year of Harvard lectures was published in January 2021. So far, these new materials have excited little scholarly comment and attention, with the most major piece of scholarship done on the first volume of lectures being published by edition staff themselves based on papers delivered at a 2017 Whitehead Research Project (WRP) conference. While some of the materials are admittedly of little philosophical use—the project holds hundreds of letters of birthday best wishes from Whitehead's various acquaintances, for instance—other materials, such as the student lecture notes and a number of never-before-seen Whitehead essays, reveal a previously unknown Whitehead, and it is high time for someone to expound on their significance.

As it happens, I find myself in a uniquely advantageous position to do just that. Hired as an editorial assistant for the Whitehead Research Project and

Critical Edition of Whitehead in February 2013, my responsibilities have since expanded into being WRP's chief archivist and the associate editor of the Critical Edition. In those roles, I have personally cataloged most of the thousands of items that the Critical Edition of Whitehead has collected and had a major hand in transcribing and editing the student notes that make up the first two volumes of the edition. This being the case, there is literally no one in the world who is more intimately familiar with these materials than I am.

My goal in this book is to show why the new material being published as part of the Critical Edition of Whitehead is important and why scholars should engage with it. In other words, I am aiming to stir up interest. It is in service to this goal of arousing interest that I have chosen the specific materials that I have. I did not focus on the first volume of Harvard lectures alone, or the second volume alone, or both together, or only on the papers donated by Whitehead's grandson in 2019. Instead, I have written on a mix of all of them. Some might say that this means the book lacks focus or lacks thematic consistency. In one sense, they would not be entirely wrong. But to this I would only say that if the goal is to arouse scholarly interest and engagement, then one should in fact try to highlight the most *interesting* pieces. Thematic consistency is a wonderful attribute, but it is not always the point.

Thus, the book examines materials that range almost thirty years, from 1911 letters to Whitehead's colleague Bertrand Russell on the one hand, to a 1939 address to a religious society on the other. They each meet the criteria of being individually fascinating and individually important, but Whitehead's interests and expertise were quite broad, and so it would be somewhat astonishing if there was an obvious, non-contrived way to tie them all together thematically in a neat little bow. That bow, that unifying factor, such as it is, can only be that we are seeing these materials for the first time, and seeing a previously unknown Whitehead as a result. When Whitehead left no *Nachlass* for scholars to pick over upon his death in 1947, he effectively erased his tracks for decades. We are only now, in the past five years, beginning to pick up the trail on the way to a new understanding of him.

Chapter 1 begins by investigating the foundational question of the accuracy of the notes taken by Whitehead's students and colleagues in his classroom. If these accounts which make up the text of *HL1* and *HL2* cannot be trusted, then the whole project of publishing them is of dubious value. The chapter argues that there are methods for testing accuracy which make *HL1* and *HL2* largely trustworthy and reliable sources (with a few exceptions, such as the notes of Paul Weiss).

Chapter 2 is an analysis of the extent to which Whitehead's Harvard lectures can be viewed as drafts of his published books. Though in some cases Whitehead did present such draft material to his students—as was the case with *Process and Reality*—the chapter concludes that this idea is mostly a misnomer. While the Harvard lectures undoubtedly contain many of the ideas (and specific terms) that would later appear in Whitehead's books, he did not simply revise his Harvard lectures for publication even in a loose sense. The relationship between Harvard lectures and books is more complex than this and is explored further in the concluding chapter.

Chapter 3 takes up the topic of the mutual influence of Whitehead and C. D. Broad. Broad is only mentioned once in Whitehead's books—in a footnote. Yet Whitehead assigned Broad's books to his students for at least the first half of his Harvard tenure. The chapter thus examines their early interactions at Trinity College and the Aristotelian Society and then looks for influence in later publications. It is argued that Whitehead took one-half of Broad's "critical" vs. "speculative" philosophy distinction as a jumping-off point for writing *Process and Reality*.

Chapter 4 examines Whitehead's presentation in Richard Clarke Cabot's Social Ethics seminar of October 1926, in which he was asked to outline what he believed were the "fundamentals of the social sciences," including social ethics. It argues that the presentation is an important document for understanding Whitehead's ethics (a topic which he seldom addressed), as it gives ethics an explicitly metaphysical basis.

Chapter 5 investigates an unpublished Whitehead essay entitled "Religious Psychology of the Western Peoples," arguing that it is the most sustained criticism of religion that he would ever make. The essay is put in conversation with Whitehead's "An Appeal to Sanity"—a contemporaneous article that appeared in *The Atlantic* exploring the international situation of the late 1930s—which provides necessary context for Whitehead's feelings toward religious extremism, anti-Semitism, and hypernationalism.

Chapter 6 explores another unpublished Whitehead essay entitled "Freedom and Order." This essay is not dated, but the chapter argues that it is likely a transitional piece in Whitehead's philosophy embodying a failed terminological experiment: the dyad of "freedom" and "order" put in conversation with the dyad of "wit" and "humour." Though these are not terms that Whitehead would continue to use in later writings, they show signs of being embryonic forms of "permanence" and "flux."

Chapter 7 returns to Whitehead's early life, education, and correspondence in order to try to determine his earliest philosophical influences and development, and to try to identify the point at which he transitioned from mathematics to philosophy. The most key source here is a long letter to Bertrand Russell written in 1911 in which Whitehead levels some criticisms at Russell's manuscript for *The Problems of Philosophy*. It also examines some of Whitehead's earliest papers delivered to the Aristotelian Society in the mid-1910s.

Chapter 8 turns to the question of how best to characterize the Harvard lectures in relation to Whitehead's books. It argues that the Harvard lectures actually contain the truest record of the development of his philosophy—including the false starts and dead ends that the published works obscure—a development which previously could only be inferred as taking place in the gaps between his books. It then calls for a complete reconsideration of Whitehead's philosophical corpus, with his published works put in a new perspective as marker buoys in the wider philosophical ocean of his Harvard classroom.

My hope is that readers will be left with a better sense of exactly why these new materials are so important to the future of Whitehead scholarship and stand to turn some of what we think we know of him on its head. It is an exciting time to be studying Whitehead; the Critical Edition project has in one sense only barely begun, having produced two volumes of previously unpublished materials with at least another eight to go. Who knows what we might discover in the years to come?

Chapter 1

The Gospels according to Whitehead's Students

No professional biographer in his right mind would touch him.

—Whitehead's biographer[1]

The basic question that this book seeks to answer might be summed up as, "What do the archival materials collected by the Critical Edition of Whitehead (CEW) reveal about Whitehead and his philosophy that we did not already know? How does the new material change how Whitehead and his philosophy are interpreted?" In the case of the newly discovered original Whitehead essays discussed in chapters 5 and 6, we can jump more or less directly to this question of their significance within Whitehead's corpus.

But the material discussed in the first four chapters is of a different sort: it is not written by Whitehead per se. Instead, it is Whitehead's Harvard lectures as recorded by his students and colleagues. George R. Lucas Jr. was the first person in my hearing to compare the various sets of student notes to the gospel accounts of the Christian Bible. And while these student notes certainly do not have quite the same difficulties as the accounts of Matthew, Mark, Luke, and John that were written some thirty to eighty years after Jesus of Nazareth had already died, they *do* have their own problems.

In all but one case, none of the note-takers were endeavoring to record Whitehead's every word, and most were not taking notes for anyone but themselves. They were interested in passing their exams, not serving as research assistants for future scholars. As such, most often they summarized or paraphrased Whitehead's words, only occasionally giving us what seem to be exact quotations. Most students did not record all of Whitehead's points even in a summarized form, either because they found these points uninteresting or unimportant, or because they missed hearing them or did not understand them. Some students made changes, comments, or references in their notes that we know were not Whitehead's, and not all of them were diligent about distinguishing their own thoughts from Whitehead's words. And in a few cases, the notes are hopelessly misleading such that they are almost literally worse than useless, serving only to confuse rather than enlighten.[2]

For these reasons, the value of these student notes has been called into question. In evaluating the CEW's 2019 application for a National Endowment for the Humanities (NEH) grant, one panelist wrote:

> How reliable are the notes of his students? . . . How helpful will they really be? Even Lowe's notes, which require extensive expansion to be comprehensible, are of questionable value (at least to me) . . . I'm still not sure how useful the final product will be. How exactly will scholars make use of student notes?[3]

Nor do such doubts come only from a first-blush reaction to the idea of relying on student notes—with all their attendant problems—to illuminate the development of Whitehead's philosophy. Adam Scarfe expresses similar sentiments in his review of the first volume of Whitehead's Harvard lectures (*HL1*) in *Process Studies* 48.1, saying that

> the book cannot be said to be completely successful in providing an unobstructed view of Whitehead's thinking . . . [the notes] are often very sketchy, at times incoherent, and on occasion render unclear the complex ideas that Whitehead attempted to convey . . . Whitehead scholars employing the volume in their work must be careful to remember that the status of the notes is that of an indirect representation of the proceedings—namely, what Whitehead *appears* to have said or discussed.[4]

These sorts of doubts and criticisms of the value and usefulness of the material that makes up the two edited volumes of Whitehead's Harvard lectures (*HL1* and *HL2*)—and the four additional volumes that are planned—must be taken very seriously. Thus the question of how the student notes that make up these volumes changes our understanding of Whitehead cannot be undertaken until their reliability and trustworthiness are scrutinized. At least three questions must be answered:

(1) How *accurate* are the notes? Do the note-takers often make mistakes? To what extent do they paraphrase? To what extent do they understand what they are recording?
(2) How *complete* are the notes? Beyond paraphrasing, do they omit portions of Whitehead's lectures? If so, to what extent does this hurt their intelligibility and usefulness?

(3) How *unique* are the notes? Did Whitehead simply read portions of his published works aloud to his classes? Did he repeat the same material from one year to the next? In short, do Whitehead's classroom lectures contain original material, or just a recapitulation of things that can be seen in a more polished form in his published monographs?

The first two are the most key questions for this chapter, not only because a lack of accuracy and completeness would seem to render the question of uniqueness irrelevant, but because it is the job of chapters 2, 3, 4, and 8 to address the question of uniqueness in more detail. I will only gesture at it here.

One obvious fact must be acknowledged at the outset: the answers to these questions will necessarily be different for each individual note-taker. Some will prove to have a high degree of accuracy and completeness, and others considerably less so. But this is not the place to evaluate *every* set of notes individually; fourteen different people recorded notes for *HL2* alone. The goal here is to examine some key examples in order to come to some general conclusions about the trustworthiness and usefulness of the two edited volumes of Harvard lectures.

The stakes here are high for the Critical Edition project in particular and Whitehead scholarship generally. If we conclude that the notes are not generally accurate, complete, or unique, then, as Scarfe puts it,

> researchers and scholars who may choose to employ the notes that are contained in th[ese] volume[s] as support for their claims will still have to corroborate almost any assertion Whitehead seems to have made therein with more direct statements contained in his more polished, formally published works.[5]

In short, if the notes in these volumes are not trustworthy, then we must be suspicious of any novel elements that appear in them which are not corroborated by Whitehead's published work. This would in turn make it much more difficult to argue for their utility and importance in Whitehead scholarship moving forward, limited as we would be to identifying a timeline of pre-existing ideas in Whitehead's philosophy, as opposed to wholly original elements.

WHY USE LECTURE NOTES AT ALL?

A first rebuttal to criticisms that student[6] notes are an unreliable and untrustworthy source of additional insight into Whitehead's thought—that is, beyond what can be found in his published books and articles—is that

Whitehead scholars really have little choice in the matter. Whitehead's biographer, Victor Lowe, starts his biography by stating that "no professional biographer in his right mind would touch him."[7] The reason for this is a lack of extant materials, a problem that creates equal difficulties for scholars interested in Whitehead's philosophical development.

The first volume of Lowe's biography, published in 1985, explicitly claims that Whitehead asked for his papers to be destroyed upon his death.

> In his will Whitehead directed that his letters to his wife be destroyed . . . [and] as he requested, his widow destroyed (along with the letters he had received) his unpublished papers and drafts of books, and the manuscripts of the published writings.[8]

Lowe also gave a few explanations for why he thought this was done:

> [Whitehead] held an almost fanatical belief in the right to privacy, and thought that the only subject of rightful public interest in him was the work that he had published . . . He idealized youth and wanted young thinkers to develop their own ideas, not spend their best years on a *Nachlass*.[9]

For more than thirty years, there was no real reason to doubt this narrative. After all, Lowe was a diligent researcher who spent more than twenty years of his life interviewing family and friends about Whitehead, and searching for whatever extant materials he could find, including student notes. It was even T. North Whitehead himself (Whitehead's son) who first suggested the biography project to Lowe in 1965, providing as much help to Lowe as he could in the project.[10]

Things were turned somewhat upside-down in 2019, when George Whitehead—T. North Whitehead's son—donated boxes containing more than six hundred items to the Whitehead Research Project (WRP). In handing over the papers to George R. Lucas Jr., George Whitehead told a somewhat different story than the one Lowe had given us. He recalled times when Lowe would call the house, which "caused my father's face to fall." The overall impression he conveyed was that, while T. North may well have encouraged Lowe to write Whitehead's biography, toward the end of his life he and the rest of the Whitehead family considered Lowe something of a pest, and deliberately withheld materials that they knew Lowe would have wanted for his project. We have found no documentary evidence that either supports or denies this attitude of Whitehead's family toward Lowe, though a snippy letter to Lowe from Whitehead himself in 1942 said that "You must not take my random statements as evidence of my original meaning at the time of writing. And I am not prepared to sit down and comment on my past work.

The Gospels according to Whitehead's Students   9

Please do <u>not</u> quote my letters."[11] It seems that Whitehead did indeed value his privacy.

But given the newfound cache of materials, we began to wonder if the story of Whitehead's papers being destroyed was entirely a fabrication for Lowe's benefit. This thought was strengthened by the presence in his papers of Whitehead's will, dated March 27, 1891—shortly after his marriage to Evelyn—which left everything to his wife, while making no reference to the destruction of any documents.[12]

However, Lowe was apparently not the only person who was told this story, nor even the first one. Kenneth Blackwell, who works with the Bertrand Russell Papers at McMaster University, told me in an email conversation that Dr. Andrew D. Osborn was the assistant chief librarian of Harvard's Widener Library from 1938 to 1958, where Whitehead's daughter, Jessie, also worked, and that one day Jessie told him, apparently unprompted, that "My mother and I have just been destroying my father's papers."[13] Jessie was known for stretching the truth at times,[14] but unprompted lies in this case seem unlikely.

I believe that the truth here, as is so often the case, is somewhere in the middle. Much of Whitehead's papers probably *were* destroyed, including all of the manuscripts for his books, as none of these has ever been found. It is likely to remain forever unclear why some items were preserved and others destroyed. But the Whitehead family also clearly did withhold items from Lowe that would have helped him in his project, including, for example, the original letter from Mark Barr informing Whitehead of a possible position at Harvard, which Lowe alludes to, but never actually saw, not to mention public lectures that were never published, the manuscript for Whitehead's first Harvard lecture, essays being emended for publication in anthologies, and other documents that would have had significant bearing on Lowe's work.[15]

Of course, none of this really answers any of our urgent questions about the accuracy, completeness, and uniqueness of the lecture notes taken by Whitehead's students. Just because they are some of the only material that might provide us additional insight into Whitehead's philosophy, it does not actually *make* them a good option for such research (it does, however, aside from the two essays discussed in chapters 5 and 6 and a few philosophical letters, make them our *only* option). Hence, we must leave this consideration aside and move forward with an analysis of the notes themselves.

THE CRUCIAL IMPORTANCE OF MULTIPLE ACCOUNTS

It is all well and good to talk about evaluating the accuracy and completeness of these student notes, but how does one actually go about it? After all, there are no known voice recordings of Whitehead's lectures, nor do we often possess Whitehead's own manuscripts as points of comparison.[16] How does one evaluate the success of note-takers in capturing Whitehead's words when there is no "control" against which to measure them?

The truth is that in cases in which we can find only a single account of Whitehead's lecture, there is often very little that can be done to assess it. One tool that can still be employed is to look at the raw word count. We know that Whitehead's Philosophy 3b lectures were slated for an hour,[17] and this gives a general sense of the sort of length to look for in a thorough account of a lecture. A basic knowledge of Whitehead's philosophy and common sense can also help to correct some of the grossest errors that may pop up; we can be fairly certain, for instance, that Whitehead probably did not say "idiocentric," but more likely "heliocentric" in his discussion of Galileo and the Copernican hypothesis.[18] One can also compare the material with Whitehead's published work in order to assess how closely it mirrors his existing philosophy, though this sort of evaluation carries the danger of predisposing us to throw the baby out with the bathwater in dismissing novel material as inherently more suspicious, when novel material is just what scholars most hope to find. But in the end, absent any other ways of robustly assessing the trustworthiness of the material, it is right and proper to be somewhat suspicious of solitary accounts in the way that Scarfe argues we must be for *all* material found in *HL1*.

However, happily, in the case of both *HL1* and *HL2*, this is not usually the situation in which we find ourselves. For most of Whitehead's lectures in his first three years, we were able to locate at least two accounts, and sometimes as many as five. By comparing the various accounts to each other, we can come to much clearer conclusions about their relative accuracy and completeness, as well as avoid many pitfalls in which we might otherwise find ourselves mired, and thus approach Whitehead's true words asymptotically. The importance of careful comparison of these "redundant" accounts of lectures, and the extent to which such comparisons can aid us in assessing their worth, cannot be overstated.

I have already discussed one extended example of just how much multiple sets of notes can help us in this task in my introductory chapter to *Whitehead at Harvard, 1924–1925*, complete with illustrations of the original manuscripts; the material discussed is slated for *HL3*.[19] Certain elements of this example are worth recapitulating here as an introduction to just how much such careful comparison can really tell us.

The lecture in question took place on October 21, 1930, about three weeks into the fall term. The class was "Philosophy 3b: Cosmologies Ancient and Modern," a phrase that would later appear in Whitehead's *Adventures of Ideas* (1933). In this lecture, Whitehead was discussing "transitions in philosophy" from one era to the next and gave students a chronology of key philosophical figures in a roughly thousand-year period from Democritus to Augustine.

There is an interesting divergence in one detail that Whitehead provided about Augustine: the city in which he died. Charles Dewey Tenney did not list any specific city; Furman G. McLarty wrote "Nollo" (a misspelling of "Nola"), but he struck this out and wrote "Hippo"; W. V. O. Quine wrote "Nola" but struck this out and wrote "Thagaste."[20] That one of the three note-takers did not bother to record this rather minor detail is not surprising, but that two students struck out the original and made *different* corrections is curious.

McLarty's notes from October 28, a week later, help to clear up some of the confusion. At the top of his notes for this day, McLarty records Whitehead as saying that he made a mistake the week prior when he said that Augustine died in Nola; in fact, it was Augustus Caesar who died in Nola, in southern Italy, while Augustine died in Hippo, in the northern part of Africa. This being the case, McLarty dutifully went back to his notes for October 21 and made the correction. But why, then, does Quine have "Thagaste" instead? It seems like a somewhat bizarre and inexplicable thing until one looks even more carefully at other portions of the notes in order to assess the character and habits of the note-takers themselves; by carefully observing the differences and inconsistencies over the whole of different sets of notes, we can make more accurate judgments about the many specific dilemmas within them.

So, observe now the different dates that these three note-takers have for Philo's birth. Quine has "26 B.C." McLarty has "20 B.C.?" Note the question mark. Based on these two sets of notes alone, the most reasonable explanation would appear to be that Quine was sure of his date, while McLarty was not; perhaps McLarty did not hear Whitehead clearly. We would then tend to think that Quine's account was more likely to be what Whitehead actually said. However, Tenney *also* has "20 B.C.?" with a question mark. And suddenly the best explanation of the divergence is very different. That two of three note-takers have a question mark here would seem to indicate *Whitehead's* uncertainty, not McLarty's or Tenney's.[21]

The two examples together tell us something important about Quine and his note-taking habits. While McLarty and Tenney seemed to be intent only on recording what Whitehead said, Quine apparently felt little compunction about "correcting" Whitehead in his own notes when he thought it merited. Hence, when Whitehead expressed uncertainty about the date of Philo's birth, Quine filled in his own—26 B.C. is, in fact, an estimate for Philo's date of birth advanced by some historical scholars—and did likewise when he realized Whitehead had erred in saying that Augustine had died in Nola. This is most likely where Quine's "Thagaste" came from—which is in fact the place of Augustine's *birth*, but not his death.

We can make a few general observations from these examples. First, besides the obvious fact that having more accounts is always better, because it allows for more cross-checking and hence more accuracy, sometimes even two accounts are not enough to untangle thorny issues of interpretation. In the case of McLarty's and Tenney's question marks, it is not just *helpful* that a two-versus-one situation has been created (i.e., McLarty and Tenney versus Quine) in which we can conservatively side with the two, it turns out that in this case it *changes our interpretation of what McLarty and Tenney wrote*. It is a prime example of both the dangers inherent in trying to parse notes of this kind and of the great power of this kind of comparison to verify exactly what was going on in Whitehead's classroom.

Second, beyond untangling specific problems of interpretation, undertaking such comparisons can lead us back to more general conclusions about a note-taker's character and habits and, by extension, lead us to conclusions about the reliability of their notes. The irony in this case is that Quine—who assuredly became the most famous and successful of the three men—was possessed of an intellectual confidence (or perhaps, less flatteringly, an intellectual arrogance) which led him to edit Whitehead's words. While McLarty and Tenney were simply trying to record what Whitehead said, Quine was evaluating it on the fly and making what he believed to be corrections. That he was able to do this may well indicate that Quine had an easier time understanding Whitehead's lectures than the other two, but his habit of making such corrections makes his notes inherently less reliable. This sort of insight is especially helpful in scenarios where multiple accounts of a lecture suddenly shrink to a single account—for example, two of three note-takers suddenly stop taking notes after a specific date in the term (a thing which happens a number of times in *HL2*). In these cases, though we may no longer have other lecture notes with which to make direct comparisons for a given date, we have a better sense of each person's trustworthiness as a whole.

Rarely are such comparisons simple or easy. In this case, for instance, Quine's account cannot simply be dismissed, for there are times when he caught detail that the other two did not.[22] All accounts should be carefully examined in order to extract whatever value might be in them, even if it is only to verify the correctness of other accounts. Successfully "combining" them in order to come up with the most thorough and accurate composite account of Whitehead's words as possible is slow and painstaking work. But it *can* be done, and the more accounts that are available, the more we can justify confidence in their accuracy.

MISUNDERSTANDINGS, MISHEARINGS, ABBREVIATIONS, AND CONFUSIONS

Now, after looking at this example from material slated to appear in *HL3*, it is time to look more closely at the already-published volumes, *HL1* and *HL2*. The best place to start may be to look at the most suspect material first.

There is no denying that at times Whitehead's students experienced great difficulty in understanding him. Stories of confusion abound. Upon being assigned as his first assistant, Whitehead spent an hour walking with Raphael Demos around Emerson Hall explaining his philosophy; Demos did not tell him that he did not understand it at all.[23] Lester King, one of our student note-takers, wrote in a letter to Lewis Ford that "[Whitehead] was up from time to time with a cherubic smile, as if to ask whether everything was clear (which it wasn't) ... I certainly had only the most confused notions of what Whitehead was trying to say."[24] And as for Paul Weiss, he often could not even understand what words Whitehead was uttering, let alone begin to parse their meaning; the difference in accents between a native Brooklyn New Yorker who had just arrived at Harvard in February 1927 and a recently emigrated Englishman was apparently too great.

> I sat right in the front row and couldn't understand a single word. Years later I spoke to Whitehead and told him this. He laughed and said, "I couldn't understand a single word you said when you spoke." Our syllabifications or emphases were so radically distinct that we couldn't understand one another.[25]

Weiss's notes, upon which we were forced to rely for portions of the spring 1927 term, may in fact be the best example of notes that are pretty thoroughly inadequate, especially when it comes to completeness. The introduction to *The Harvard Lectures of Alfred North Whitehead, 1925–1927: General Metaphysical Problems of Science* (*HL2*), which I co-authored, provides a grim assessment:

> Weiss was our only option after 19 March, and so we use his account as primary for 13 lectures only because we had no other choice. Frankly, if the rest of the notes in this volume were of a similar quality to these notes of Weiss, then the volume itself would not have been worth publishing, but we present them here in the interest of giving as complete an account of Whitehead's lectures for 1925–6 and 1926–7 as we possibly can.[26]

In at least one case, Weiss's notes were not just woefully incomplete but dangerously misleading. On the fifth page of Weiss's notes for the spring 1927 term (page 54),[27] he had written nineteen equations/expressions of symbolic logic and numbered them consecutively from 1.0 to 1.18. As Brian Henning and I were largely untrained and unfamiliar with this kind of material, we consulted with three others who had advanced training in mathematics and logic, and a familiarity with Whitehead and his notation in the *Principia*. None of them could make any sense of it. We had thought only to check for errors in the symbolism itself, but we were told that the whole thing did not actually make any sense at all and that Weiss himself must have been hopelessly confused.

As it turned out, Weiss certainly was confused, but not quite in the way our math and logic experts thought. By comparing Weiss's notes with the notes of George Conger and others, we discovered that the nineteen expressions were actually from three entirely separate lectures. The first four (1.0–1.3) were from March 3, the next seven (1.4–1.10) were from March 5, and the last 8 (1.11–1.18) were from March 8. Further, many of the expressions were never intended to have anything to do with one another, as Weiss's numbering strongly implies. Weiss had copied down the expressions absent any of the context which would have rendered them intelligible, the context which we found in the notes of Conger.

Why exactly did Weiss do this? A likely explanation is that Whitehead did occasionally write figures and formulas on the blackboard, and Weiss—who we have established often did not understand what Whitehead was saying—dutifully copied down the only thing he knew was correct, namely the stuff that Whitehead had written on the board for all to see. No trouble with accents there! His numbering, which was certainly not Whitehead's, may have simply been intended to make extra-clear to himself the order in which the expressions were written, or he may have been so befuddled as to their meaning that he believed they actually *were* all related when they clearly were not. In any case, Weiss's shortcomings here created a situation in which we were looking for a unity in these nineteen expressions that simply did not exist, and was never intended to.

Thankfully, as the references to Conger's notes imply, for some portions of the spring 1927 term, we had other options and did not need to rely on Weiss's notes. That changed following Whitehead's lecture of March 19, after which Conger left Whitehead's class and returned to the University of Minnesota. For thirteen lectures in the second half of this term, Weiss's account was all we had. Beyond their suspect accuracy, their sheer brevity renders them nearly useless; Weiss's notes most often consisted of one long paragraph or a few short ones. For the lecture of May 10, he records only sixteen words. Beyond a very general summary of some of the topics discussed, it is hard to see where they could be of much use. They are enough, for instance, for us to know that immediately after his return from delivering the Barbour-Page lectures at the University of Virginia over Harvard's spring break, Whitehead repeated those lectures over a period of about two weeks.[28] But they are not enough to provide us with the kind of spontaneous critiques which Whitehead had made of his own work in other class sessions[29] that would have made such an exercise worthwhile.

Weiss's notes are not the only set that might be described as grossly inadequate and unreliable—the notes of George Burch also come to mind in this regard[30]—but they are, importantly, the only such set of notes across *HL1* or *HL2* which we have been forced to present for lack of any better alternatives, though this does not make them either good or trustworthy. I am not a blanket apologist for the notes that appear in these volumes, nor should anyone be, and here I think I can say that Scarfe's reticence is well and truly justified and that scholars would do well not to trust them beyond what can be verified in Whitehead's published works, or in more trustworthy sets of Harvard lectures notes. But thankfully, Weiss's notes are not at all representative of the whole.

HL1 AND THE SPECIAL CASE OF WHITEHEAD'S FIRST LECTURE

The discovery of a manuscript for Whitehead's first Harvard lecture[31] in the papers donated by George Whitehead presents a unique opportunity for assessing the accuracy of the notes published in *HL1*. It is not the only time that this sort of opportunity presents itself—as we will see with Whitehead's "Time" paper and his quoting of C. D. Broad in *HL2*—but it is probably the most exciting one. Discovered too late to include in *HL1* itself, Paul Bogaard has already undertaken a comparative analysis of the texts.[32] I want to expand a little here on what Bogaard has already done.

One thing not mentioned in Bogaard's article is that the manuscript itself has been marked in such a way that suggests Whitehead was editing it for inclusion in a monograph.[33] This is supported by the facts that it was found together with several other Whitehead essays that had also been edited for inclusion in a book—in some cases with new titles added at the top and roman numeral chapter numbers—and that the one paragraph marked off makes reference to what Whitehead planned to discuss in a second lecture. Such a paragraph does not make sense to include in a book when said second lecture was not going to be included. That it remains in the document argues for it being the original, unedited manuscript, even if it may have been re-typed.

How close do the student notes—particularly Winthrop Bell's—match up with this manuscript? The first few pages are an interesting study in themselves. Lowe had noted in his biography that James Woods introduced him and that Whitehead started by saying "what an honor it was to be at Harvard—the university of William James. He probably mentioned other famous names."[34] This recollection of James Wilkinson Miller seems entirely accurate, for the manuscript does in fact mention James, Hugo Munsterberg, and Josiah Royce.[35] But neither Bell nor Heath records anything like this. This certainly confirms that neither student was taking down every word that Whitehead said. On the other hand, that this material is missing from the student accounts should not surprise us, for as students looking to pass

16   Chapter 1

exams and write essays based on what Whitehead presented, the fact that he felt honored and dropped a few famous names was not really a thing worth recording. It is another reminder that these students were not thinking of posterity as they recorded their notes.

Bell begins taking notes toward the end of the second page of the manuscript, while Heath actually begins somewhat sooner, near the beginning of the second page. One thing that is immediately apparent is that Bell was often endeavoring to record Whitehead's exact phrasing, even though he did not nearly record everything. Compare, for instance, Whitehead's manuscript with the first lines of Bell's notes:

> *Whitehead's manuscript:* Now every philosophy is dominated by some type of difficulty which is in the mind of those who put forward the system. A philosophy is a solution of some ultimate problem which is crying aloud for explanation. There is some wonder, some puzzle which disturbs the rationality of thought and demands the evolution of a point of view capable of reintroducing harmony. It is useless to expound philosophy to |3| those who have never wondered, or to those who are exclusively occupied with other aspects of the great mystery of things. Conversely, from the point of view of those who enter upon an examination of a system of philosophy, the first question to ask is, what are the peculiar difficulties of everyday thought which this philosophy is designed to resolve?[36]
>
> *Bell's notes:* Every Philosophy dominated by some type of difficulty. – Some problem of fundamental kind lying at root of it. What are peculiar difficulties of daily life which "this" Philosophy is calculated to solve? is the question.[37]

Two lines from the manuscript correspond almost exactly to Bell's notes (the first and last bits). There are minor differences here: a missing "is" from the first line and a rephrasing from "designed to solve" to "calculated to solve," both of which carry the same sense. Early signs are that accuracy is looking pretty good. How important is the material in the middle that Bell missed, assuming that Whitehead delivered it as written? Arguably little other than poetry, so to speak; mostly it concerns "wonder" and the idea that philosophers must have a sense of it. Meanwhile, Heath's notes are both shorter and less likely to capture Whitehead's phrasing, an unsurprising fact considering Bell recorded about 1,200 words while Heath only had 750.

But am I just cherry-picking a good bit from Bell? Let's look at one more example.

> *Whitehead's manuscript:* There are degrees of reality according to the completeness of realizations of togetherness. It is the connections which are realized. In a sense the idea of reality does not apply absolutely to the things thus connected, but only relatively. Thus, by reason of the realization of a type

of togetherness between A and B, A is real for B and B is real for A. But it is nonsense to speak of A as absolutely real in itself, or of B as absolutely real in itself. A and B are individual existents with a relative reality each for the other. This relative reality of B for A is the becoming of B for A: namely B becomes a reality for A: that is to say, |18| the individual quality of B—what B is in itself—becomes significant for A, and affects the character of A's experience.[38]

Bell's notes: Ideal of objective togetherness of things is becoming realized—in varying degrees—Thus there are varying degrees of reality. A may be real for B. B for A. But it's nonsense to say that either A or B is absolutely real. B's becoming real for A = B's inherent, individual qualitative character becoming significant for A.[39]

Heath's notes: Reality applies to connections and only relatively to the things connected. a is real for b & b is real for a but not absolutely real independent of each other.[40]

There is not much that might be considered "poetry" here. These are highly specific and technical points that Whitehead is making. To my eye, Bell again is not missing any crucial elements. Heath's summary is sparser; it captures the general idea but makes no mention of "degrees of reality," which is a key element of what Whitehead is driving at.

All of this is further complicated by the fact that the manuscript of Whitehead's lecture is almost certainly not fully reflective of the lecture that Whitehead actually delivered. There are quite a number of factors that support this idea. First, the manuscript is 6,600 words, which is a lot to deliver in an hour (actually, fifty minutes, from noon to 12:50 p.m.). Second, both Bell and Heath have material that is not present in the manuscript; for example, both mention Spinoza toward the end, which the manuscript never does.[41] Third, both note-takers are missing material of a kind that it seems they almost certainly would have recorded, at least in part, including two whole pages on the extended metaphor of a boy and his cricket ball; this example shows up weeks later in Whitehead's October lectures. It seems, in fact, that Whitehead probably did not deliver anything at all from roughly his last four pages of manuscript. But in comparing the student notes with the remainder of the manuscript (i.e., excepting the first two pages and the last four), it does not seem that Bell omitted any major idea completely, though as the examples have demonstrated, he did not record every word.

Where does this leave us on the questions of accuracy and completeness? Bell's notes appear impressive, especially considering that the 1,200 words he recorded for this lecture are less than the typical 1,500–1,900 per lecture that he recorded for the rest of the term.[42] He does not seem to miss any key points, nor could I find any instance where Whitehead's point seems to have become grossly distorted, confusing, or ambiguous. Further, Hocking's presence for all but the first month provides a corroborating account, though a considerably less detailed one.

Given the detailed and accurate nature of Bell's notes, which constitute the core of the volume, I am not sure that Scarfe's criticism of *HL1* as occasionally "sketchy" and "incoherent" is necessarily justified. He tries to justify the criticism by providing five quotations related to autopoiesis, then simply asserting that "the usefulness of these quotations is somewhat marred by the facts of their sketchiness and, at times, incoherence, as displayed above."[43] Now, to be fair, this is a review of the book, and not meant to be a detailed analysis. Still, he does not attempt to justify this assertion, apparently regarding it as self-evidently true. It is not self-evidently true to me. I see nothing incoherent in the provided quotations. The "sketchiness," of course, is harder to judge and quantify absent a text for comparison. But it does not help that the three longer quotations Scarfe cites are all from Heath and Hocking, rather than Bell, both of whose accounts were unquestionably more abbreviated. I very much allow that these two omitted more detail, and hence they are indeed "sketchier," but I do not see the incoherence, nor does the criticism really seem to touch Bell. I also think it is a little presumptuous to attribute the sketchiness and incoherence solely to the students, rather than Whitehead himself, for he himself admits that he was sometimes confused in his lectures and apt to change his mind. We will see examples of this in the final section of this chapter.

THE "COMPOSITE" APPROACH OF *HL2*

HL2 took a different approach than *HL1* partly due to necessity. As we were covering two academic years instead of one, and at times had as many as five different accounts of a single lecture, simply editing and presenting each separate account was not a realistic proposition for a print volume. Instead, we adopted the approach of choosing a single "primary" account for each lecture (based largely on comprehensiveness) and using the other accounts to corroborate and/or augment that primary account through footnotes when necessary—for instance, adding a footnote that provides some detail a second student caught that the primary account missed. The result is a volume that minimizes the impact of the non-primary accounts but surfaces salient differences in detail and interpretation to readers, which both creates a constant awareness of the status of the material as recorded notes, while doing much to reinforce its accuracy.

The volume can be split into two academic years, 1925–1926 and 1926–1927.[44] The inadequacy of Weiss's notes in the last few months of 1927 has already been assessed, so I will start first with the rest of the 1926–1927 year, which is rather easier to size up anyway. It is largely dominated by the notes of George Perrigo Conger, a visiting professor of philosophy from the University of Minnesota who was spending his sabbatical at Harvard and seemingly attending almost every one of Whitehead's class sessions that he possibly could. The raw word count of his notes is impressive, typically ranging from around 1,000 to 1,500 words, comparing favorably with Bell from *HL1*. We used his account as the primary one in almost every instance, and there were lectures for which nothing from the other note sets was used to supplement Conger at all.[45]

As we point out in the introduction to the volume, there were times when all note-takers had almost exactly the same material, such as this one:

> *Conger:* But process of knowing ought to be something general of which we are only particular modes.
> *Nelson:* The process of knowing has obviously got to be something general of which we are particular modes.
> *King:* The process of knowing is obviously something general of which we are only particular modes.
> *Jackson:* Process of knowing must be general of which you and I are particular molds.[46]

Jackson made an overt error in writing "molds" instead of "modes." Such mishearings were not unprecedented, but the availability of so many different accounts made it a lot less likely that such distortions made it into the final product uncorrected or unremarked. And even when Conger's account was the only one available, there are other reasons to have confidence in its accuracy.

While we have no manuscripts from Whitehead with which to compare Conger's notes, what we do have are a number of instances in which it is clear that Whitehead was reading aloud from a published book or article, providing an important opportunity to check the general fidelity of Conger's note-taking ability. For instance, Whitehead re-presented his "Time" paper on October 1 in his seminary, and again in an expanded form in Philosophy 3b over multiple lectures in early December 1926. He also at times read fairly extensively from his own *Principle of Relativity* and Broad's *Scientific Thought*. A direct comparison of them is instructive:

> *Broad's book*: These two branches of Philosophy—the analysis and definition of our fundamental concepts, and the clear statement and resolute criticism of our fundamental beliefs—I call *Critical Philosophy*. It is obviously a necessary and a possible task, and it is not performed by any other science. The other sciences *use* the concepts and *assume* the beliefs; Critical Philosophy tries to analyse the former and to criticise the latter.[47]

> *Conger's notes*: Critical Philosophy. Analysis and definition of fundamental concepts. A necessary and possible task. Other sciences use concepts and assume beliefs—Critical philosophy tries to analyze former and criticize the latter.[48]

Here again, much as with Bell, we have an instance of a note-taker recording almost the exact phrasing that was actually used. Like Bell, Conger omits some detail from the quotation, but not enough to short-change the meaning. This is not to say that he was perfect. At times other students caught details that he did not—just as when Bell started recording his notes for Whitehead's first lecture at a slightly later point than Heath did—but in these places we have supplied that content in the appropriate place. The overall picture is again of a very meticulous note-taker who had occasional lapses of either concentration or selective interest (as we all do). They are not Whitehead's exact words, and they are not without omissions. But they appear to be very close indeed.

Lastly, there are the notes for 1925–1926, which comprise the other half of *HL2*. This material falls somewhere in the middle ground between the highs of Bell and Conger and the low of Weiss. The notes of Fritz Roethlisberger, our most frequent primary account, typically consisted of about 400 words, a far cry from the 1,000+ from Bell and Conger. Edward S. Robinson did better at about 700 words per lecture, but we only had his account for eighteen lectures, and the original has been lost, leaving us with an unverified typescript done by the Yale Philosophy Club in the mid-1960s, which had their own difficulties.[49] And the notes of Charles Hartshorne, the most famous of the three in the process philosophy world, were an absolute mess, having been incorrectly reordered to an impressive degree that we were only able to clear up through comparison with Roethlisberger's notes.[50] Moreover, the number of differences between the Roethlisberger and Hartshorne accounts, and the amount of material we had to footnote into the one from the other, suggests a more selective attention for both men when compared to Bell and Conger. There are also no easy points of comparison to any external texts that would help us assess general accuracy.

My own sense of these materials, having spent years editing them, is that the comparison and compositing work we have done in *HL2* provides a reasonably accurate and complete account of Whitehead's lectures for 1925–1926. But I cannot pretend that my own private intuition here is conclusive. Lacking a more detailed account, we were forced to rely on sparser notes and try to combine them into a whole that is more revealing than the parts. There certainly can be no doubt that together they are both more complete and more accurate than any one account would have been alone. But "better" does not necessarily mean "good."

CONCLUSIONS ON THE ACCURACY, COMPLETENESS, AND UNIQUENESS OF *HL1* AND *HL2*

I stated the self-evident point at the beginning of this chapter that an assessment of the trustworthiness and value of student notes is necessarily an assessment of each individual account, both against one another and against a control (where available). And so, in an analysis of the most important constituent parts of *HL1* and *HL2*, of course, we are left with a split conclusion. The Bell notes for *HL1* and the Conger notes for *HL2* are as complete and accurate as we are likely to get for notes of this kind, and I am confident in asserting that Whitehead scholarship would do well to be more trusting than suspicious of them. In contrast, the notes of Weiss for *HL2* should be regarded with a good deal of suspicion. The Heath and Hocking portions of *HL1* and the Roethlisberger/Hartshorne/Robinson/Heath portions of *HL2* are somewhere in the middle; their mutually corroborating portions should be trusted, while details appearing in only one account might well be regarded with more skepticism.

The larger point I want to make here is that Whitehead scholars do themselves and the scholarly community an injustice if they feel they must "corroborate almost any assertion Whitehead seems to have made therein with more direct statements contained in his more polished, formally published works."[51] New ideas, or at least new ways of stating or supporting the old ideas, are exactly what we most hope to find, and in the case of large swaths of both *HL1* and *HL2*, there is simply no great reason to distrust these notes, and lots of reasons to regard them as completely adequate accounts of the ideas Whitehead wanted to convey.

Even the confusions, where they can be seen, are potentially revealing. I mentioned earlier that Whitehead was sometimes confused or prone to change his mind. We know that Whitehead was sometimes confused because he literally *tells his students* that he is confused, such as at the top of the April 6, 1926, lecture: "Durations. I was very confused last time. I should have stated it negatively and not positively."[52] Nor was he slow to change his mind when he saw a potential problem. One easy example of this occurring is in the October 7, 1926, lecture. In the previous lecture, Whitehead had provided his students with six standards for rational criticism, but in this class he gave a new list of seven standards (he had not simply added one, but changed some of the others); in short, in the space of only a few days he had already come to the conclusion that what he had just presented was inadequate and returned to tell his students exactly why.[53]

This is partly why I take issue with Scarfe charging *HL1* with occasional incoherence (beyond the fact that I do not see any in the passages that he cites). If incoherence was introduced by the student taking notes, then clearly it is problematic, but in such cases the incoherence may well be Whitehead's. Such things tend to happen to a philosopher who is genuinely working through problems in his classroom rather than repeating the same polished material year after year.

This was Whitehead's plan all along when he first came to Harvard. He said quite pointedly in response to the idea of a position at Harvard that:

> The post might give me a welcome opportunity of developing in systematic form my ideas on Logic, the Philosophy of Science, Metaphysics . . . I do not feel inclined to undertake the systematic training of students in the critical study of other philosophers.[54]

In short, he never wanted and never planned to simply teach what other great thinkers thought. He wanted to teach what *he* was thinking about at the moment. And it is quite clear that this is exactly what happened. It is why Louise Heath—the only student whose notes we possess who took Whitehead's class for the first two years—wrote at the top of her notes for fall 1925 that it was "Theoretically same course as 1924, but I credited it because actually it was quite different."[55] Of course, there were some repetitions of ideas in order to make things somewhat coherent for each new crop of students, but each year was more different than similar to the others. At times he even re-presented material in his Philosophy 3b that he had recently delivered elsewhere, such as his essay on "Time"—nor is this sort of repetition a waste for scholars, because he most often commented and further elaborated on such materials in the classroom setting.

He would also quite cheerily admit to problems and inconsistencies with his philosophy. For instance, he admitted many such shortcomings to A. H. Johnson when the latter was working with him to write his thesis on Whitehead's philosophy. When Johnson pointed out that God cannot seem to provide data to other entities since it is apparently an actual entity that never perishes, Whitehead answered that "this is a genuine problem. I have not attempted to solve it."[56] William Ernest Hocking—Whitehead's colleague at Harvard, with whom he co-taught two seminars in metaphysics—similarly paints Whitehead as someone more than willing both to take criticism and to change his mind in the classroom.

> When a student modestly suggested that his point of criticism "may be superficial," Whitehead's swift word was, "Don't be polite to me." After accusing me on one occasion of having spoken from a Hegelian standpoint, he added, "Don't be afraid of exposing my ignorance before the class—say anything you like—I speak in complete ignorance of Hegel."[57]

Not only was Whitehead willing to be criticized, but he also seemed more willing to criticize and discuss others than he was in his published books.

Whitehead, it must be said, was always bad at referencing the work of his contemporaries; for instance, he wrote in the preface to *Science and the Modern World* (*SMW*) that "there has been no occasion in the text to make detailed reference to Lloyd Morgan's *Emergent Evolution* or to Alexander's *Space, Time and Deity*. It will be obvious to readers that I have found them very suggestive."[58] In the lectures, he takes more care to cite and discuss such references more thoroughly. For instance, Whitehead mentions C. D. Broad only once in his published writings but assigned Broad's books to his students for at least the first half of his career at Harvard. Broad's philosophy seems to have provided a more crucial foil for Whitehead than anyone could have previously realized.

In short, partial as I may be as an editor of the Critical Edition, I would argue that these volumes of Harvard lectures provide a marvelous resource to scholars that is set to enrich and change our understanding of Whitehead forever more. The novel elements that we find in them should not be discarded for lack of corroboration in his published works, but more often embraced and verified internally against parallel sets of notes whenever possible (which, as I hope I have shown, is often) and explored as fully as we are able. Hopefully, this book, following the anthology of essays on *HL1*, will help provide a beginning of that enrichment and change.

NOTES

1. Victor Lowe, *Alfred North Whitehead: The Man and His Work*, vol. 1, *1861–1910* (Baltimore: Johns Hopkins University Press, 1985), 2. Reprinted with permission of Johns Hopkins University Press.

2. Here I am thinking particularly of Paul Weiss's numbered list of symbolic expressions. See below.

3. Lydia Medici, email to Brian G. Henning, August 17, 2020. This anonymous panelist was one of four; the other three enthusiastically endorsed the project and awarded it their highest rating.

4. Adam C. Scarfe, review of *The Harvard Lectures of Alfred North Whitehead, 1924–1925: Philosophical Presuppositions of Science*, edited by Paul A. Bogaard and Jason Bell, *Process Studies* 48, no. 1 (Spring–Summer 2019): 144–147.

5. Scarfe, Review of *HL1*, 147.

6. It should be noted that the term "student" is here used to distinguish *Whitehead's own lecture notes* (which, aside from the manuscript of his first lecture, appear to be lost to time) from *lecture notes taken by those listening to his lectures*. However, some of these "students" were actually assistants in the department (Bell, Hartshorne), or even full professors (Hocking) or visiting scholars (Conger).

7. Lowe, *Alfred North Whitehead*, vol. 1, 2.

8. Lowe, *Alfred North Whitehead*, vol. 1, 7.

9. Lowe, *Alfred North Whitehead*, vol. 1, 7.
10. Lowe, *Alfred North Whitehead*, vol. 1, 7–8.
11. Alfred North Whitehead, "Letter from Alfred North Whitehead to Victor Lowe, August 21, 1942," Alfred North Whitehead Collection, MS-0282, Box 2, Special Collections, Johns Hopkins University. https://aspace.library.jhu.edu/repositories/3/resources/282.
12. Alfred North Whitehead, "Whitehead's Will," March 27, 1891, DOC332, Whitehead Research Library. http://wrl.whiteheadresearch.org/items/show/2739. It is possible that the will found in the papers donated by George Whitehead was not his final will, or that he verbally expressed a wish to have his papers destroyed later in life, but we have no evidence of this.

[As this book was in the process of being edited for publication, a more recent will of Whitehead's was discovered in Lowe's papers—apparently the one that was actually executed. It is dated December 26, 1934. It specifically requests the destruction of his wife Evelyn's letters to him, but there is no request for the destruction of any other documents.]

13. Kenneth Blackwell, emails to Joseph Petek, January 15 and 17, 2020.
14. See Paul Weiss, *Philosophy in Process, Volume 10* (Carbondale: Southern Illinois University Press, 1966), 232, and Brian G. Henning, "Whitehead's Daughter, Jessie," Whitehead Research Project, January 15, 2020, http://whiteheadresearch.org/2020/01/15/jessie-marie-whitehead/.
15. Victor Lowe, *Alfred North Whitehead: The Man and His Work, Volume II: 1910–1947* (Baltimore: Johns Hopkins University Press, 1990), 134. WRP now holds this letter: Mark Barr, "Letter from Mark Barr to Whitehead," January 2, 1924, LET1052, Whitehead Research Library, http://wrl.whiteheadresearch.org/items/show/1418. See also Alfred North Whitehead, "First Lecture," September 25, 1924, ADD020, Whitehead Research Library, http://wrl.whiteheadresearch.org/items/show/2093; Alfred North Whitehead, "Religious Psychology of the Western Peoples," March 30, 1939, ADD020, Whitehead Research Library, http://wrl.whiteheadresearch.org/items/show/1414 (discussed in chapter 5); Alfred North Whitehead, "Freedom and Order," n.d., ADD019, Whitehead Research Library, http://wrl.whiteheadresearch.org/items/show/1413 (discussed in chapter 6); Joseph Petek, "The Whitehead book that never was," Whitehead Research Project, April 16, 2020, http://whiteheadresearch.org/2020/04/16/the-whitehead-book-that-never-was/. For more on the significance of the papers donated by Whitehead's grandson, see Brian G. Henning, "Preface: A Brief History of the Critical Edition of Whitehead," in *Whitehead at Harvard, 1924–1925*, ed. Brian G. Henning and Joseph Petek (Edinburgh: Edinburgh University Press, 2020), xvii–xviii; Brian G. Henning, "On the Recently Discovered Whitehead Papers," Whitehead Research Project, January 14, 2019, http://whiteheadresearch.org/2019/01/14/on-the-recently-discovered-whitehead-papers/; and Joseph Petek, "Whitehead Papers Now Available Online," Whitehead Research Project, April 9, 2020, http://whiteheadresearch.org/2020/04/09/whitehead-papers-now-available-online/.
16. An exception is the manuscript of Whitehead's first lecture, which provides a useful comparison point with the notes of Winthrop Bell and Louise Heath in *HL1*,

a comparison which has already been undertaken: Paul A. Bogaard, "Examining Whitehead's 'First Lecture: September, 1924,'" in *Whitehead at Harvard, 1924–1925*, ed. Brian G. Henning and Joseph Petek (Edinburgh: Edinburgh University Press, 2020), 56–72. More on this later. Another exception is the notes of Whitehead's appearance in Cabot's social ethics seminar, which appear to have been done by a stenographer, whose account we have little reason to doubt (see chapter 4).

17. Whitehead lectured at Radcliffe from 9:00 a.m. to 10:00 a.m. and from noon to 1:00 p.m. at Harvard.

18. This mistake was made by the stenographer recording Whitehead's words in Cabot's social ethics seminar. It actually reinforces the idea that it was a professional stenographer taking notes, for a graduate student in Emerson Hall likely would not have made an error of this kind.

19. Joseph Petek, "Introduction: Tales from the Whitehead Mines – On Whitehead, His Students and the Challenges of Editing the Critical Edition," in *Whitehead at Harvard, 1924–1925*, ed. Brian G. Henning and Joseph Petek (Edinburgh: Edinburgh University Press, 2020), 22–29.

20. Petek, "Introduction: Tales from the Whitehead Mines," 22.

21. Petek, "Introduction: Tales from the Whitehead Mines," 26.

22. Petek, "Introduction: Tales from the Whitehead Mines," 27.

23. Lowe, *Alfred North Whitehead*, vol. 2, 140.

24. Lester S. King, "Letter from Lester S. King to Lewis S. Ford," May 3, 1978, LET322, Whitehead Research Library, http://wrl.whiteheadresearch.org/items/show/565.

25. Paul Weiss, "Recollections of Alfred North Whitehead," *Process Studies* 10, no. 1–2 (1980): 44.

26. Brian G. Henning, Joseph Petek, and George Lucas, eds., *The Harvard Lectures of Alfred North Whitehead, 1925–1927: General Metaphysical Problems of Science* (Edinburgh: Edinburgh University Press, 2021), lii.

27. Available online at the Whitehead Research Library (WRL): Paul Weiss, "Whitehead Lecture Notes: Seminary in Metaphysics," 1927, STU063, Whitehead Research Library, http://wrl.whiteheadresearch.org/items/show/590.

28. *HL2*, 336–337.

29. Chapters 6 and 7 of *An Enquiry Concerning the Principles of Natural Knowledge* (*PNK*) are "frightfully confused chapters," while chapter 3 of *The Concept of Nature* (*CN*) is "better, but one gets out of a confused state by cropping the difficulty [of change, motion, time], so in some sense this is not so good" (*HL1*, 69); "*Principle of Relativity* (*R*) doesn't make distinction between physical concrescence and conceptual analyses" (*HL2*, 236); "Obviously left out something [of *PNK*]—then wanted to define what we should mean by a point. Couldn't define it properly—without bringing in further question of how measured time, idea of a duration . . . Fairly obvious that that was because I left out some element" (*HL2*, 304); "Epochal physical occasion—becomes as one divisible but not divided in its becoming. In *The Concept of Nature*, no epochal view, nor of relationship of physical and mental" (HL2, 351).

30. *HL2*, lv.

31. Whitehead, "First Lecture."

32. Bogaard, "Examining Whitehead's 'First Lecture.'"
33. Petek, "The Whitehead book that never was."
34. Lowe, *Alfred North Whitehead*, vol. 2, 141.
35. Whitehead, "First Lecture," 1.
36. Whitehead, "First Lecture," 2–3.
37. *HL1*, 3.
38. Whitehead, "First Lecture," 17–18.
39. *HL1*, 5.
40. *HL1*, 413.
41. Bogaard, "Examining Whitehead's 'First Lecture,'" 67.
42. Bogaard, "Examining Whitehead's 'First Lecture,'" 69.
43. Scarfe, Review of *HL1*, 145–46.
44. I will focus on the "Philosophy 3b" portions and ignore the seminar/seminary portions for now; the peculiar status of Whitehead's appearance in Cabot's social ethics seminar is the topic of chapter 4.
45. See, for instance, the December 21, 1926 lecture (*HL2*, 265–68).
46. *HL2*, xxxiv.
47. C. D. Broad, *Scientific Thought* (London: Kegan Paul, Trench, Trubner & Co., 1923), 18.
48. *HL2*, 189.
49. *HL2*, xliv–xlvi.
50. "To give the reader a sense of the extent of the disorder, what we now know to be the first six pages of Hartshorne's notes had been labelled in Ford's version as pages 1, 2, 6, 72, 22 and 19" (*HL2*, xlii).
51. Scarfe, Review of *HL1*, 147.
52. *HL2*, 155.
53. *HL2*, 179.
54. Lowe, *Alfred North Whitehead*, vol. 2, 134.
55. *HL2*, 3.
56. A. H. Johnson, *Whitehead and His Philosophy* (Lanham: University Press of America, 1963), 47.
57. William Ernest Hocking, "Whitehead as I Knew Him," *The Journal of Philosophy* 58, no. 19 (September 14, 1961): 512.
58. Alfred North Whitehead, *Science and the Modern World* (New York: The Free Press, 1967), vii.

Chapter 2

Whitehead's Lectures as Book Drafts

> *In the lecture room [Whitehead] gave the appearance of complete spontaneity. He did not deliver a set piece; his lecture was thought in action. Those who know him only from his books have missed something of his mind; for he was happier, easier, freer in speech than in writing. The listener had the experience of being taken behind the scenes and witnessing the very process of creative thinking, with its doubts and queries, its problems genuinely felt, in an unfinished but living form.*
>
> –Obituary by Whitehead's
> colleagues and students[1]

If Whitehead had taken care to preserve the drafts of his books and essays, his lecture notes, and his correspondence—in short, left behind the sort of *Nachlass* that important scholars often do—then a Critical Edition of his writings would no doubt have taken place long before now. As it stands, the idea of a Critical Edition of Whitehead was ignored for many years partly because it seemed so readily apparent that there was nothing substantive left to pick over. As mentioned in the previous chapter, stories that he had asked for his papers to be burned began to circulate shortly after his death, and this appeared to be confirmed in the first volume of Victor Lowe's Whitehead biography in 1985. And even though we now know that this story is not completely true, we nonetheless have never found an original manuscript for any of Whitehead's books, only a few articles with emendations.

But what few people had suspected until recently is that the substance of the missing drafts for Whitehead's books might still exist in the form of notes of his Harvard and Radcliffe lectures. In retrospect, such a possibility should have been obvious. For one, Whitehead comes right out and says in the preface to *Process and Reality* (*PR*) that "in the expansion of these lectures to dimensions of the present book, I have been greatly indebted to the critical difficulties suggested by the members of my Harvard classes."[2] There does not appear to be much room for interpretation here: Whitehead is saying that he tested out his philosophical ideas in his Harvard classroom and received feedback which he integrated into his published writings.

Then there are the descriptions of his lecturing style, such as the one above, which suggest spontaneity and "thought in action." Further, with the publication in 1990 of the second volume of Lowe's biography, more evidence of what went on in Whitehead's classroom was given in the form of a letter to Mark Barr, in which Whitehead wrote that

> I do not feel inclined to undertake the systematic training of students in the critical study of other philosophers . . . [but] I should greatly value the opportunity of expressing in lectures and in less formal manner the philosophical ideas which have accumulated in my mind.[3]

And lastly, of course, in actually examining the notes themselves, we have Louise Heath's observation at the top of her notes for fall 1925 that "Theoretically [this was the] same course as 1924, but I credited it because actually it was quite different."[4]

All of these things provide evidence that Whitehead was lecturing his Harvard students on whatever philosophical ideas he was currently thinking about, rather than a static curriculum that remained the same from year to year and that he was using his classroom as a forum to develop his ideas prior to formalizing them for public lectures that would become his published books. In this sense, we might surmise that Whitehead's Harvard lectures could be seen as the "drafts" of his books whose absence scholars have so long lamented.

The object of this chapter is to examine the truth of this idea. To what extent can Whitehead's lectures be seen as "drafts" of his books? How easily can specific passages be correlated? And what might the changes from classroom to page tell us about the development of Whitehead's philosophy?

The focus will be mostly on the already-published volumes of the edition covering Whitehead's first three years of teaching at Harvard, from 1924 to 1927, though I will also look at year four for evidence of early "drafts" of Whitehead's Gifford lectures, since this is likely to be of special interest to Whitehead scholars. Books published during this period include *Science and the Modern World* (1925), *Religion in the Making* (1926), *Symbolism* (1927), and *Process and Reality* (1929).[5] We will start with the last book first and work our way backward, since the latter two works are actually easier and cleaner candidates for this analysis than the former two.

PROCESS AND REALITY

Whitehead got the invitation to deliver the Gifford lectures on January 17, 1927, two days after he had delivered his last lecture of the term, and accepted on February 27.[6] From that point, he had a little more than a year to prepare the lectures before their delivery in June of 1928. The obvious time to start was during the summer of 1927, and it appears that this is exactly what he did.[7] A letter of August 22, 1927, to his son, North, confirms that by that time he had "9 ½ chapters finished out of a projected plan of 20 or 25 chapters."[8] We might then expect that Whitehead would test some of this work out in his Harvard classes during the 1927–1928 school year, which began in late September, about a month after his letter.

Lo and behold, during the second and third lectures of the term, Whitehead would dictate eight "principles . . . to be expounded in the course"[9] of what he would later call his "categories of explanation," of which there would eventually be twenty-seven. (Note that Whitehead's lectures for the fall of 1927 are recorded by Edwin Marvin,[10] Sinclair Kerby-Miller,[11] and Susanne Langer,[12] but Marvin's notes are often the most thorough and complete, so these are the notes I will usually reference.) The eight principles that he presented to his students would become categories 1, 2, 4, 19, 7, 8, 9, and 18, in that order. The fact that he presented less than a third of the categories to his students, and in a different order than the one in which they would ultimately appear in *PR*, certainly suggests that Whitehead did not have his categoreal scheme in anything like a final form yet, even though what he *did* present seems almost word-perfect with *PR* in many cases.

Interestingly, in a letter to Lewis Ford which accompanied Edwin Marvin's notes, Lowe opined that probably Whitehead "had made a draft of [the full scheme] in the summer, but wanted to talk to his students instead of losing them with its formal presentation" as an explanation for why the rest of the categories weren't presented, and then goes on to argue against the significance of the notes and against the value of their publication. Though the closeness of these principles as they appear in Marvin's and Kerby-Miller's notes is an argument in favor of this theory, Lowe's explanation still strikes me as half-baked and somewhat bizarre, since it seems unlikely that Whitehead would have not just truncated his categories of explanation for his students, but also called them something else ("principles") and presented them in a different order. The simpler explanation is that Whitehead's Giffords were incomplete, and Whitehead was presenting what he had. Ford himself, in his preliminary notes on the material, says he is "skeptical that this represents only a partial list of W's principles. I suspect we can see a genetic development here."[13] I am with Ford in this instance.

The first sentence of principle 1 *is* word-perfect with the first category of explanation in *PR*, though the rest is not the same at all. *PR* has a second sentence which says that "thus actual entities are creatures; they are also termed 'actual occasions,'"[14] while principle 1 as recorded by Marvin makes no mention of creatures or occasions, instead mentioning pluralism and overcoming Zeno.[15]

There is not space here to slog through *all* the differences between the notes and the published book for these eight principles, but let us take principle/category 2 as a representative example and discuss what can be gleaned from it.

> *Process and Reality*: (ii) That in the becoming of an actual entity, the *potential* unity of many entities in disjunctive diversity—actual and non-actual—acquires the *real* unity of the one actual entity; so that the actual entity is the real concrescence of many potentials.[16]
>
> *Marvin's notes:* 2. That in the becoming of an actual entity, the <u>potential</u> unity of many entities acquires the actual unity of the one entity—the whole process is the many becoming one, and the one is what becomes. Actual entity is the real unity of many components. Physics—<u>potential</u> is what would happen in actual circumstances. (This principle gets us in touch with modern physics.)[17]
>
> *Kerby-Miller's notes:* 2. In the becoming of an actual entity. The <u>potential</u> unity of many entities acquires the <u>real</u> unity of the actual entity. So the actual entity is the real unity of many potentials.[18]

The closeness of the language here shows that Whitehead had this category of explanation in something very like its final form. Differences between the notes of Marvin and Kerby-Miller again remind us that wording of notes is not always exact; though Marvin's notes are generally more thorough, he has "actual unity of the one entity" while Kerby-Miller has "<u>real</u> unity of the actual entity," which more closely reflects the published form. Likewise, Kerby-Miller's notes more accurately reflect the final line in talking of "potentials" rather than Marvin's "components." But both agree that Whitehead spoke of a "real *unity*" rather than a "real *concrescence*."

Further, the rest of Marvin's notes under principle 2 record some material either not present in *PR* or that appears in a different place or different form. He says that "the whole process is the many becoming one, and the one is what becomes," which resembles a famous Whitehead line from his explanation of the category of the ultimate in *PR*: "The many become one, and are increased by one."[19] The other lines on "potential" read like an aside, an extra bit of explanation to Whitehead's students (an idea supported somewhat by the parentheses).

Concerns about the accuracy of the notes aside, it seems clear that Whitehead was well on his way to establishing his categoreal scheme, was still in the process of organizing it into its final form and distinguishing between various species of categories, and had not even formulated all of its most basic principles; that is, the notes appear to show an early and half-formed category of the ultimate, though it yet lacks the notion of creativity, which is not mentioned in any of these eight principles at all.[20] I take this as yet another argument against Lowe's idea that Whitehead had composed a complete draft of his scheme at this point in the term; if he had, it seems unthinkable that he would make no mention of creativity even in a truncated list. It seems, therefore, quite clear that these eight principles delivered in his fall 1927 lectures constitute an early draft of *PR*'s categoreal scheme and reveal some of the lines of development of Whitehead's thought.

Before moving on a few other deviations of these "principles" from *PR* are worth mentioning. Principle 6 as recorded by Marvin[21] (which would become category of explanation 19) again contains much that would come slightly later in *PR*, including talk of "superjects"—which would first appear in *PR* in discussing the nine categoreal obligations[22]—and an insistence that entities "never change" but are "superceded." This resembles discussions of the unchanging nature of actual entities on pages 28 and 35 of *PR*. Second, both Marvin[23] and Kerby-Miller[24] record Whitehead's "ontological principle" as having another name that never appears in *PR*: the "principle of extrinsic reference" (i.e., the definition is the same, but Whitehead calls it something else here).

Moving beyond these eight principles, it seems clear from further examination of Marvin's fall 1927 notes that there are elements of Whitehead's Giffords scattered throughout, though rarely in a form in which whole pages or even whole paragraphs can be easily correlated. But here are some striking examples of similarities (the second example is particularly exact):

Process and Reality: The primary method of mathematics is deduction; the primary method of philosophy is descriptive generalization. Under the influence of mathematics, deduction has been foisted onto philosophy as its standard method, instead of taking its true place as an essential auxiliary mode of verification whereby to test the scope of generalities.[25]

Marvin's notes, page 13: Descriptive generalization is the task of philosophy. Deduction is a subordinate method of verification.[26]

Process and Reality: For "theory" itself requires that there be "given" elements so as to form the material for theorizing . . . I quote from Professor A. E. Taylor's summary of the *Timaeus:* In the real world there is always, over and above "law," a factor of the "simply given" or "brute fact," not accounted for and to be accepted simply as given.

This element of "givenness" in things implies some activity procuring limitation . . . The ontological principle declares that every decision is referable to one or more actual entities, because in separation from actual entities there is nothing, merely nonentity—"The rest is silence." The ontological principle asserts the relativity of decision; whereby every decision expresses the relation of the actual thing, *for which* a decision is made, to an actual thing *by which* that decision is made.[27]

Marvin's notes: There must be material for theorizing. (A.E. Taylor in new book on Plato: Brute fact given. Some always remains after rationalizing process.) Givenness implies limitation. Every decision is referable to one or more actual entities. Apart from actuality "the rest is silence." The apparent world has actuality. Ontological principle asserts the relativity of decisions—every decision expresses relation of the actual thing for which a decision is made to another actual thing by which a decision is made.[28]

Process and Reality: The notion of one ideal arises from the disastrous over moralization of thought under the influence of fanaticism, or pedantry.[29]

Marvin's notes: Nonsense that there is one Ideal which a thing ought to be. This due to overzealous religious leaders. Want all the congregation to conform. Over-moralization means rigid conformity to some form of mores, customs.[30]

Many more examples could be given, but suffice it to say that it is quite clear that Whitehead presented what amounted to drafts of portions of his Gifford lectures to his Harvard classes.

Moreover, though I tend to think that the most interesting and truest sense of "drafts of Whitehead's books" in effect means material that was delivered *before the public lectures* that would *become* Whitehead's books, Dorothy Emmet confirms another definition:

> Whitehead had given the Gifford Lectures in Edinburgh in 1928, and when I was in his classes in 1929 he was turning them into *Process and Reality*. He believed that he could sometimes say what he wanted better in verbal exposition than when writing, so sometimes when he came to a hard passage he would signal to me to get it down *verbatim* and afterwards asked for my notes. I recognize some of these passages in *Process and Reality;* I take no responsibility except as an amanuensis.[31]

So we can say that not only was Whitehead presenting parts of what would become his Gifford lectures to his Harvard classes before he delivered them but also recapitulating them in his Harvard classroom after completion and, in some cases, using his verbatim classroom delivery to finalize the finished text.

SYMBOLISM

Whitehead's Giffords are certainly not the only instance of public lectures that Whitehead would later repeat in his classroom. In the case of *Symbolism*—which he delivered as the Barbour-Page lectures at the University of Virginia during Harvard's spring break in the second half of April 1927—he delivered the lectures again to his Harvard students immediately upon his return in early May.

This is clear from the notes of Weiss. For instance, he recorded Whitehead saying that "we go from the perception of a colored object to a colored chair," which mirrors Whitehead's discussion on pages 2–3 of *Symbolism*. Likewise, Weiss recorded him as saying that "direct experience is infallible," which is a direct quote from page 6 of the published work. Unfortunately, however, Weiss's notes are so sparse that they are of little use in showing us the *differences* between his classroom presentation and the ensuing book. And if he had someone like Emmet in his class at this time, who he asked to take down his words exactly, then we do not know it.

But when returning to the more interesting question of the extent to which Whitehead's Harvard lectures prefigured his Barbour-Page lectures, the answer is not nearly so clear as it is for *Process and Reality*. It appears that the Giffords may have been a special case to the extent that he wrote large portions of them over the summer and proceeded to share the fruits of his labors with his students—work that had been specifically written for delivery in Edinburgh, but which he wished to refine. For *Symbolism*, and for Whitehead's two other American books that we are set to examine, there does not appear to be a strong case for the idea that whole passages of his Harvard lectures were simply adopted for the public lectures. Instead, he was writing them in parallel, drawing from ideas that he had presented to his students, but nonetheless writing something new.

One might think that the relatively narrow range of *Symbolism*'s topics compared to some of Whitehead's other works, however—paired with some of its unique terminologies—provides an advantage. For instance, "causal efficacy" and "presentational immediacy" were both terms that feature prominently, and *Symbolism* is the first book in which they appear. Therefore, searching for instances of these terms in the Harvard lectures in the period leading up to the Barbour-Page lectures would seem to be a good strategy.

But as it turns out, this approach gets us less than one would hope. First, while the term "presentational immediacy" had not appeared in Whitehead's previous *books*, it *did* appear in his paper "Time," which Whitehead delivered at Sixth International Congress of Philosophy in September of 1926, just before the beginning of the 1926–1927 academic year, and which he would later present to his Harvard classes. His first use of "presentational immediacy" is important, so I quote it at length:

> But A does prehend these occasions in the mode of *presentational immediacy*. The eternal objects functioning in this prehensive mode are termed the *sense-data*.

> This presentational immediacy of the world simultaneous with *A* embodies the originative character of *A*. It is the self-creative self-enjoyment of *A* in its character of a concretion. . . . Thus presentational immediacy has the character of physical imagination, in a generalized sense of that word. This physical imagination has normally to conform to the physical memories of the immediate past; it is then called sense-perception, and is non-delusive. It may conform to the physical memories of the more remote past: it is then called the image associated with memory. It may conform to some special intrusive element in the immediate past such as, in the case of human beings, drugs, emotions, or conceptual relationships in antecedent mental occasions: it is then variously called delusion, or ecstatic vision, or imagination.[32]

We can see some parallels here with the way the term is later used in Whitehead's Barbour-Page lectures. For instance, the whole discussion of it as "non-delusive" is consistent with its definition in *Symbolism* (*S*) as a "pure mode" which is by itself free from error. But "presentational immediacy" as used here has a slightly different meaning—or at least a slightly different connotation—than it does in *Symbolism*. The paper Whitehead was presenting was on time, and as such the stress is on the "immediacy" side; it is a concept designed to deal with the problem of simultaneity, because it is the same regardless of whether the "conformation" of the "physical imagination" (a term that would not appear in *Symbolism*) is to the sense perception of the immediate past, or to memory, or to some delusive element.

Now, this element certainly is not *absent* from the Barbour-Page lectures; Whitehead says when introducing the term that it "expresses how contemporary events are relevant to each other, and yet preserve a mutual independence. This relevance amid independence is the peculiar character of contemporaneousness."[33] The difference lies in the fact that Whitehead had not yet conceived of causal efficacy as a second pure perceptive mode, which together with presentational immediacy becomes "symbolic reference." Being one half of a whole gives the term a whole different flavor in which it becomes the hallmark of a "high-grade mentality." Moreover, the emphasis that we see above on the bringing of memory into immediacy is less prominent in *Symbolism*; Whitehead says that "By 'presentational immediacy' I mean what is usually termed 'sense-perception.' . . . [It] is our immediate perception of the contemporary external world, appearing as an element constitutive of our own experience."[34] Further, the second sentence speaks of presentational immediacy as a "prehensive mode," with the term "prehension" being notably absent from *Symbolism*.

The larger point, though, in terms of the question we are asking about the extent to which Whitehead's Harvard lectures amount to drafts of his books, is that it can be hard to distinguish between instances when Whitehead is simply repeating thoughts from his paper "Time" and instances where there is a genuine evolution toward his use of the term as found in *Symbolism*. The best indication would be, in fact, its appearance as a double-act with "causal efficacy."

As it turns out, however, the term "causal efficacy" is largely missing in action during Whitehead's third year of lectures. It appears exactly twice,[35] with both of them—maddeningly—in the undated seminar notes of Conger.[36] By process of elimination, these undated notes must fall somewhere in the period between October 22 and December 17, 1926. That the term appears only here suggests that Whitehead may have been experimenting with and developing his philosophy to an even greater extent in the discussion-focused seminars than he was in his lectures. But in this case, the record we have is sparse just when we want more detail. At the very least, his first use of the term pretty well reflects *Symbolism*'s themes:

> Language takes sense data, gives artificial, sophisticated external reference, but make it do same sort of work which the sight of Boston does. If no knowledge of past—self as entering into or issuing out of it—then we have no knowledge. In making it precise, we are often misled by functioning in wrong way. Likely to have concept first of causal efficacy of past and from concept presuming that we have a definite knowledge of it. Unless have some perceptual knowledge, have no knowledge, and whole talk of past and present is fictitious. Classification so elaborate. Why not talk about patches of color? Sense data give last term of historic route of that book—but book with its past more abstract than any one occasion.[37]

The first sentence recalls Whitehead's observation in *Symbolism* that words are "handy" in the sense that they can summon up the image of a forest without the need to have a forest in front of us.[38] And his warning regarding classification and conceptions of abstract enduring entities as knowledge recalls his warning in *Symbolism* that "our judgments on causal efficacy are almost inextricably warped by the acceptance of the symbolic reference between the two modes as the completion of our direct knowledge."[39] Yet even here, Whitehead does not discuss "symbolism," but rather "language," nor does "presentational immediacy" appear along with it.

If we move on to looking for "presentational immediacy," it appears sporadically throughout his 1926–1927 lectures, including near the end of Whitehead's October 14, 1926, lecture: "Representation of all our Knowledge and conceptual feelings in terms of presentational immediacy—the natural symbolism of knowledge—shared no doubt by animals."[40] He follows this by noting that "language [is] a conventional narrowing of this process by which knowledge is rendered vivid, distinct, often erroneous."[41] Here, clearly, is some of *Symbolism*'s terminology and some of its major themes. But it is also not a very substantive mention; it comes at the end of the lecture with no real follow-up during the next session. Likewise, there is a somewhat striking though specious connection in the October 23 lecture in which Whitehead is discussing "redness" and says "Maybe I'm an artist and interested in color patch. Maybe interested in wall." Both color patches and walls are examples used in *Symbolism*,[42] but again, the connection is otherwise fairly weak. The same thing could be said of Whitehead's use of Aesop's dog with a leg of mutton as an example of error in a late February seminar.[43] I could cite more instances, but none shows a clear genetic development in the Barbour-Page lectures.

I would love to be able to argue that Whitehead's Harvard lectures provide what amounts to a draft or blueprint of *Symbolism*. But in the end, this simply does not seem to be supported by the evidence. The very fact that Whitehead immediately repeated his whole course of Barbour-Page lectures to his Harvard classes upon his return argues against the idea that the substance of them had already been given, for if so they would have been redundant. He appears to have written his Barbour-Page lectures in parallel with his Harvard lectures, rather than using the latter to directly construct the former.

SCIENCE AND THE MODERN WORLD AND RELIGION IN THE MAKING

As for Whitehead's first two American books—both delivered as Lowell lectures a year apart—they bear a closer resemblance to *Symbolism* than they do to *PR* in the extent to which the Harvard lectures preceding them might be considered some type of draft. Finding passages in the Harvard lectures that could be considered clear precursors to *Science and the Modern World (SMW)* and *Religion in the Making (RM)* is actually even harder than it is for *Symbolism*, given their relative width of scope (especially *SMW*). This is not to say that Whitehead's Harvard lectures have nothing to do with his books at all. Besides covering many of the same subjects and themes, there are passages that can be seen as seeds for his books, but whether they constitute a straight line of development is open to interpretation and seems likely to remain ambiguous.

For example, Whitehead offers the following conception of evil on October 22, 1925, about three months before his Lowell lectures that would become *RM*: "Ethically evil is always by comparison with something else. (1. lack of survival power 2. diminish another's survival power 3. hindering progress)."[44] In relation to *RM*, this formulation is only half complete: it states that evil is only evil relative to some other outcome, but does not positively state that evils, to some degree, are also goods in themselves, something which he would clarify in *RM*: "Evil, triumphant in its enjoyment, is so far good in itself; but beyond itself it is evil in its character of a destructive agent among things greater than itself."[45]

Further, in at least one case Whitehead seemed to hint at material that would appear in *RM* without actually sharing it. Charles Hartshorne recorded the following in his notes for Whitehead's October 20, 1925, lecture: "Art vs. ethics. Art for the immediate good. Ethics looks beyond given. Solution in concept of God."[46] Incredibly Whitehead says nothing more on the matter, and yet it seems to prefigure his discussion of "God and the moral order" in *Religion in the Making*, in which God is "the measure of the aesthetic consistency of the world,"[47] whose purpose is "the attainment of value in the temporal world,"[48] an actual entity of "unchanged consistency of character . . . [a] definite determination which imposes ordered balance on the world."[49] God is the "solution" to the "problem" of art as the immediate good versus ethics as looking beyond, in the sense that God's immanence grounds aesthetic order[50] while God's internal consistency promotes a maximum of creative order in preference to the inherently unstable destructiveness of evil.

But for every instance in which we can draw some sort of line from the Harvard lectures to *RM*, there are five more that seem to have no parallel. For instance, *RM* makes much of Christianity and Buddhism as "two main rational religions . . . the two Catholic religions of civilization" which are both "in decay . . . [and] have lost their ancient hold upon the world."[51] He spends pages and pages comparing them, at one point famously noting that Christianity "has always been a religion seeking a metaphysic, in contrast to Buddhism which is a metaphysic generating a religion."[52] Yet in the year leading up to his 1926 Lowell lectures, Whitehead did not mention Buddhism at all,[53] and when he mentioned Christianity—which was seldom—it was usually to make an assertion about medieval philosophy: "Authority of mediaeval age was the authority of a harmonious whole, a successful harmony—successful fusion of Aristotelean doctrines with Christian religion."[54] While this point itself has some parallel in *RM*,[55] it is more of an aside rather than the main thrust of what Whitehead was talking about in his comparison of Buddhism and Christianity, which simply does not appear in the Harvard lectures.

Finally, finding parallels in the Harvard lectures that prefigure *Science and the Modern World* is the thorniest comparison of them all, since *SMW* has such a wide scope. Again there are hints, weak connections which prove little, yet suggest much. For instance, in his chapter on "The Romantic Reaction," he makes much of the poetry of Wordsworth and Shelley.[56] And if we look at *HL1*, we do in fact find both men mentioned a few times prior to the beginning of the Lowell lectures, with the first being at the very end (literally the last line that Bell recorded) of the October 18, 1924 lecture: "Contrast between Wordsworth and Shelley in attitude to science."[57] This line can be seen as a summary of Whitehead's extended discussion of the two men in

SMW, in which he says: "Wordsworth was passionately absorbed in nature . . . He weakens his evidence by his dislike of science,"[58] while "Shelley's attitude to science was at the opposite pole to that of Wordsworth. He loved it, and is never tired of expressing in poetry the thoughts which it suggests."[59]

This seems like a good connection, but what does it really tell us? Six pages of *SMW* have been reduced to a single line. Or more accurately, one line of Whitehead's Harvard lectures was expanded to half a dozen pages in his Lowell lectures. Does this represent a genetic development from one to the other? It is a question complicated by the fact that our records of Whitehead's lectures come from the notes of others. Bell was generally a thorough note-taker, and yet it seems hard to credit the idea that Whitehead spoke the line as Bell recorded it without specifying what the contrast between them *actually was*. Nevertheless, if it had been an extended discussion such as appears in *SMW*, it also seems safe to assume that Bell would have recorded more than this. Could this be the sort of thing that occurred to Whitehead on the fly right at the end of his lecture, which he thought was such a good idea that he paused to write it down as he dismissed his class, thinking that he had found an excellent idea for his forthcoming Lowell lectures, three months hence?

Let us look at one more example of a possible linkage to drive the point home. Whitehead mentions Albert Michelson in two places in his Harvard lectures on January 17, about two weeks before his Lowell lectures would begin:

> One or two men of genius—Michelson and his inventions. There is now possible a series of Experiments comparing total Event A and total one B.—Of two objects. The difference expresses itself in motion with respect to each other. The meaning of Motion is a difference between Space-Time systems.

This parallels an extended discussion of the Michelson-Morley experiments that appear on pages 114–118 of *SMW*. Yet once again we are left to question the usefulness of comparing a single paragraph to half a dozen pages.

CONCLUDING THOUGHTS

When I began writing this chapter, I felt certain that I would quickly find easy correspondences between Whitehead's Harvard lectures and his books. I had, after all, completed the editing of *HL2* not so long ago, and I saw much in the Harvard lectures that seemed familiar. The idea that strong connections and parallels could be made was reinforced by what I consider to be the very strong evidence that Whitehead's Gifford lectures were shared and developed in his Harvard classroom well before their delivery in Edinburgh.

But in the final analysis, I think we must conclude that while Whitehead did indeed develop his philosophy and nurture ideas in his Harvard lectures, much of what we find later in his books was written and developed in parallel with his Harvard teaching, rather than—as I first thought might be the case—transferred directly from the one to the other. *PR* appears to have been a special case in which Whitehead spent a significant portion of his time over the summer preparing for lectures taking place a year hence, while the preceding three books seem to have been written during the academic term.[60] I genuinely have no idea whether Whitehead's later books follow the pattern of *PR* or his preceding three works; we will have to wait for the transcription of later materials (at least) or the publication of the rest of the Harvard lectures to know for sure.

The silver lining in what might be a disappointing conclusion as concerns *SMW*, *RM*, and *Symbolism* is that while the Harvard lectures as "drafts" may be a harder line to draw than might be hoped, we also know that something like the reverse *was* the case: Whitehead was prone to bringing his published works into the classroom, and then commenting on them. We can find quite a number of instances of this, including comments that he was "confused" in *PNK*,[61] or his remark that *"Principle of Relativity* doesn't make distinction between physical concrescence and conceptual analyses,"[62] or his extended discussion of Lloyd Morgan's critique of *SMW*.[63] In the end, what we are really wanting to find in the newly published Harvard lectures is insight into the line of Whitehead's philosophical development, and this can be accomplished by his metacommentary on his published works as much as by early drafts. Nor would we be correct to be overly discouraged at the idea that the Harvard lectures are relatively unique pieces of philosophy unto themselves, and not simply partially formed and incomplete drafts which have been wholly superseded by published work.

NOTES

1. Raphael Demos et al., "Proceedings of the American Philosophical Association 1948–1949," *The Philosophical Review* 58, no. 5 (September 1949): 469. Copyright 1949, Cornell University. All rights reserved. Reprinted by permission of the publisher, Duke University Press. www.dukeupress.edu

2. Alfred North Whitehead, *Process and Reality* (New York: The Free Press, 1978), xiv–xv.

3. Lowe, *Alfred North Whitehead*, vol. 2, 134.

4. *HL2*, 3.

5. Though the book was published in 1929, Whitehead delivered his Gifford lectures in June of 1928.

6. *HL2*, xxxii.

7. Victor Lowe, "Whitehead's Gifford Lectures," *Southern Journal of Philosophy* 7, no. 4 (Winter 1969): 332.

8. Lowe, *Alfred North Whitehead*, vol. 2, 328.

9. Edwin L. Marvin, "Whitehead Lecture Notes, 1927–1928," Victor Lowe papers, MS-0284, Series 2, Box 2.9, Special Collections, Johns Hopkins University, 9. Langer has them as "eight principles of metaphysics" (Susanne K. Langer, "Notes on Whitehead's Course on Philosophy of Nature, 1927," Susanne Langer papers, MS Am 3110, Box 5, Houghton Library, Harvard University, 2).

10. Marvin, "Whitehead Lecture Notes."

11. Sinclair Kerby-Miller, "Notes on Whitehead's Fall 1927 Philosophy 3b course and other related materials," 1927, STU060, Whitehead Research Library.

12. Langer, "Notes."

13. Marvin, "Whitehead Lecture Notes," 6.

14. *PR*, 22.

15. Marvin, "Whitehead Lecture Notes," 10.

16. *PR*, 22.

17. Marvin, "Whitehead Lecture Notes," 10.

18. Kerby-Miller, "Notes," 12.

19. *PR*, 21.

20. Though Whitehead did use the term "creativity" in a somewhat technical sense ("creative activity of the intellect") as early as his February 19, 1925, lecture (*HL1*, 213), this instance is rather lean compared to the more robust idea of creativity that appears in *PR*. A better one is in the May 2, 1925, lecture, in which Whitehead says that "Experient Self, Whitehead looks on as embodiment of Creative Activity whose law of being is Self-creative" (*HL1*, 356).

21. Marvin, "Whitehead Lecture Notes," 11.

22. *PR*, 28.

23. Marvin, "Whitehead Lecture Notes," 12.

24. Kerby-Miller, "Notes," 15.

25. *PR*, 10.

26. Marvin, "Whitehead Lecture Notes," 13.

27. *PR*, 42–43.

28. Marvin, "Whitehead Lecture Notes," 22.

29. *PR*, 84.

30. Marvin, "Whitehead Lecture Notes," 87.

31. Dorothy Emmet, *Philosophers and Friends: Reminiscences of Seventy Years in Philosophy* (Houndmills: Macmillan, 1996), 36–37.

32. Alfred North Whitehead, "Time," in *Proceedings of the Sixth International Congress of Philosophy*, ed. Edgar Sheffield Brightman (New York: Longmans, Green & Co., 1927), 63.

33. Alfred North Whitehead, *Symbolism: Its Meaning and Effect* (New York: Fordham University Press, 1985), 16.

34. *S*, 21.

35. Not counting its appearance during the classes immediately following the delivery of the Barbour-Page lectures, in which he seems to have re-delivered them to his students.

36. *HL2*, 361–362.
37. *HL2*, 361.
38. *S*, 56.
39. *S*, 54.
40. *HL2*, 186.
41. *HL2*, 187.
42. The artist on *S*, 3–4, the wall on *S*, 14–16, both in relation to color.
43. *HL2*, 374.
44. *HL2*, 63. This is from Roethlisberger's notes, but Hartshorne has a fourth example which Roethlisberger missed: "it might have (freely) made itself better."
45. Alfred North Whitehead. *Religion in the Making* (New York: Fordham University Press, 1996), 95–96.
46. *HL2*, 60.
47. *RM*, 99.
48. *RM*, 100.
49. *RM*, 94.
50. *RM*, 105.
51. *RM*, 44.
52. *RM*, 50.
53. Though there is reason to suspect that he was learning of Buddhism from his colleague in the Philosophy Department, James Haughton Woods. See Joseph Petek, "Whitehead and James Haughton Woods," Whitehead Research Project, October 8, 2018, http://whiteheadresearch.org/2018/10/08/whitehead-and-james-haughton-woods/.
54. *HL2*, 87.
55. "Modern European philosophy, which had its origin in Plato and Aristotle, after sixteen hundred years of Christianity reformulated its problems with increased attention to the importance of the individual subject of experience" (*RM*, 140).
56. "In English literature, the deepest thinkers of this school were Coleridge, Wordsworth, and Shelley . . . For our purposes Coleridge is only important by his influence on Wordsworth. Thus Wordsworth and Shelley remain" (*SMW*, 82–83). Whitehead would go on to discuss the poetry of these two men from pages 83–88.
57. *HL1*, 41.
58. *SMW*, 83.
59. *SMW*, 84.
60. For instance, in a letter to his son, North, Whitehead wrote of his 1925 public lectures (*SMW*) that "The Lowell Lectures—eight of them—amounted to writing a book in about two months" (Lowe, *Alfred North Whitehead*, vol. 2, 303). He does not specify which two months, but it seems safe to assume that the lectures were not composed before he left England.
61. *HL1*, 185.
62. *HL2*, 236.
63. *HL2*, 372–375.

Chapter 3

Muddle-Headedness versus Simple-Mindedness, Round 2

At the best Speculative Philosophy can only consist of more or less happy guesses, made on a very slender basis. . . . Now speculative philosophers as a class have been the most dogmatic of men. They have been more certain of everything than they had a right to be of anything.

—C. D. Broad[1]

If you don't go into metaphysics, you assume an uncritical metaphysics. . . . Every scientific man in order to preserve his reputation has to say he dislikes metaphysics. What he means is he dislikes having his metaphysics criticized.

—Alfred North Whitehead[2]

As was already noted at the end of chapter 1, Whitehead was not particularly good about referencing the work of his contemporaries in his published books but did so with considerably more frequency during his Harvard lectures, sometimes reading whole pages of works by others aloud to his classes. While Whitehead references quite a number of people in his Harvard lectures that he seldom or never discussed elsewhere, possibly the most intriguing is C. D. Broad. Mentioned only once in Whitehead's books,[3] Broad nonetheless featured prominently in Whitehead's teaching, and he routinely assigned Broad's *Scientific Thought* (1923) and/or *The Mind and Its Place in Nature* (1925) to the students of his Philosophy 3b lecture course from his arrival in the fall of 1924 through at least the spring of 1933. Broad is somewhat less remembered today, but he was an important philosopher in the early to mid-1900s—important enough to warrant an entry in Paul Schilpp's *Library of Living Philosophers* books series in 1959, sandwiched between volumes dedicated to Karl Jaspers (1957) and Rudolf Carnap (1963).

This chapter is divided into four sections. The first lays out Whitehead's and Broad's interactions in England from the time of Broad's enrollment at Trinity College, Cambridge, in 1906 to Whitehead's departure for America in August 1924. The second looks at Whitehead's influence on Broad, which is largely acknowledged and explicit. The third surveys what Whitehead said of Broad and his philosophy in his Harvard classes. Finally, the fourth section examines the influence of Broad in Whitehead's published works.

INTERACTIONS BETWEEN WHITEHEAD AND BROAD

Their association began at Trinity College, Cambridge. Whitehead had been elected a Fellow of Trinity in 1884 and would teach there until 1910, when he departed for London in the wake of his friend Andrew Forsyth's resignation. Broad attended Trinity on scholarship from 1906 to 1910 and was elected a Fellow of Trinity in 1911, just after Whitehead's departure. It is not clear whether Broad, who wrote his dissertation under J. M. E. McTaggart, attended any of Whitehead's mathematics courses, but Broad's work demonstrates a strong enough grounding in mathematics and symbolic logic that it is entirely possible.

The first documented interaction that I could find between the two is an indirect one. Whitehead wrote a letter to Russell on September 20, 1911, in which he apologized for keeping the *Principia* proofs too long and also shared some recent ideas on time and space. But there is also a line in it in which Whitehead says, "Please send me Broad's dissertation, I shall like to tackle it."[4] Russell must have mentioned the dissertation to Whitehead in a letter of his own, but sadly this letter is not in evidence. Broad's dissertation would be published in 1914 as his first book: *Perception, physics, and reality; an enquiry into the information that physical science can supply about the real.*[5] One can see from the title why Whitehead may have been intrigued.

Five years later came another indirect interaction. Both co-signed (along with twenty other Fellows) a statement expressing dissatisfaction that Bertrand Russell had been stripped of his Trinity lectureship following his decision to refuse conscription as a conscientious objector in WWI. The statement was sent out for signatures by F. M. Cornford in October 1916[6] and formally submitted to the Trinity College Council in January 1917.[7]

More significant than these in terms of possibly influencing one another's thought were their interactions in meetings of the Aristotelian Society, to which Broad had been elected in 1914, with Whitehead following a year later.[8] The abstracts of the minutes for the proceedings[9] reveal that both men were fairly frequent attendees of these meetings—Whitehead somewhat more than Broad—and that there are indeed a half dozen times over these ten years when the minutes confirm that they interacted directly. It seems likely that they participated together in discussions more than the minutes can confirm, for in listing the names of people who responded to a paper, the list often ends with "and others." There also would have been ample opportunity before and after sessions for them to speak more informally.

To give a brief listing of their confirmed interactions at the Aristotelian Society meetings:

- On January 8, 1917, Broad presented a paper on "Hume's Theory of the Credibility of Miracles," with Whitehead listed as taking place in the discussion.[10]
- On December 16, 1918, John Laird presented a paper on "Synthesis and Discovery in Knowledge," with Broad and Whitehead both listed as taking place in the discussion.[11]
- On January 6, 1919, Broad's paper "Mechanical Explanation and its Alternatives" was read by Chairman H. Wildon Carr due to Broad's illness, with Whitehead taking part in the discussion.[12]
- On September 25, 1920, Whitehead chaired a symposium on "The Philosophical Aspect of the General Theory of Relativity" by Broad and others at the Congress of Philosophy at Oxford.[13]
- On April 9, 1923, Broad read a paper on "Various Meanings of the Term 'Unconscious,'" with Whitehead listed as the chair.[14]
- On July 12, 1924—only a month before Whitehead's mid-August departure for America—Broad was part of a symposium at a joint session of the Aristotelian Society and the Mind Association entitled "Critical Realism: Can the Difficulty of Affirming a Nature Independent of Mind Be Overcome by the Distinction between Essence and Existence?" Whitehead is listed as taking part in the discussion.[15]

In addition to their conversations at the Aristotelian Society, they also seemed to be aware of each other's published work, as evidenced by the fact that Broad reviewed two of Whitehead's books in the journal *Mind* (*An Enquiry Concerning the Principles of Natural Knowledge* in 1920[16] and *The Principle of Relativity* in 1923)[17] while Whitehead, as previously noted, must have read Broad's article in *Mind* on "The External World," as he adapted Broad's term "historical section' to "historical route" for his *Principle of Relativity*. And these are of course only the cases for which we have direct evidence; it seems safe to assume that the two men often read each other's work, even when we cannot definitively prove it.

They shared another indirect connection through the Tarner lectureship at Trinity College. Whitehead delivered the inaugural series of Tarner lectures in 1919, which would be published as *The Concept of Nature* (*CN*) in 1920, while Broad gave the second set of Tarner lectures in 1923 on "The borderline between physics and psychology," which would be published as *The Mind and Its Place in Nature* in 1925. It is unfortunate that I have been unable to confirm that Whitehead and Broad attended one another's lectures, but it seems somewhat likely to me; Broad's reviews of Whitehead's books showed him to be an admirer of Whitehead's work, and Whitehead, for his part, would undoubtedly have been interested in the follow-up act to his inaugural series of lectures, as his assigning of the ensuing book to his students at Harvard would seem to suggest.

It is perhaps worth noting that Lowe, in his biography of Whitehead, characterizes Broad as "a friend of Whitehead's."[18] I have been unable to find any documentary evidence that definitely confirms this characterization beyond the professional interactions which I have just laid out; WRP has never found any letters between the two men, only their comments on one another's work. It may well be that in this case, Lowe knew more of Whitehead's relationship with Broad than he ever wrote down before he (Lowe) died.

But a final mention of Broad by Whitehead is worth highlighting here and may be the closest we can get to confirming their friendship. Paul Schilpp had written to Whitehead in 1939 to try to convince him to be his next subject in his newly begun *Library of Living Philosophers* series. Initially Whitehead refused,[19] but in early 1941 he agreed and sent Schilpp a list of possible contributors. Broad is one of the first two men that he mentions—the other being A.E. Taylor—and he cited both as particularly important:

> First, as to my work in England before I came to Harvard, at the age of 63—and my relation to some English philosophers and men of science.
>
> Prof A. E. Taylor of Edinburgh University has taken great interest in my relationship to Platonic thought and to modern religious thought:
>
> Profr C. D. Broad, Trinity College, Cambridge, was very interested in my philosophic work published before I came to Harvard.
>
> I should particularly value contributions, however short, from these two men. I guess that Broad may be somewhat critical of my later work.[20]

Unfortunately, in the end neither man would contribute to Whitehead's LLP volume, due largely to extra duties they had undertaken in the midst of WWII.[21] Nonetheless, Whitehead's strong recommendation of Broad in this letter suggests much about their mutual regard.

WHITEHEAD'S INFLUENCE ON BROAD

Now that we have looked at the occasions on which we know that Whitehead and Broad interacted, what can be said about how they influenced each other's philosophies? I will start with Whitehead's influence on Broad, for the simple reason that, unlike the reverse, Broad was not at all shy about crediting Whitehead in his work, and so tracing influence in this direction is fairly simple.

First, it is perhaps worth noting at the outset that though Broad was younger than Whitehead by twenty-six years, and did not become a Fellow at Trinity until the year after Whitehead's long tenure at Trinity was over, in their philosophical careers they might be considered contemporaries in a certain sense, for of course the focus of Whitehead's early career was mathematics, and he did not start to seriously engage with philosophy until at least 1910, when he was finishing the *Principia* and departing Trinity for London. As already noted, Broad actually preceded Whitehead in membership in the Aristotelian Society by a year. That the two men were entering professional philosophical circles at roughly the same time and place likely contributed to their mutual interest and respect. But there was also the weight of Whitehead's accomplishments in the math and physics worlds in the background of this, something of which Broad was only too aware.

This can be seen as early as Broad's 1918 paper "A General Notation for the Logic of Relations." Broad describes it as an effort to "offer a consistent system of notation which shall be extensible to relations of any degree of polyadicity," while saying that the notation in Whitehead's *Principia Mathematica*

> is highly convenient for dyadic relations, . . . [but] is not readily extensible to triadic, and higher relations . . . I venture to put forward the following sketch in the hope that it may be at least temporarily useful till Dr. Whitehead publishes the fourth volume of *Principia*.[22]

The fourth volume of *Principia* would, of course, ultimately never appear, but it speaks to Broad's deference in this area that he saw his efforts as merely a stopgap measure until Whitehead himself had a real go at it.

I have already noted that Broad reviewed Whitehead's *An Enquiry Concerning the Principles of Natural Knowledge* (*PNK*) in 1920, taking more than thirty pages of detailed handwritten notes in order to write a lengthy sixteen-page review of an "almost wholly expository character," which he intended to be a "first aid to critics."[23] Indeed, the review lauds the book's importance while refraining from any sharp criticism; it is evident that Broad found it very convincing. The only thing that amounts to criticism appeared a year later in Broad's "The External World," when he commented that Whitehead understood the importance of the notion of "place" but "[found] his actual statements on the subject extremely difficult to understand."[24] Yet he went on to argue for Whitehead's understanding of sensa and physical objects over Bertrand Russell's, saying that "I think that some such theory as Whitehead's forms a very promising basis for further advance."[25]

Then came 1923, a crucial year for this discussion, in which Broad published his *Scientific Thought*, reviewed Whitehead's *Principle of Relativity*, and delivered his Tarner lectures, which would subsequently be published in 1925 as *The Mind and Its Place in Nature*. It is the time period in which Broad was most deferential to Whitehead even as he became more critical of him than he had ever been before.

Broad says in the preface to his *Scientific Thought* that he considers Whitehead's principle of extensive abstraction (from *PNK*) to be the "prolegomena to every future Philosophy of Nature" and that "my obligations to [G.E.] Moore, Russell, Whitehead and [G.F.] Stout are continual, and will be perfectly obvious to anyone acquainted with the literature of the subject."[26]

In the first chapter on "the traditional conception of space," Broad notes that

> The method by which such difficulties as these [having to do with the conceptions of points] have been overcome is due to Whitehead, who has lately worked it out in full detail in his *Principles of Natural Knowledge* and his *Concept of Nature*, two epoch-making works.[27]

In the chapter on space-time, Broad takes virtually no credit for his work at all, instead saying that "in the section that follows I am more than usually indebted to Whitehead, and I shall be contented if I provide the reader with 'first aid' to the study of Whitehead's two great works on the philosophy of Nature."[28] He points out that his given definitions of points, straight lines, planes, and timeless space are "wholly due to Whitehead."[29]

All the while, Broad provides at the end of each chapter a list of "works that may be consulted with profit," frequently pointing readers toward both Whitehead's *PNK* and *CN*; for the first chapter on space and extensive abstraction, they are the *only* books that Broad lists. In the final two chapters on space-time and sensa, Broad also lists Whitehead's *Principle of Relativity*, while noting that "this most important work appeared while the present book was in the press."[30]

Broad's review of Whitehead's *Relativity*, in contrast to his wholly complimentary appraisals of *PNK* and *CN*, was somewhat mixed. He acknowledged its great importance while saying that it consists too much of "isolated snippets" lacking "connective tissue"[31] and criticized Whitehead for electing to simply publish his unedited lectures without further fleshing them out, leading to what he saw as occasional incoherence.[32]

In a section in which Broad lays out Whitehead's alternative method of deducing the transformation equations of the special theory of relativity, he notes that Whitehead cites three advantages to it, the third and last of which

Muddle-Headedness versus Simple-Mindedness, Round 2 49

is that "the notion of time-systems has given a clear meaning to the notion of a Newtonian frame of reference, and has solved the old philosophical difficulties about absolute rotation."[33] Broad is quite suspicious of this claim:

> It is greatly to be wished that Whitehead had entered more into detail about this last claim. He has now made it in an incidental paragraph three times over in successive works. If it be true, it is of the utmost importance, and it ought to be discussed in some detail. At present I cannot see that Whitehead has accomplished anything more in this matter than the old doctrine of absolute Space and Time.[34]

Much of the rest of Broad's review is similarly critical. Of Whitehead's argument for the uniformity of space-time, he says that "I must confess that I should be greatly surprised if so concrete a result can be reached from such abstract premises,"[35] not explicitly invoking yet nonetheless echoing his "critical" versus "speculative" philosophy distinction from *Scientific Thought* (a distinction that would become very important for Whitehead; see the next section). He is likewise "not persuaded" by Whitehead's argument that space-time must be homaloidal.[36] He ends the review by again asserting the book's importance while lamenting its difficulty and lack of polish:

> It would be impossible to over-estimate the importance and interest of this book. It shows Whitehead's powers of original thought and detailed mathematical application at their highest. But I am very much afraid that it will not have the influence which it ought to have. From the nature of its subject-matter it cannot be easy, and I cannot but think that it has been made quite needlessly difficult by excessive condensation.[37]

Broad's remarks about Whitehead in *The Mind and Its Place in Nature* make a return to being wholly complimentary, though this is to be expected given the setting and Whitehead's status as the first Tarner lecturer, whom Broad was attempting to follow. Indeed, Broad makes it clear that he is specifically endeavoring to "overlap [Whitehead's lectures] as little as possible," noting that Whitehead's most recent books constituted

> the most important contribution which has been made for many years to the philosophy of mathematical physics, [and that] for me to attempt to cover the same ground again in these lectures would be to expose myself to the most unflattering comparisons.[38]

It is almost as if Broad was waving the white flag of surrender and ceding the mathematics and physics discussions to Whitehead as he moved on to other pursuits. And, indeed, Broad's next books would be on the philosophy of Francis Bacon, followed by two books on ethics.

Beyond all these places in which Broad explicitly acknowledges Whitehead, at least one more deserves a look. In 1924, Broad contributed a chapter to a book titled *Contemporary British Philosophy: Personal Statements*, the idea being that philosophy grows both from the spirit of an age and from the personality of the philosopher. Broad titled his chapter "Critical and Speculative Philosophy," the very distinction which would later enter wider circulation, and which Whitehead himself took up to a certain extent.[39]

Broad's discussion of his two types of philosophy in that chapter largely echoes what he had written a year earlier in *Scientific Thought*. However, it contains some important new qualifications and softening of his previous position. There is too little evidence to conclude that these came directly from Whitehead; any number of people could have influenced Broad to these concessions. But they are remarkably reflective of the criticisms that Whitehead made to his students in his Harvard classroom.

In this chapter, Broad begins the discussion of his distinction thus:

> It seems to me that under the name of "Philosophy" two very different subjects are included. They are pursued by different methods, and can expect to reach quite different degrees of certainty. I am wont to call them *Critical* and *Speculative* Philosophy. I do not assert that either can be wholly separated from the other. The second quite certainly presupposes the first, and it is probable that in the first we tacitly assume some things that belong to the second. But they certainly can be separated to a considerable extent.[40]

This is considerably different than the description that is found in *Scientific Thought* (discussed at length in the next section). In that book, there is no acknowledgment at all that the two cannot be wholly separated, or that critical philosophy in any way presupposes speculative philosophy; in fact, Broad points out in *Scientific Thought* that the time to practice speculative philosophy may have not yet come at all and is wholly premature.[41] Compare Broad's new, qualified account with Whitehead's Harvard lectures, in which he tells his students that the two types "can't be sharply separated"[42] and that one must also start with some "speculative" synoptic vision—a metaphysics—while allowing that one will almost certainly need to adjust one's world view along the way.[43]

Likewise, compare Whitehead's criticism in his Harvard lectures of Broad's jettisoning of religious experience:

> Broad's objection to putting religious and ethical experience with the others. Why not? Who is Broad and who are we to put Experience into these

compartments (really abstractions)? There are surely ideas and relevant factors of situation to be found by cutting across the lines.[44]

with Broad's newly discovered respect for such experience:

> There is one thing which Speculative Philosophy must take into most serious consideration, and that is the religious and mystical experiences of mankind. These form a vast mass of facts which obviously deserve at least as careful attention as the sensations of mankind . . . It seems reasonable to suppose at the outset that the whole mass of mystical and religious experience brings us into contact with an aspect of Reality which is not revealed in ordinary sense perception, and that any system of Speculative Philosophy which ignores it will be extremely one-sided. In fact it cannot safely be ignored.[45]

Again, this is much different than what is found in *Scientific Thought*, where the word "religious" is only used twice, the second, more substantive of which Broad uses to opine that "it is useless to take over masses of uncriticised detail from the sciences and from the ethical and religious experiences of men."[46]

Is it possible that some of this qualifying and back-tracking of Broad's was due to conversation with Whitehead? Again, we cannot know. But Whitehead did have a year together with Broad in England after the publication of *Scientific Thought* and prior to his departure to America during which they attended conferences and Aristotelian Society meetings together, plenty of time to make some of his thoughts known. It is a plausible idea.

BROAD IN WHITEHEAD'S CLASSROOM

First, to give a very broad overview (no pun intended) of the extent to which Whitehead referred to Broad's work over the course of his Harvard tenure, Whitehead discussed Broad most heavily in his first three years at Harvard but continued to assign one or both of Broad's *Scientific Thought* and *The Mind and Its Place in Nature* through at least the spring of 1933, typically the first few chapters of each.

Neither Winthrop Bell nor William Ernest Hocking record reading lists for 1924, but Louise Heath does, showing that Whitehead assigned *Scientific Thought* on the first day of class.[47] Fritz Roethlisberger[48] and Heath[49] confirm the same for fall 1925, and George Conger for spring 1927,[50] and student notes continue to confirm these books as required reading in fall 1927,[51] spring 1928,[52] fall 1928,[53] and fall 1929.[54] A lack of any student notes leaves us unable to know whether Whitehead still assigned Broad's books in the spring of 1930, but based on ensuing patterns, it seems safe to assume that he did. Starting with spring 1931, Whitehead began writing down his assigned reading lists in his grading notebook, revealing that he had stopped assigning Broad for the fall terms but assigned *The Mind and Its Place in Nature* for 1931, 1932, and 1933 spring terms.[55] There is no evidence that Whitehead continued to assign Broad's work for his last four years of teaching at Harvard.

What did Whitehead actually say about Broad to the students in his classroom? Generally speaking, Whitehead most often brought up Broad to disagree with him. Brian G. Henning has already characterized Broad's influence as "an important foil for Whitehead in [the] first year of lectures,"[56] an observation that holds for most of the occasions in which we find Whitehead discussing him.

The first time that Whitehead references Broad directly is in his Harvard lecture of October 11, 1924, his eighth Harvard lecture overall. He starts out the lecture discussing the status of perceptual objects, and eventually gets into "control theory" as an alternative to "class theory," saying that he was under the influence of the latter in *Principles of Natural Knowledge* ("Was in a muddle") but had moved to the former in *The Concept of Nature* and *The Principle of Relativity*.[57] He then says that there is a "very acute discussion of whole subject in Broad's book . . . p. 266–283," which corresponds to two sections of chapter 8 ("Theory of Sensa") in *Scientific Thought* titled "How are Sensa related to Physical Objects?" and "The Critical Scientific Theory."[58] Whitehead contends that Broad is on the side of control theory but oversimplifies the argument and fails to extricate himself from Berkeley:

> Broad himself comes down on side of control theory—but doesn't handle his arguments rightly.—Doesn't quite extricate Self from Berkeley, and whole point of Control Theory is to enable you to do this. Theory of multiple relations would have helped him here to do it better. Real fact is much more complex than Broad allows for.
>
> "Ingression" is Whitehead's term for this complexity of situation. Broad does refer to a multiple relation theory of Dawes Hicks and George Moore—On right lines but have oversimplified things and therefore get into all sorts of difficulties . . . When you try really to see what you're apprehending in moment of stress—the classification of display is not what's interesting you.[59]

It is worth noting that, like Whitehead and Broad, both G. E. Moore and G. Dawes Hicks were Aristotelian Society members, and all four, in fact, would serve terms as president. It suggests once again that Whitehead's time in the Aristotelian Society seems to have been more influential on his thought than is sometimes realized.

Whitehead's second substantive discussion of Broad in his Philosophy 3b lectures[60] is the criticism that he would most often repeat throughout his

Harvard tenure, a distinction of Broad's around which Whitehead appears to have framed his entire metaphysical project: the difference between "critical philosophy" and "speculative philosophy." It is a distinction that Broad draws in the introduction to *Scientific Thought*; in *HL1*, Whitehead cites pages 18–25 in particular,[61] and in *HL2* Conger's notes make it apparent that he read much of pages 18–21 aloud with breaks for commentary.[62]

For Broad, "critical philosophy" is "the analysis and definition of our fundamental concepts, and the clear statement and resolute criticism of our fundamental beliefs . . . [It is] concerned, not with remote conclusions, but with the analysis and appraisement of the original premises."[63] "Speculative philosophy," on the other hand, aims "to take over the results of the various sciences, to add to them the results of the religious and ethical experiences of mankind, and then to reflect upon the whole."[64] Broad sees himself to be chiefly a critical philosopher and emphasizes the virtues of critical philosophy, while largely denigrating speculative philosophy. He says that the latter has produced "elaborate systems which may quite fairly be described as moonshine," that at best it "can only consist of more or less happy guesses, made on a very slender basis," and that it is "peculiarly liable to be biased by his hopes and fears, his likes and dislikes, and his judgments of value."[65] Broad's only real praise for speculative philosophy is that its synoptic vision reminds us of the complexity of the world and teaches us to reject overly neat, simple solutions to philosophical problems.[66]

That Whitehead would be critical of this kind of distinction is no great surprise. As Henning notes, "Whitehead never met a bifurcation he didn't question."[67] Whitehead told his Harvard students that

> Broad's book and others of the kind sometimes fail to elucidate the very points they're considering by refusing to see the real breadth of the problem they're considering . . . We mustn't give up anything because Broad thinks it a bit dangerous.[68]

In Whitehead's view, Broad is being too safe, too afraid of error, and failing to acknowledge the crucial place of speculation in philosophy and, indeed, in science, which is driven by speculative hypotheses. Whitehead passionately defends this idea in a later lecture in the spring term:

> In trying to get Concepts of allied Sciences into harmony, you point the way to a reorganization within each branch of science. You will not get something you Know is true. But you will get "well-grounded" hypothesis; and you've taught yourself to be imaginative without any danger of running wild. The difficulty is to have firmness of mind to discard what won't hold water. Who is Broad to say where you're to stop in that way? Intense distrust of any wide metaphysical view – You've got to mistrust it; but it is one way of getting to truth. To refuse

any of these is to do what Dante called the "great refusal." To think is most dangerous operation—First thing you do is to think wrong. But to think is our business. Refusal is cowardice. Constant Criticism of course is necessary. The way to correct is to speculate more. Constantly speculate and constantly verify.[69]

Broad sees speculative philosophy as presupposing critical philosophy[70]—a statement with which Whitehead agrees[71]—but for Whitehead, the presupposing also goes in the other direction, and the two "types" of philosophy "can't be sharply separated."[72] Nor does Whitehead agree with Broad's cordoning off of religious and ethical experiences from philosophy:

> Broad's objection to putting religious and ethical experience with the others. Why not? Who is Broad and who are we to put Experience into these compartments (really abstractions)? There are surely ideas and relevant factors of situation to be found by cutting across the lines: ∧– by the synoptic view∧. You can't even keep the various sciences apart—chemistry running into physics. You can't keep mentality and physical world apart. Philosophy ought to cut across lines and get new points of view—gets things together in a new way and thus get a new and illuminating abstraction.[73]

It is interesting that Whitehead explicitly says that Broad's two "types" of philosophy "can't be sharply separated," and yet he appears drawn to the word "speculative" and frames the entirety of his *Process and Reality* as "an essay in Speculative Philosophy." Put another way, he rejects the bifurcation even as he cheerfully adopts the terminology.

But Whitehead's enthusiastic defense of speculative philosophy is not even his harshest criticism of Broad—that is reserved for Broad's conception of perceptual objects. Whitehead began his November 20, 1924, lecture by trying to define "basic objects." In doing so, he notes their highly complex character and that objects are not merely in a single location in time and space—what he would later call the "fallacy of simple location." In the midst of this, he notes that Broad's discussion in *Scientific Thought* "[isn't] worth the paper it's written on":

> ∧Relevance of∧ a pure object to Space-Time in any occasion of realization is of a highly complex character. Idea that:—It is "there," isn't really stating facts of the case. It's assuming that there is a meaning of "being there," *simpliciter*. There are senses in which the object is everywhere—only it's everywhere in varying senses. The discussion of the perceptual object in Broad's *Scientific Thought*. Whitehead's own opinion is that it's not worth the paper it's written on—doesn't have regard to Complexity of relation of pure object to Space-Time. When we consider that this is the first thing that ought to strike us. A pure object is "all over the shop."[74]

Similarly, Whitehead also takes issue with Broad's view of the future, which the latter holds is "nothing at all."[75] For Whitehead, in a certain sense the future already exists in the present because entities are incomplete and have an appetition for the future, that is, have final causes, though his vocabulary surrounding these ideas in 1924 had not yet fully developed to the extent that it did in *Process and Reality*. But we get the sense of what Whitehead means when he says in his December 2, 1924, Harvard lecture that "in very being of Q there is the Future (and the Past);—and that's why can talk of fitting on subsequent Experiences—You see the R as the realisation, for own sake, of what was modally and particularly already in Q for Q's sake."[76]

It appears that most of Whitehead's overt discussion and criticism of Broad happened in these first three years that constitute *HL1* and *HL2*. Keyword searches for Broad's name in student notes covering Whitehead's lectures from fall 1927 to spring 1933 reveal nothing beyond Whitehead assigning Broad's books, and discussions of the critical vs. speculative distinction. Though it seems entirely possible that Whitehead continued to discuss certain philosophical topics with Broad in mind while failing to specifically cite him, this fact does seem to paint a picture of Whitehead gradually moving on in his philosophical project, with Broad's voice slowly fading in importance. I believe, too, that it is fair to speculate that a lack of physical vicinity to and interaction with Broad and the rest of his Aristotelian Society friends in England contributed to their decreasing relevance for him.

But there is at least one other mention of Broad worth noting, one far removed from Whitehead's first three years of lectures. In a final exam for the spring 1933 term—the last term in which Whitehead assigned a book of Broad's, so far as we can tell—there is a question on Whitehead's final exam that reads as follows:

> 12. Discuss the following quotation [Broad's *Mind and Its Place in Nature*, Ch. II]: "Every system which is *certainly known* to be at once teleological and mechanistic is an artificial machine; and, if we follow its history far enough backwards, we always come to one or more *organisms*, which are teleological but not *certainly* mechanistic systems."[77]

First, it is important to note that we do not have copies of the majority of Whitehead's exams—WRP has discovered only about half a dozen of these, when (assuming one exam at the end of each semester) there should be at least twenty-six. Thus, we cannot say whether or not Whitehead had similar questions concerning Broad's work during the other semesters in the late 1920s and early 1930s. However, the above exam question, while not overt praise, can certainly be read as praise, for Whitehead was surely in full agreement with this statement. He called his own philosophy a "philosophy of organism," and one in which teleology played a part, with each actual entity holding an appetite for the future. The question shows that Whitehead did not assign and discuss Broad's work *only* to criticize him.

BROAD'S INFLUENCE ON WHITEHEAD

Now we come to Broad's influence on Whitehead, and here, of course, the task is more difficult and more uncertain than the reverse. First, it would be well to begin with the few explicit mentions of Broad that Whitehead made outside of his lectures.

As noted at the beginning of this chapter, in chapter 2 of *The Principle of Relativity* (1922), Whitehead writes that "a route lying entirely in one moment is called a spatial route, and a route which lies entirely in the past and future of each one of its event-particles is called a historical route."[78] A footnote to "historical" says that "I borrow the term 'historical' from Prof. C. D. Broad." This reference is to Broad's article "The External World," wherein he distinguishes between simultaneous and non-simultaneous event-particles as "momentary sections" versus "historical sections":

> If pennies do persist through time there must be non-simultaneous sections of their history and these sections will be parts of their history . . . Let us call such sections *Historical Sections*, and let us call sections consisting entirely of simultaneous event-particles *Momentary Sections* . . . It is obvious however that a momentary section is a limit of a series of historical sections as the time-lapse between the earliest and latest event-particle in the section becomes smaller and smaller.[79]

It is an article in which Broad himself was already explicitly relying heavily on Whitehead's theories of place and space-time, and the cited passage does not seem to have affected Whitehead's thought so much as it simply gave him more apt vocabulary. While this is Whitehead's first use of the term "historical route"—a term that he would continue to use in his later books, including *Process and Reality*—he had already been using the term "route" heavily in *PNK* (1919), and all the same concepts were already there.

> The procedure of the method of extensive abstraction is to formulate the law by which the approximation is achieved and can be indefinitely continued. The complete series is then defined and we have a "route of approximation." These routes of approximation according to the variation of the details of their formation are the points of instantaneous space (here called "event-particles"), linear segments (straight or curved) between event-particles (here called "routes"), the moments of time (each of which is all instantaneous nature), and the volumes incident in moments.[80]

Whitehead also defines a moment in *PNK* as "a route of approximation to all nature which has lost its (essential) temporal extension."[81] So Whitehead had already reached the conclusion that "half a sheep is mutton," that instantaneous moments are abstractions. Broad's term seems to have helped Whitehead clarify his own thought rather than contribute anything genuinely new to it.

The only other time that Whitehead mentions Broad by name in a published essay is in the speech he gave at his seventieth birthday celebration in February of 1931—something which he likely did not actually intend for publication. He is discussing the notion of becoming and perpetual perishing and says, "The world is always becoming, and as it becomes, it passes away and perishes. Now that notion of perishing is covered up as a sort of scandal. Broad even goes so far as to say, in effect, that the past is nothing, simpliciter."[82]

It is not clear what Whitehead is referring to here. Broad had stated quite clearly in his *Scientific Thought* (1923) that the future is nothing, while the past is quite real:

> It will be observed that such a theory as this accepts the reality of the present and the past, but holds that the future is simply nothing at all. Nothing has happened to the present by becoming past except that fresh slices of existence have been added to the total history of the world. The past is thus as real as the present.[83]

Further, in a 1928 symposium on "Time and Change" that appeared in the Aristotelian Society Supplementary volumes, Broad repeats this same argument,[84] and I have been unable to find anything in the intervening years in which he argues differently. Aside from the obvious difference that Whitehead argues strongly for the reality of the future, Broad's summation of his philosophy of time as "slices of existence" being added to the "total history of the world" sounds similar to Whitehead's idea in *Process and Reality* (*PR*) that "the many become one, and are increased by one."[85]

But besides these two brief mentions, there are other places where traces of Broad's influence can be found. The obvious and undeniable one is Whitehead's adoption of the term "speculative philosophy." It is curious that Whitehead fundamentally rejected the notion that Critical and Speculative Philosophy as defined by Broad could ever be fully separated and yet takes up one-half of the faulty bifurcation as expressive of his own philosophical project/approach. Admittedly, he only mentions the "other half" ("critical") in one place in his books—on the second-to-last page of *Modes of Thought* (*MT*), originally a series of lectures delivered shortly after his retirement from Harvard:

> The fallacy of the perfect dictionary divides philosophers into two schools, namely, the "Critical School," which repudiates speculative philosophy, and the "Speculative School" which includes it. The critical school confines itself to verbal analysis within the limits of the dictionary. The speculative school appeals to direct insight, and endeavours to indicate its meanings by further appeal to situations which promote such specific insights. It then enlarges the dictionary. The divergence between the schools is the quarrel between safety and adventure.[86]

There is no doubt at all that this is Broad's formulation all over again. It should be noticed that Whitehead's comments here do not really depart from what he had told his students in his Harvard classroom more than ten years prior when he said that Broad's view embodied "cowardice" and "the great refusal."[87]

But Whitehead's most striking use of Broad's terminology is in the opening pages of his most famous book, *Process and Reality*. Its first part is "The Speculative Scheme," its first chapter is "Speculative Philosophy," and its first two sentences note that "This course of lectures is designed as an essay in Speculative Philosophy. Its first task must be to define 'speculative philosophy,' and to defend it as a method productive of important knowledge." It is rather astonishing to realize that in this sense, the entire book can be seen as a response to Broad's criticism of this type of metaphysics as "more or less happy guesses, made on a very slender basis."[88]

Whitehead, of course, takes pains to argue that this is not true at all and that "speculative philosophy" is a wholly necessary endeavor. The fact that the history of philosophy is "littered with metaphysical systems" does not make speculative philosophy "over-ambitious," for "we no more retain the physics of the seventeenth century than we do the Cartesian philosophy of that century."[89] A system of metaphysics, then, acts as a wholly necessary "working hypothesis," one that philosophers cannot actually abandon even if they pretend to, or deceive themselves into believing they have escaped from, for "to venture upon productive thought without such an explicit theory is to abandon oneself to the doctrines derived from one's grandfather."[90] This again echoes what he had told his students years earlier in a spring 1927 seminary:

> If you don't go into metaphysics, you assume an uncritical metaphysics. Spatial-temporal matter point of view always assumed and expressed in those terms. Every scientific man in order to preserve his reputation has to say he dislikes metaphysics. What he means is he dislikes having his metaphysics criticized.[91]

So, we can be sure that Broad influenced the way that Whitehead framed his later philosophy, broadly speaking. But beyond this framing, are there other things in Whitehead's philosophy that can be pointed to as being certainly influenced by Broad?

The answer, so far as my own investigations have shown, is "probably not." There are number of places in which we might *surmise* that Broad influenced Whitehead, but there will probably never be enough evidence to definitively confirm such influence as coming specifically from Broad, and not some of their shared influences, like Samuel Alexander. Still, it seems that it may be a worthwhile exercise to at least touch on a few of the plausible possibilities.

One other possible terminological influence—though not a very significant one, it seems to me—may have been the pregnant phrase "shadow of truth." Broad ends his chapter on "time and change" in his 1923 *Scientific Thought* by saying that "I can hardly hope that what I have been saying about Time and Change will satisfy most of my readers, or indeed, that it is more than a shadow of the truth, if that." It is a phrase that would never appear in Whitehead's books but that he used with some frequency in his first year of Harvard lectures, and about which George Allan has written a penetrating analysis.[92] On the other hand, the idea embodied in this phrase can be traced back to at least Plato's cave metaphor, and there are other places Whitehead may have heard it, including lectures on Plato by Harvard philosophy department chair James H. Woods, some of whose classes Whitehead appears to have attended during his early years at Harvard.[93]

Another possible influence can be found in one of Broad's Aristotelian Society papers on which we know Whitehead commented at the time of its presentation: his 1919 "Mechanical Explanation and Its Alternatives." Broad's concern in the article is that the term "mechanical explanation"—especially as it was being applied to biology—is ill-defined. In pursuing this goal, Broad begins by "suppos[ing] that it is a necessary condition of a mechanical explanation that the laws employed shall be those of Mechanics, *i.e.*, Newton's three laws of motion or some substitutes for them," and then quickly moves to present these laws by way of Joseph-Louis Lagrange's equations.[94]

Then, in 1925, we find this paragraph in Whitehead's *Science and the Modern World*:

> In this century the notion of the mechanical explanation of all the processes of nature finally hardened into a dogma of science. The notion won through on its merits by reason of an almost miraculous series of triumphs achieved by the mathematical physicists, culminating in the *Méchanique Analytique* of Lagrange, which was published in 1787. Newton's *Principia* was published in 1687, so that exactly one hundred years separates the two great books. This century contains the first period of mathematical physics of the modern type.[95]

Other than a throw-away mention in *The Concept of Nature*,[96] pages 60–62 of *Science and the Modern World* (*SMW*) is the only place where Whitehead discusses Lagrange in his philosophical works.

However, this is again certainly nothing close to conclusive evidence of direct influence. For both men to discuss an extremely famous and influential mathematician as an exemplar of the "mechanical explanation" of nature six years apart should be no surprise to anyone, and the fact that Whitehead's ensuing discussion in *SMW* focuses not only on Lagrange but also Pierre Louis Maupertuis—whom Broad does not mention in his article at all—should amply demonstrate that Whitehead's thoughts here are very much his own.

Then there is the passage from page 87 of *The Mind and Its Place in Nature* which Whitehead later turned into a 1933 exam question.[97] It is from the second chapter of the book, titled "Mechanism and its Alternatives," in which Broad attempts to clarify and adjudicate different species of mechanistic and vitalistic theories of matter and living organisms. Broad shows that he is quite suspicious of mechanist explanations, for the reason that "matter has no natural tendency to arrange itself in the form of *machines* (i.e., of teleological systems whose characteristic behaviour is *mechanistically* explicable)." He favors, instead, what he calls an "emergent vitalism," a term used by both Samuel Alexander and Lloyd Morgan[98] (to whom Whitehead likewise acknowledges an indebtedness) and which he takes to be the position of J.S. Haldane.[99] Broad sums up his opinion thusly:

> It is perfectly consistent for a man to hold that matter has *no* tendency to fall spontaneously into the form of *machines* and that it *has* a natural tendency to fall into the form of *organisms*; provided he holds, as the Emergent Vitalist does, that organisms are not machines but are systems whose characteristic behaviour is emergent and not mechanistically explicable. Thus the real difference is that a possibility is open to the Emergent Vitalist, who recognises two fundamentally different kinds of teleological system, and that this possibility is closed to the Biological Mechanist, who recognises only one kind.[100]

Though Whitehead would, of course, ultimately argue that *all* "actual entities" contain some form of rudimentary awareness in the form of causal efficacy, if nothing else, he would certainly agree with Broad that an organism is a fundamentally different kind of beast than an artificial machine. And, like Broad does here, he took teleology seriously—more seriously, in fact, since he took the appetition of the future to guarantee the future's existence, while Broad continued to maintain that it was "nothing at all."[101]

Yet we are again left with the question of whether Whitehead's philosophy was directly influenced by Broad, or if instead both were influenced together by others. In this example, we have as close to an ideal situation as we are likely to get in trying to ascertain influence, since we know that Whitehead had not only assigned this book to his classes frequently but also cited a passage from this very chapter as an exam question. And yet evidence of influence is hazy at best. On the one hand, Broad's overall argument for the inadequacy of the language of "mechanism" in analyzing organisms echoes Whitehead's sentiments in *HL1* that the most important advances in the sciences in the ensuing decades would be made in biology.[102] But as for his published works, we know that Whitehead acknowledges his indebtedness to Morgan and Alexander in the preface to his *SMW*, but not Broad, and that in it, he rejects vitalism as an "unsatisfactory compromise" while terming his own theory "*organic* mechanism," in which "molecules differ in their intrinsic characters according to the general organic plans of the situations in which they find themselves."[103] This does not really sound much like Broad at all.

So, to conclude, why does Broad feature so prominently in Whitehead's Harvard lectures—and, indeed, uncredited in some of Whitehead's books in the form of the "critical" vs. "speculative" distinction—while only receiving a single mention in *The Principle of Relativity*? There are a number of possible reasons. The first, as already stated, is that Whitehead was simply bad at citing contemporary philosophers in his work. Related to this is that the most crucial element that Whitehead adopted from Broad—the "critical" versus "speculative" distinction and particularly his adoption of "speculative philosophy" to describe his own work—seems to have become fairly common parlance shortly after Broad wrote about it, so that Whitehead may have simply assumed that it needed no attribution.[104] Another factor is that Whitehead was usually not keen to criticize his contemporaries in public—that is, in published writings—even as he was more frank in both delivering and receiving criticism in a classroom setting.[105]

Lastly, though I almost hesitate to say it, it cannot be denied that in *Scientific Thought* in particular, Broad is hugely complimentary of Whitehead's importance. I do not mean to suggest vanity on Whitehead's part, for my sense garnered from years sifting through his personal letters and documents is that vanity was not a large part of his character. Broad wrote as much in his obituary for Whitehead when he said that

> A lesser man than he might easily have been spoiled by the adulation which his later work received and by being treated as a kind of Messiah by many of his more foolish admirers. Nothing of the kind happened. He remained simple, natural, modest, humorous, and intensely human.[106]

It may, in fact, be fairer to conclude that Whitehead regarded Broad's explication of his theories laid out in *PNK* and *Relativity* as in some ways preferable to his own, which Broad, recall, had criticized in his review of

Relativity as "isolated snippets" lacking "connective tissue,"[107] and "needlessly difficult."[108] Recall, too, that Broad even described some of his efforts in *Scientific Thought* as an attempt at "'first aid' [for] the study of Whitehead's two great works on the philosophy of Nature."[109] Broad even said in his obituary for Whitehead: "I cannot pretend to understand much of [*Process and Reality*], and I cannot help thinking that many of its enthusiastic admirers must simply be counted among those who 'wonder with a foolish face of praise.'"[110]

So Broad's usefulness in the classroom was that while Whitehead often thought his theories were wrong, he *expressed himself clearly*. Whitehead was a great believer in the usefulness of clarity, even when—or perhaps even *especially* when—the theory in question was wrong. Whitehead once famously said that he was "muddle-headed" while his former student and collaborator, Bertrand Russell, was "simple-minded."[111] As the title of this chapter suggests, I tend to think of Broad as something of a second coming of Russell for Whitehead, a philosopher who was "simple-minded" and, hence, one with great explanatory power on the path to a more complex and nuanced philosophical truth.

NOTES

1. Broad, *Scientific Thought*, 21.
2. *HL2*, 375.
3. In chapter 2 of *The Principle of Relativity*, Whitehead writes that "A route lying entirely in one moment is called a spatial route, and a route which lies entirely in the past and future of each one of its event-particles is called a historical route" (Alfred North Whitehead, *The Principle of Relativity with applications to Physical Science* (Cambridge: Cambridge University Press, 2011), 30). A footnote to "historical" says that "I borrow the term 'historical' from Prof. C. D. Broad." This is clearly a reference to Broad's article "The External World," wherein he distinguishes between simultaneous and non-simultaneous event particles as "momentary sections" versus "historical sections." More on this later. See C.D. Broad, "The External World," *Mind* 30, no. 120 (October 1921), 385–408.
4. Alfred North Whitehead, "Letter from Alfred North Whitehead to Bertrand Russell, September 20, 1911," Box 5.54, Bertrand Russell Archives, 81682, McMaster University.
5. C. D. Broad, *Perception, Physics, and Reality; an Enquiry into the Information that Physical Science Can Supply About the Real* (Cambridge: Cambridge University Press, 1914).
6. Alfred North Whitehead, "To the Council of Trinity College, October 18, 1916," Bertrand Russell Archives, Rec. Acq. 912, 60904, McMaster University.
7. Alfred North Whitehead et al, "To the Council of Trinity College, January 1917," Bertrand Russell Archives, Rec. Acq. 710, 81732, McMaster University.

8. Aristotelian Society, "Back Matter," *Proceedings of the Aristotelian Society*, New Series 15 (1914–15): 438, 441.

9. The actual minutes did not survive German bombings of London during WWII (Lowe, *Alfred North Whitehead*, vol. 2, 90).

10. C. D. Broad, "Hume's Theory of the Credibility of Miracles," *Proceedings of the Aristotelian Society*, New Series 17 (1916–17): 77–94.

11. John Laird, "Synthesis and Discovery in Knowledge," *Proceedings of the Aristotelian Society*, New Series 19 (1918–19): 46–85.

12. C. D. Broad, "Mechanical Explanation and Its Alternatives," *Proceedings of the Aristotelian Society*, New Series 19 (1918–19): 86–124.

13. A. S. Eddington, W. D. Ross, C. D. Broad, and F. A. Lindemann, "The Philosophical Aspect of the Theory of Relativity: A Symposium," *Mind*, New Series 29, no. 116 (October 1920): 415–445.

14. Aristotelian Society, "Abstract of the Minutes of the Proceedings of the Aristotelian Society for the Forty-Fourth Session," *Proceedings of the Aristotelian Society*, New Series 23, (October 1922–23): 275.

15. J. Loewenberg, C. D. Broad, and C. J. Shebbeare, "Symposium: Critical Realism: Can the Difficulty of Affirming a Nature Independent of Mind Be Overcome by the Distinction between Essence and Existence?" *Proceedings of the Aristotelian Society, Supplementary Volumes* 4 (1924): 86–129.

16. C. D. Broad, review of *An Enquiry Concerning the Principles of Natural Knowledge*, by Alfred North Whitehead, *Mind*, New Series 29, no. 114 (April 1920): 216–231. There are also more than thirty pages of detailed handwritten notes by Broad on *PNK* in the Trinity College Archives, presumably taken in preparation for writing the lengthy fifteen-page review: C. D. Broad, "Whitehead notes: Principles of Natural Knowledge (Philosophical Part)," 1919–20, Papers of C.D. Broad, C1/17, Trinity College Cambridge Archives; C. D. Broad, "Whitehead notes: Principles of Natural Knowledge (Mathematical Part)," 1919–20, Papers of C.D. Broad, C1/18, Trinity College Cambridge Archives.

17. C. D. Broad, review of *The Principle of Relativity, with Applications to Physical Science*, by Alfred North Whitehead, *Mind*, New Series 32, no. 126 (April 1923): 211–219.

18. Lowe, vol. 2, 177.

19. Alfred North Whitehead, "Letter from Alfred North Whitehead to Paul Schilpp, September 12, 1939," Library of Living Philosophers records, Series 3, Box 5, Folder 1, Southern Illinois University, Carbondale.

20. Alfred North Whitehead, "Letter from Alfred North Whitehead to Paul Schilpp, January 29, 1941," Library of Living Philosophers records, Series 3, Box 5, Folder 1, Southern Illinois University, Carbondale.

21. Paul Schilpp, "Letter from Paul Schilpp to Alfred North Whitehead, April 5, 1941," Library of Living Philosophers records, Series 3, Box 5, Folder 1, Southern Illinois University, Carbondale.

22. C. D. Broad, "A General Notation for the Logic of Relations," *Mind*, 27, no. 107 (July 1918): 284.

23. Broad, Review of *PNK*, 216.

24. Broad, "The External World," 404.

25. Broad, "The External World," 405–408. In writing the entry for "Time" in the 1921 *Encyclopedia of Religion and Ethics*, Broad also cites Whitehead's understanding in *PNK* as foundational to understanding time as events: C. D. Broad, "Time," in *Encyclopedia of Religion and Ethics*, ed. James Hastings (Edinburgh: T. & T. Clark, 1921), 343.

26. Broad, *Scientific Thought*, 4–5.

27. Broad, *Scientific Thought*, 38–39.

28. Broad, *Scientific Thought*, 460.

29. Broad, *Scientific Thought*, 465–466.

30. Broad, *Scientific Thought*, 487.

31. A criticism that is softened slightly by his acknowledgment that some of the consequences of Whitehead's theories are "below the limits of our present powers of observation." Broad, Review of *R*, 211.

32. Broad, Review of *R*, 211–212.

33. Broad, Review of *R*, 213.

34. Broad, Review of *R*, 214.

35. Broad, Review of *R*, 215.

36. Broad, Review of *R*, 217.

37. Broad, Review of *R*, 219.

38. C D. Broad, *The Mind and Its Place in Nature* (London: Kegan Paul, Trench, Trubner & Co., 1925), 3.

39. It should be noted here that Broad did not *invent* either term. In fact, there had been a *Journal of Speculative Philosophy* in existence since 1867. And "critical philosophy," of course, can be traced all the way back to Kant. However, Broad appears to have been the philosopher who popularized the juxtaposition.

40. C. D. Broad, "Critical and Speculative Philosophy," in *Contemporary British Philosophy: Personal Statements*, ed. J. H. Muirhead (London: George Allen & Unwin, 1924), 82.

41. Broad, *Scientific Thought*, 20.

42. *HL2*, 190.

43. *HL1*, 248.

44. *HL1*, 81.

45. Broad, "Critical and Speculative Philosophy," 99–100.

46. Broad, *Scientific Thought*, 20.

47. *HL1*, 413.

48. *HL2*, 46.

49. *HL2*, 3.

50. *HL2*, 293.

51. Kerby-Miller, Notes, 7.

52. Sinclair Kerby-Miller, "Notes on Whitehead's Spring 1928 course on Mathematics - Extension," 1928, STU061, Whitehead Research Library, 1.

53. Sinclair Kerby-Miller, "Notes on Whitehead's 1928 Philosophy of Science course in Metaphysics (non-mathematical part)," 1928, STU059, Whitehead Research Library, 3–4.

54. J. Raymond Cope, "Philosophy of Science," 1929–1930, MS Am 2079, Houghton Library, Harvard University, 1. Cope's notes actually do not provide a reading list, but Whitehead discusses Broad and critical vs. speculative philosophy on the first day of class.

55. Alfred North Whitehead, "Whitehead's Grading Notebook," 1924–1937, Papers of Alfred North Whitehead, HUG 4877.10, Harvard University Archives, 115, 141, 173. The notes of W.V.O. Quine also confirm the book assignment for 1931 (W. V. O. Quine, "Whitehead lecture notes: Philosophy and the Sciences," Victor Lowe papers, MS-0284, Series 2, Box 2.9, Folder 52, Special Collections, Johns Hopkins University, P1).

56. Brian G. Henning, "Whitehead in Class: Do the Harvard-Radcliffe Course Notes Change How We Understand Whitehead's Thought?" in *Whitehead at Harvard, 1924–1925*, ed. Brian G. Henning and Joseph Petek (Edinburgh: Edinburgh University Press, 2020), 345.

57. *HL1*, 31–32.

58. *HL1*, 32.

59. *HL1*, 32.

60. Excepting a couple of occasions at which Whitehead assigned Broad's work as a necessary source for assigned student essays. See *HL1*, 36, 69.

61. *HL1*, 79.

62. *HL2*, 189–190.

63. Broad, *Scientific Thought*, 18, 20.

64. Broad, *Scientific Thought*, 20.

65. Broad, *Scientific Thought*, 20–21.

66. Broad, *Scientific Thought*, 22.

67. Henning, "Whitehead in Class," 344.

68. *HL1*, 80–81.

69. *HL1*, 248.

70. Broad, *Scientific Thought*, 20.

71. *HL2*, 189.

72. *HL2*, 190.

73. *HL1*, 81.

74. *HL1*, 102.

75. Broad, *Scientific Thought*, 56.

76. *HL1*, 125.

77. David Loeb Krupsaw, "Philosophy 3 notes and exams," 1932–1933, David Loeb Krupsaw personal archive, HUD 930.46, Folder 10, Box 2, Harvard University Archives, 2. The quotation is from page 87 of *The Mind and Its Place in Nature*.

78. *R*, 30.

79. Broad, "The External World," 400.

80. *PNK*, 76.

81. *PNK*, 112.

82. Alfred North Whitehead, *The Interpretation of Science. Selected Essays*, ed. A. H. Johnson (Indianapolis: Bobbs-Merrill, 1961), 218.

83. Broad, *Scientific Thought*, 56.

84. J. Macmurray, R. B. Braithwaite, and C. D. Broad, "Symposium: Time and Change," *Proceedings of the Aristotelian Society, Supplementary Volumes* 8 (1928): 188.

85. *PR*, 21.

86. Alfred North Whitehead, *Modes of Thought* (New York: Free Press, 1966), 173.

87. *HL1*, 248.

88. Broad, *Scientific Thought*, 21.

89. *PR*, 14.

90. Alfred North Whitehead, *Adventures of Ideas* (New York: The Free Press, 1967), 222.

91. *HL2*, 375.

92. George Allan, "Diagrams and Myths," in *Whitehead at Harvard, 1924–1925*, ed. Brian G. Henning and Joseph Petek (Edinburgh: Edinburgh University Press, 2020), 283–306.

93. See *HL2*, xxix, and Petek, "Whitehead and James Haughton Woods."

94. Broad, "Mechanical Explanation and Its Alternatives," 89–90.

95. *SMW*, 60.

96. Alfred North Whitehead, *The Concept of Nature* (Cambridge: Cambridge University Press, 2000), 140.

97. Krupsaw, "Philosophy 3 notes and exams," 2.

98. Broad, *The Mind and Its Place in Nature*, 58

99. Broad, *The Mind and Its Place in Nature*, 69.

100. Broad, *The Mind and Its Place in Nature*, 92–93.

101. Broad, *Scientific Thought*, 66.

102. *HL1*, 12.

103. *SMW*, 79–80.

104. See, for instance, R. E. Stedman, "A Defence of Speculative Philosophy," *Proceedings of the Aristotelian Society*, New Series 38 (1937–38): 113–142.

105. See, for instance, the diary entry of George Conger in *HL2*, 435–437.

106. Broad, "Alfred North Whitehead," 145.

107. Broad, Review of *R*, 211.

108. Broad, Review of *R*, 219. Broad would go even further in this criticism in the obituary he wrote for Whitehead, saying the fact that he seemed little-read "was largely [the fault] of Whitehead himself. He was an abominably obscure and careless writer, and this fault certainly grew on him as he became older. It is the more deplorable, since he certainly possessed at one time the power to write clearly" (Broad, "Alfred North Whitehead," 144).

109. Broad, *Scientific Thought*, 460.

110. C. D. Broad, "Alfred North Whitehead (1861–1947)," *Mind* 57, no. 2 (April 1948): 144.

111. For the origin of this, see George Lucas, "'Muddleheadedness' vs. 'simplemindedness'—comparisons of Whitehead and Russell," *Process Studies* 17, no. 1 (Spring 1988): 26–39.

Chapter 4

Conciliating Privacy and Socialism

> *As for finding a ground for an ethic, Whitehead confessed his inability to think the complexity of the situation through ... The key to an ethic, he said, is perhaps so simple that we fail to find it for its simplicity.*
>
> —Notes from John Goheen on a talk
> with Whitehead on November 7, 1933[1]

For all that Whitehead criticized C. D. Broad for a lack of adventurousness, he himself tended toward caution when expressing his thoughts in areas in which he considered his position to be less than fully comprehensive. In fact, in a letter to Bertrand Russell in 1895, after wondering at the propriety of the term "absolute," and musing that such propriety seemed to hang on whether one considered science to be explanatory or merely descriptive, he noted that "this further question lands us in the ocean of metaphysic, onto which my profound ignorance of that science forbids me to enter."[2] A little more than thirty years later, he would deliver his Gifford lectures that would be published as *Process and Reality*, one of the most important books on metaphysics of the twentieth century.

Perhaps if Whitehead had lived another decade, he might finally have felt comfortable about pontificating at length on ethics, as he eventually did about metaphysics. As it stands, he seldom addressed ethics at all in his published works, and when he did, it was in passing, never the main subject of what he was getting at. In November 1933, he even confessed to one of his teaching assistants that he felt unable to find the ground for an ethic.[3]

The object of this chapter is chiefly to examine a previously unseen typescript of Whitehead's remarks during a seminar on social ethics, delivered on October 18, 1926, his third fall semester at Harvard, and see how it affects our understanding of Whitehead's ethics. This centerpiece will be supplemented with a few other brief discussions of ethics in lecture notes, and a comparison to some of Whitehead's remarks on ethics in his published works. The upshot is that Whitehead's presentation in Cabot's class devotes more time to metaphysics than it does to ethics in a way that seems to show his uncertainty, and he comes to only fairly preliminary ethical conclusions.

I will begin by looking at Whitehead's discussions of ethics prior to Cabot's seminar.

EARLIEST DISCUSSIONS OF ETHICS

As has already been mentioned in the previous chapter, Whitehead was a relative latecomer to philosophy—having spent the first quarter-century of his academic career on mathematics, logic, and physics—and the first decade of his philosophical efforts followed these same general lines, that is, philosophy of science. Early on, he seems to have been both a little intimidated at the idea of making any ethical assertions and unconvinced that philosophy had much to do with it. In discussing a liberal education in his 1917 *Organisation of Thought (OT)*, he wrote that "one is reminded of the calculation in a dialogue of Lucian that, before a man could be justified in practising any one of the current ethical systems, he should have spent a hundred and fifty years in examining their credentials."[4] Five years later, in *The Principle of Relativity*, he asserted that philosophy "has nothing to do with ethics or theology or the theory of aesthetics. It is solely engaged in determining the most general conceptions which apply to things observed by the senses."[5] Clearly, it was not a topic with which he wished to engage at that time.

But after his arrival at Harvard, Whitehead's reticence toward making ethical statements—or statements with ethical implications—began to thaw a little. In his Lowell lectures of early 1925, he made a few statements that would help to set the tone of remarks to come. The first is this paragraph:

> It is this realised extension of eternal relatedness beyond the mutual relatedness of the actual occasions, which prehends into each occasion the full sweep of eternal relatedness. I term this abrupt realisation the "graded envisagement" which each occasion prehends into its synthesis. This graded envisagement is how the actual includes what (in one sense) is not-being as a positive factor in its own achievement. It is the source of error, of truth, of art, of ethics, and of religion. By it, fact is confronted with alternatives.[6]

That Whitehead himself considered this formulation important can be seen in the fact that he subsequently quoted it verbatim in his Gifford lectures three years later, speaking of it in connection with the idea of God as a "lure for feeling."[7] This "synthesis" or "graded envisagement" served as Whitehead's technical, metaphysical explanation for the phenomenon of freedom: that each entity reacts to the whole of the universe in which it finds itself in its own way, creating "alternatives." For Whitehead, this metaphysical freedom serves as a precondition for ethics, since a total determinism would mean that ethics could never get off the ground.

To this idea of graded envisagement, he added a statement about evil:

> The two evils are: one, the ignoration of the true relation of each organism to its environment; and the other, the habit of ignoring the intrinsic worth of the environment which must be allowed its weight in any consideration of final ends.[8]

We can say, then, that for Whitehead an occasion's graded envisagement should take proper account of the true relations of other organisms to one another and recognize their intrinsic value in considering its own final ends; evil consists in ignoring the true nature of relations and discounting the worth of the environment. This is not much to go on, but it is a start, an assertion of not only the metaphysical primacy of relations but also the importance of social solidarity.

His discussion of ethics—and evil—would become more explicit during his second year at Harvard and come to involve God for the first time. First, he made some remarks about the "antagonism between art and ethics"[9] which appear to be the basis of material that would later appear in his Lowell lectures the following spring (*Religion in the Making*).

> Aesthetic considerations are more fundamental than those of ethics in their philosophical implications. Because art has to do with immediate value as an end in itself, i.e. as isolatable unity (the superject from the immediate prehension), but ethics has to do with the comparison of occasions, whereby the status of occasions ⟨?⟩ ∨among∨ realized values may or may not lead to endurance. i.e. ⟨ethics⟩ is concerned with survival power and progress. Art, with immediate value of achievement for its own sake. Thus ethics presupposes art, and art requires an ethics derivative from itself. Thus ethics should not be made fundamental in metaphysics.[10]

This paragraph amounts to Whitehead's first formulation of a principle that he would state more pithily eight years later in *Adventures of Ideas*: "The teleology of the Universe is directed to the production of Beauty."[11] Beauty, as Whitehead says, is a good in itself, while ethics is concerned with some future achievement, or lack thereof. This primacy of aesthetics over ethics is, of course, a familiar idea for Whiteheadians.

To this, he again added a short mention of evil: "Ethically evil is always by comparison with something else. (1. lack of survival power 2. diminish another('s) survival power 3. hindering progress)."[12] This formulation is in one sense only half-complete. It states that evil is only evil relative to some other outcome, but does not positively state that evils, to some degree, are also goods in themselves, something which he would clarify in his Lowell lectures months later.

Most intriguing of all, Hartshorne recorded the following in his notes for Whitehead's October 20, 1925, lecture: "Art vs. ethics. Art for the immediate good. Ethics looks beyond given. Solution in concept of God."[13] Incredibly, Whitehead neglects to explain this statement about God at all, but apparently just teased his students with it.[14] Perhaps Whitehead was still formulating this solution and did not yet feel prepared to share it with his students, but it would prefigure his discussion of "God and the moral order" in *Religion in the Making*.

The parallels between these Harvard lectures and his February Lowell lectures are quite remarkable. The main differences are that Whitehead drops all references to "art" in favor of the words "aesthetic(s)" and "value," his formulation of evil becomes more nuanced, and he introduces God as the element of consistency and completion in the world.

To start, just as he had told his students four months earlier that aesthetic considerations are more fundamental than ethical ones, he writes that

> The metaphysical doctrine, here expounded, finds the foundations of the world in the aesthetic experience, rather than as with Kant in the cognitive and conceptive experience. All order is therefore aesthetic order, and the moral order is merely certain aspects of aesthetic order.[15]

Likewise, his statements about evil are more voluminous and more developed than those recorded by his Harvard students, but nonetheless follow from the seed of his earlier statement:

> The common character of all evil is that its realization in fact involves that there is some concurrent realization of a purpose towards elimination. The purpose is to secure the avoidance of evil. The fact of the instability of evil is the moral order in the world.
>
> Evil, triumphant in its enjoyment, is so far good in itself; but beyond itself it is evil in its character of a destructive agent among things greater than itself. In the summation of the more complete fact it has secured a descent towards nothingness, in contrast to the creativeness of what can without qualification be termed good. Evil is positive and destructive; what is good is positive and creative.
>
> This instability of evil does not necessarily lead to progress. On the contrary, the evil in itself leads to the world losing forms of attainment in which that evil manifests itself.[16]

In this passage, Whitehead has teased out the further implications of his earlier statements. Evil remains a good in itself so far as it is an enjoyment and is only evil relative to some other outcome. He no longer talks of "diminishing survival power," true, but does say that it is "destructive" and "a descent towards nothingness," which would seem to amount to the same thing. He mentions the hindering of progress in both formulations. Additionally, he identifies all evil, in being destructive, as *aiming to eliminate some other evil*, a circular notion that makes it inherently unstable and therefore leads to a moral order.[17]

He also, of course, introduces God into the equation, the "solution" to "art vs. ethics" which he had teased to his students. He had not yet formulated the language of God being a "lure for feeling," and yet most of the rest of Whitehead's concept of God as found in *Process and Reality* can be found in his second series of Lowell lectures. God is "the measure of the aesthetic consistency of the world,"[18] whose purpose is "the attainment of value in the temporal world,"[19] an actual entity of "unchanged consistency of character . . . [a] definite determination which imposes ordered balance on the world."[20] God is the "solution" to the "problem" of art as the immediate good versus ethics as looking beyond, in the sense that God's immanence grounds aesthetic order[21] while God's internal consistency promotes a maximum of creative order in preference to the inherently unstable destructiveness of evil.

This was the state of Whitehead's ethics heading into the fall 1926 term—ethics grounded in a metaphysical understanding of the primacy of aesthetics, an understanding of evil as fundamentally good, yet destructive, all tied together through the newly important concept of God as the measure of determinate order amid creativity. Given all of this, his subsequent lecture in Richard Clark Cabot's social ethics seminar is as interesting for what it omits as for what it contains.

CONTEXT FOR THE SEMINAR AND THE PECULIAR NATURE OF THE ACCOUNT

The document which records Whitehead's lecture in Cabot's seminar on October 18, 1926, is unique among all his writings and among all the recorded notes of his lectures not only in its content—it is the only document in which he is focused solely on the topic of ethics—but also in its form. It is not his own manuscript, such as we have for his "First Lecture," but neither is it student notes—taken by some student, colleague, or assistant who was seeking to capture the high points for their own purposes. It is, instead, an actual *transcript* of his words by a professional stenographer, along with the conversation that followed. Aside from a few errors and missed words, it is an almost exact account of what Whitehead actually said. In some ways, such an account might be regarded as actually preferable to Whitehead's own manuscript, because it gives us his actual words on the day and allows us to look in on the ensuing conversation, rather than leaving us stuck with a document that Whitehead may or may not have adjusted in the delivery (as he did for his first Harvard lecture).[22]

But how exactly did this come about? How is it that Whitehead's words in Cabot's class were recorded this way, when such a thing apparently was not done anywhere else? The answer comes back to Cabot himself and the unusual nature of the class he was teaching—or, more accurately, the class that he was *presiding over*.

Cabot had earned his MD from Harvard Medical School in 1892 and spent the first half of his career working in the outpatient department of Massachusetts General Hospital. Socially conscious and independently wealthy, he established the first hospital social services department in 1905, and when the hospital refused to pay for it, he himself paid the salaries of all its staff for twelve years.[23] While still at Massachusetts General Hospital, he began teaching philosophy and clinical medicine at Harvard in 1902. Then, in 1919 he took up the chair of Harvard's "Social Ethics" department,[24] which had been established in 1905 and housed on the second floor of the newly constructed Emerson Hall—the first floor of which housed (and continues to house) the philosophy department.

Fast-forward to fall 1926, Cabot was presiding over a seminar which he titled "Fundamentals Underlying the Social Sciences." It was unusual in that it was quite explicitly not designed to instruct the students who signed up for it; Cabot referred to students as being "the small end of [the] course."[25] Rather, the course was designed for professors from Harvard's various departments to come together and think collaboratively about what constituted the fundamentals of the social sciences. He said in his opening lecture for the class that

> My aspiration is to knock down some of the interdepartmental lines of Harvard or to weaken at any rate the defences and dykes that keep departments apart. I feel strongly that one of our greatest evils here is the lack of any synthesis. Each department teaches the best it knows, but with no considerable awareness of what the others are doing. I cannot help thinking, when I visited some of the courses last spring, how good it would be for other departments to be hearing that teaching.[26]

It should be no surprise at all that Whitehead was one of the professors who found himself giving a presentation in Cabot's class. Beyond the fact that both men had worked in the same building for two years,[27] Cabot's project would no doubt have been of interest to Whitehead, who had long expressed a sentiment similar to Cabot's in his writings on education—that the various school departments were too sharply separated and that a lack of co-mingling hurt their impact and effectiveness.[28]

The special nature of the class and Cabot's wealth together help to explain why there are exact transcriptions of the conversations that took place in it. It was a class in which a goodly number of "Great Men" of Harvard were parading through and contributing their own esteemed opinions to the conversation, and it is clear that Cabot thought that having an accurate record of what was said was going to be important. To that end, he must have hired a stenographer to record the proceedings; this is the only hypothesis that fits the situation, as there appears to be no other way that there could be such extensive records of these conversations.

WHITEHEAD'S LECTURE ON SOCIAL ETHICS

Before getting into the meat of Whitehead's presentation, it should be noted that he begins by denigrating his qualifications and speaking somewhat off-topic, then ends his presentation with a dodge.

His first words are a disclaimer that he regards it as "impertinent" to believe that he could contribute anything at all to social ethics or social science as a specialized department of thought, which requires "expert formation by years of quiet prosecution of that study" and that he had "not the slightest belief that I am qualified" in that sense.[29] He then proceeds into what might fairly be described as a lengthy account of the nature of philosophy itself having little to do with social ethics before returning (to a degree) to the actual questions at hand.

At the end, after Whitehead had finished presenting and Cabot himself had asked a few questions, Cabot asked him, "Do you care to take the questions suggested for discussion?"[30] He was referring to six questions[31] which appeared at the top of the course syllabus,[32] questions which each presenter was supposed to answer so that the responses from representatives of the various Harvard departments could be more easily synthesized into a more comprehensive view. Whitehead answered Cabot that "To tell you the truth, I should think it rather impertinent to answer those. They are just the questions I should ask you rather than to state myself."[33]

If I were Cabot, I would have been a little annoyed. In his humble and self-deprecating way, Whitehead had declined to follow the format that Cabot had laid out, avoiding questions that he apparently felt himself unqualified to answer and filling a large portion of his presentation with philosophical background of somewhat dubious applicability. As we know from his remarks to John Goheen seven years later (see the opening quotation),

Whitehead would remain reticent about making ethical assertions for years to come.

Still, at the very least, following his disclaimer Whitehead does state clearly the two basic points he wishes to develop about social ethics, before diving into the philosophical questions underlying them:

(1) I think that Social Ethics is founded on two great doctrines, one the doctrine of original sin and the other the correlative doctrine of original virtue, both in the theological sense.
(2) Then there is another two aphorisms, both of which I think are partly true and both of them partly false, and they are antagonistic aphorisms in a way, yet they have to be conciliated: one is the commandment "Thou shalt not steal," which is the great proclamation of individualism, and the other is the statement that "property is robbery." And I think they are equally true and equally false and that the conciliation between them is where law and the lawyers and social ethics and social sciences meet.[34]

As we will see, Whitehead does not really distinguish between original sin and original virtue, regarding them both as different sides of expressing the individual value of each actual entity, a value which is "infectious throughout the universe."[35] Meanwhile, the conciliation of the two statements he cites will serve as his formulation of the key *question* of ethics, a question which he never really resolves, either here or elsewhere.

But before really discussing these matters, Whitehead goes off on a long explanation of the scope and purpose of philosophy—somewhat understandable in the sense that he was presenting to a mixed group of professors and students who would not all have had philosophical training. Most of this need not be repeated, for it will be almost wholly familiar to Whitehead scholars. Some of it sounds like the "critical philosophy" championed by C. D. Broad, with Whitehead saying that philosophy is "a critic of the notions of any one science, by pointing out where its special ideas fail to fit into what seems to be the best generalization."[36] But it is still speculative, again in Broad's sense, by acting "not only [as] . . . a critic, but an aid to the imagination . . . what we may term the ⟨poetry⟩ of thought."[37] And some of Whitehead's words here sound like they could have been ripped straight out of *Process and Reality*, such as when he talks of "adequacy": "namely, are there whole regions of immediate experience which escape from any exemplification, whatever of our philosophic scheme?"[38]

After slogging through all of these preliminaries,[39] and asserting that the individual sciences are habitually overstating the scope of applicability of their method,[40] Whitehead turns to one of his favorite philosophical scapegoats, Descartes, who he says is "short and clear and definite and has the supreme merit that where he is wrong, he is clearly wrong."[41] Predictably, he cites Principle 51 from Descartes's *Principles of Philosophy*—which says that a substance is a "thing which requires nothing but itself in order to exist"—and asserts that this understanding is "absolutely fatal to any adequate understanding of the world."[42] With this understood, Whitehead finally returns to his two opening theses.

His first point in this regard is that Descartes's formulation is overly individualistic, an individualism that is also exemplified in "Protestant civilization and in the Ten Commandments."[43] He believes that this view is fatal to what he calls "original sin" and "original virtue," which are the "foundation stones" of ethics:

> The world derives from you an original sin and an original virtue, because whatever you are infects the world. Now that is exactly what is denied by Descartes, because he says each real agency requires nothing but itself in order to exist.[44]

This is, of course, wholly consistent with Whitehead's earlier metaphysical and ethical statements, though he uses different language and comes at the problem with a slightly different emphasis and direction. He had said in *Science and the Modern World* that the "graded envisagement" was "the source ... of ethics,"[45] starting from the assumption of a deterministic relatedness and asserting the graded envisagement as an expression of individual freedom and choice. Here he not only uses the religious language of sin and virtue but also comes at the problem from the opposite direction, beginning with Descartes's over-emphasis on individuality and asserting a constitutive relatedness by which each entity "infects" all the other entities in the world.

His return to his second thesis enlarges and clarifies this point and might be regarded as the key paragraph in the whole lecture:

> I look on as [*sic*] social ethics as a conciliation of the two diverse expressions by the statement "Thou shalt not steal," which is the assertion of a measured privacy, and "property is robbery," which is an assertion of the complete socialism. And both law and social ethics are engaged in conciliating these opposed statements. They are considering what principles there can be which should regulate society, in which there can be a fulfilment of private ends which do not constitute robbery. How you can have private ends in a society without robbery is really, I hold, the topic of social ethics.[46]

It is with this paragraph that Whitehead neatly defines the "topic" or "question" of social ethics, but he comes nowhere close to answering it. In fairness to Whitehead, the way that he formulated his metaphysics did not really allow for an answer, for both privacy/freedom and socialism/relatedness are wholly foundational opposing elements, with reality perhaps best described as unfolding in the interplay between them. There can be no final conciliation between these two principles, because the process of this conciliation is *life*, which is ongoing and never finished—or only "finished" in the sense of perpetual perishing.

It bears mentioning that this paragraph also holds a striking resemblance to one of the more oft-quoted passages from *Process and Reality* which has long been considered a key piece of Whitehead's ethics: "Whether or no it be for the general good, life is robbery. It is at this point that with life morals become acute. The robber requires justification."[47] Both passages talk of "robbery," which is a word that Whitehead never uses in any other place in his published writings. Sure, the robbery has become of "life" rather than "property," but this merely reflects a widening of the self-same principle of "ownership/privacy" from "external" property/goods to sustenance necessary for life. And both passages end by posing an antithesis without attempting to answer it—the robber's justification is the topic of social ethics.

After following this by expounding upon some surrounding metaphysical points with which Whitehead scholars will already be familiar—for instance, contra Descartes, that an entity for Whitehead requires *all other entities* in order to exist, it is an end in itself, it is a process terminating in itself as the result, and looks to ends beyond itself[48]—he asserts that the

> right to existence is the ultimate right that there can be, the ultimate foundation of all rights . . . [which] can be further held as the foundation of morals. So that there may be a mutual aid, a mutual intensification throughout the universe as equivalent to the intensity of attainment in the individual parts that it leads thereby.[49]

This "mutual aid" and "mutual intensification" expresses the point that Whitehead had made in *Religion in the Making* when he said that "good" was "positive and creative," while evil is "positive and destructive."[50] Mutual aid and intensification might thus be described as Whitehead's ultimate positively stated moral imperative or principle: to live and work harmoniously in one's environment in considering one's final ends.[51] And as for evil, Whitehead's answer to Cabot's first question (on his further thoughts about original sin) exactly reflects what he had written in *Religion in the Making*.[52]

But for all the resemblance that Whitehead's presentation bears to his recently delivered Lowell lectures, there is one very noticeable difference: he does not bring in God as an explanatory principle at all. In fact, his only mentions of God are derogatory, saying that sixteenth- and seventeenth-century philosophers had conformed philosophical methods to physics, and in doing so caused morals to be "imposed on an alien universe by the crude device of the will of God."⁵³ What a difference from *Religion in the Making*, in which God had become the "solution" to the questions of value, teleology, good, and evil, a being who provided to all entities a determinate order while promoting creative freedom!

We might theorize that Whitehead was reticent to promote God as a key concept in this discussion because of the setting—professors from various other departments in the university were taking part, many of whom likely regarded the idea of God as a central explanatory principle to be distinctly out of fashion. Even if Whitehead did not regard the promotion of God among such men as possibly a little embarrassing, he may have thought it would have simply been too complex or too distracting a notion for a short presentation.

But perhaps Whitehead had genuinely started to move away from God as an explanatory principle in his metaphysics? After all, his Barbour-Page lectures of the following spring term (which would become *Symbolism*) also make no mention of God at all.

Then again, Whitehead uses the religious language of "original sin" and "original virtue" in his presentation to Cabot's class. and, moreover, he would end up doubling down on God's importance a few years later when he delivered his Gifford lectures which would become *Process and Reality*.

I might say that we must remain ultimately unable to distinguish the reason behind Whitehead's exclusion of God from this presentation in Cabot's seminar, were it not for material that appears in his Philosophy 3b lectures immediately following it. For one, he mentions God as early as five days later, in his lecture of October 23.⁵⁴ But the real key is that in his lectures of October 26 and 28, he specifically contrasts his own idea of God with that of Descartes:

> Descartes: All substances require concurrence of God in order to exist.
> Whitehead: ought to have gone further—that proposition is not peculiar to God because all require each other in order to exist. If don't require each other, your idea of causality. theory of knowledge all going west.⁵⁵

We can go even further. In his lecture of October 30, it is very apparent that Whitehead is in fact repeating much of the same material that he had presented in Cabot's seminar twelve days earlier.⁵⁶ This time, however, God plays a part:

> For Descartes, God, in addition to being the only substance which has absolute independence, is only substance which is self-creative—only process for which process of creation is also the creature. But in Whitehead, this is general characteristic of all actual entities. On one hand, deny God has absolute substantial independence. On other, raise all entities to level of being self-creative. They are their own originations. Every self which is beyond them is

in itself a character of the specific creative act [in them?]. Insofar as any actual entities are creatures (result of process of activity), God ought to be called creature.[57]

This paragraph actually represents a *development* from *Religion in the Making*, in which Whitehead had never explicitly identified God as a creature; in his published writings, this point would not be made until *Process and Reality*, three years later.

So, to return to the question of why God disappears for Whitehead in Cabot's class. While his precise motive still cannot be identified, we can say definitively, thanks to the text of the Harvard lectures, that God had never truly left Whitehead's thought after *Religion in the Making*. Indeed, he was still developing it in his classroom into the form in which it appears in *Process and Reality*.

In summation, Whitehead's presentation in Cabot's seminar can be characterized as displaying his ambivalence toward moral and ethical questions. It appears to be his first stark formulation of the "topic of social ethics" as the never-ending interplay between privacy/freedom and socialism/relatedness, competing dyads which for Whitehead have a certain degree of insolubility and (in some cases) irrelevance—at least on the most fundamental, metaphysical level. For instance, he would later comment in *Process and Reality* that God and love were "a little oblivious as to morals"[58] and in *Modes of Thought* that "our enjoyment in the theatre was irrelevant to moral considerations applied to the performance . . . [W]hile they are singing their parts and dancing on the stage, morals vanish and beauty remains."[59] It is not that Whitehead did not believe in morality, or law, or ethics, but rather that for him ethics continued to be a subservient consideration to aesthetics, a secondary concern to the deeper, more fundamental philosophical questions to which he continued to devote himself.

NOTES

1. John D. Goheen, "Essays on Whitehead, 1933–35," John D. Goheen Papers, SC0267, Additional Papers, ARCH-1994-080, Subseries 3, Box 10, Folder 15, Yale University Archives, 4. Reprinted with permission.

2. Alfred North Whitehead, "Letter from Alfred North Whitehead to Bertrand Russell, 13 February 1895," Box 5.53, Bertrand Russell Archives, 81426, McMaster University, 4.

3. Goheen, "Essays on Whitehead."

4. Alfred North Whitehead, *The Organisation of Thought, Educational and Scientific* (London: Williams & Norgate, 1917), 35.

5. *R*, 4.

6. *SMW*, 176–177.
7. *PR*, 189.
8. *SMW*, 196.
9. *HL2*, 15, 62.
10. *HL2*, 15–16.
11. *AI*, 265.
12. *HL2*, 63. This is from Roethlisberger's notes, but Hartshorne has a fourth example which Roethlisberger missed: "it might have (freely) made itself better."
13. *HL2*, 60.
14. It is also possible that the two Harvard students taking notes during this session—Charles Hartshorne and Fritz Roethlisberger—simply neglected to record Whitehead's "solution." But as it presumably would have been of some interest, particularly to Hartshorne, this seems rather unlikely.
15. *RM*, 104–105.
16. *RM*, 95–96.
17. *RM*, 95.
18. *RM*, 99.
19. *RM*, 100.
20. *RM*, 94.
21. *RM*, 105.
22. See Bogaard, "Examining Whitehead's 'First Lecture.'" Bogaard's analysis shows that Whitehead was probably running low on time and cut some portions of from his manuscript in the delivery, while also adding other material.
23. *HL2*, lviii.
24. The "Social Ethics" department was an interdisciplinary department that straddled a line between philosophy, economics, and "Christian morals." In 1921, the Harvard Alumni Bulletin published an article by Cabot about the history of the department following the death of its primary benefactor, Alfred T. White. An unattributed preface to the article examined its ambiguity:

"The Department suffers from its ambiguity. It has grown up in close relations with Philosophy, and is at present a member of the same division, and a fellow-tenant of Emerson Hall. Furthermore, Social Ethics sounds like 'ethics,' and it is well known that ethics is a branch of philosophy. On the other hand, Social Ethics sounds almost equally like sociology; and that, according to our Harvard plan of organization, is a branch or dependency of Economics. Furthermore, when we come to examine the details of the Social Ethics courses we find that they deal with poverty, immigration, labor, and the like; and these topics appear also in the courses on Economics. There is even a third affinity that confuses the identity of Social Ethics. It is edifying and improving, and in that respect like Divinity. When Professor Peabody headed the Department of Social Ethics he was at the same time 'Plummer Professor of Christian Morals' and preached (as happily he still does) in Appleton Chapel.

What, then, would be left of Social Ethics if its definitions of moral standards were assigned to Philosophy, its descriptions of social facts to Economics, and its devotional spirit to the Divinity School? Nothing—that is, nothing except just that peculiar thing which you get when the three are *combined*. But the more one thinks of it the more clear one becomes that they are well worth combining" (Harvard Alumni Bulletin Staff, "Social Ethics," *Harvard Alumni Bulletin* 23, no. 30 (May 5, 1921): 688).

25. Richard Clarke Cabot, "The Fundamentals of Social Science, 1926–1927," First meeting, Papers of Richard Clarke Cabot, HUG 4255, Box 90, Harvard University Archives, 2.

26. Cabot, "The Fundamentals of Social Science," First meeting, 2.

27. We know from one of Whitehead's letters to his son, North, that he and Evelyn became friends with the Cabots during his first fall term at Harvard in 1924. The letter provides an entertaining look at Whitehead's views about Cabot's attitude toward his wealth: "[Agnes Hocking] told Richard Cabot—an overconscientious New Englander who has an important engagement for every half-hour of the day—to call for Mummy at 3:15 and take her to a school entertainment about a mile off. Accordingly Cabot turned up . . . that Mrs Hocking should have thought it possible to tell an immensely busy man of some importance to fetch Mummy in his car, and that he should of course have complied at great inconvenience, is just like them. Of course no one, not a millionaire, keeps a chauffeur. Cabot is a millionaire, via his wife, but is much too conscientious to spend money in that way. The idea of New Englanders flaunting wealth is quite wrong. They are much more likely to be living on half their incomes, and either investing the rest or giving it away—about equal chances which." Alfred North Whitehead, "Letter from Alfred North Whitehead to T. North Whitehead, December 21, 1924," Alfred North Whitehead Collection, MS-0282, Box 2, Folder 17, Special Collections, Johns Hopkins University.

28. For example, his 1916 address "Aims of Education" cautioned against teaching "too many subjects," saying that "The result of teaching small parts of a large number of subjects is the passive reception of disconnected ideas, not illumined with any spark of vitality" (193). Later on, he is even more emphatic: "The solution which I am urging, is to eradicate the fatal disconnection of subjects which kills the vitality of our modern curriculum. There is only one subject-matter for education, and that is Life in all its manifestations. Instead of this single unity, we offer children—Algebra, from which nothing follows; Geometry, from which nothing follows; Science, from which nothing follows; History, from which nothing follows; a Couple of Languages, never mastered; and lastly, most dreary of all, Literature, represented by plays of Shakespeare, with philological notes and short analyses of plot and character to be in substance committed to memory" (Alfred North Whitehead, "The Aims of Education—A Plea for Reform," *Mathematical Gazette* 8, no. 121 (January 1916): 196–197).

29. *HL2*, 391.

30. *HL2*, 402.

31. (a) What are the fundamentals of the social sciences, in your view and from the standpoint of the body of knowledge which you represent?

(b) Define: power, authority, responsibility, loyalty, equality, freedom, representation, conflict.

(c) What is the central word around which your views arrange themselves?

(d) In view of your theory, how do you deal with the problem of evil?

(e) From the point of view of your philosophy of the social sciences, what should be the reconstruction of Harvard University and the education it offers [or some other educational experiment]?

(f) What change should be made in our criminal law and in our treatment of offenders?

32. Cabot, "The Fundamentals of Social Science," Syllabus, 1.
33. *HL2*, 402.
34. *HL2*, 392.
35. *HL2*, 398–399.
36. *HL2*, 393.
37. *HL2*, 393.
38. *HL2*, 393.
39. On which he dwells for more than 2,000 words.
40. *HL2*, 395.
41. *HL2*, 395.
42. *HL2*, 396.
43. *HL2*, 396
44. *HL2*, 397.
45. *SMW*, 176–177.
46. *HL2*, 397.
47. *PR*, 105.
48. *HL2*, 398.
49. *HL2*, 399. It is worth noting that Whitehead had cited Peter Kropotkin's book *Mutual Aid* in his first year of Harvard lectures (*HL1*, 141) and that Whitehead may well have had him in mind here.
50. *RM*, 96.
51. This formulation is a simplification to the extent that for Whitehead the environment is a constitutive part of the organism, and so they cannot be neatly separated.
52. See *HL2*, 399–400.
53. *HL2*, 397–398.
54. "One thing which may be described as God. But same principle applies to God as to an electron as one occasion in its history or to ourselves" (*HL2*, 198).
55. *HL2*, 204.
56. See *HL2*, 207–210.
57. *HL2*, 210.
58. *PR*, 343.
59. To give more context for this short quotation: "About eleven years ago, a young friend of mine reached her tenth birthday . . . The child's great-aunt celebrated the day by taking her to an afternoon performance of the opera Carmen, rendered in English . . . As we came out of the opera house after the performance, she looked up at her aunt and said—'Auntie, do you think that those were *really good* people?' Both the aunt and I sidestepped the question by looking for the car which was to take us home.

The point that I now wish to make is that our enjoyment in the theatre was irrelevant to moral considerations applied to the performance. Of course, smugglers are naughty people, and Carmen is carefree as to niceties of behaviour. But while they are singing their parts and dancing on the stage, morals vanish and beauty remains" (*MT*, 12–13).

Chapter 5

Religion and Hatred

The Augustinians were not merely displeased with [Whitehead's] address; they were furious

—Paul G. Kuntz[1]

Whitehead's address "Religious Psychology of the Western Peoples" (RPWP) is breathtaking for the sheer force of its rebuke of Christian dogmatism.[2] It is an essay that is primarily concerned with the scourge of what Whitehead calls "religious hatred," which today we would call "religious extremism"—a very live issue in the twenty-first century. The topic gives the essay more emotional power than is usual for the majority of Whitehead's corpus, and according to one account, it certainly provoked a strong reaction at the time. It is the most sustained criticism of religion that Whitehead would ever make.

CONTEXT

If it hadn't been for a handwritten marginal note and a letter included with the papers donated to the Whitehead Research Project by Whitehead's grandson, George Whitehead, in 2019, we may never have been able to definitively date the essay or know the context in which he delivered it. On the eighth page of one of the drafts of the address, there is a handwritten note that reads, "Insert Pick's two quotations."[3] "Pick" was Whitehead's nickname for Edward Pickman, a Harvard-educated lawyer and historian with whom he became friends.[4] An undated letter from Pickman found in the papers donated by George Whitehead provides a quote by a fourth-century bishop named Hilary of Poitiers. Pickman said that the quote lacked a citation, but that it could be found "if you thought it appropriate enough for use in connection with your paper read to the Augustinian Society."[5] Pickman also refers to a second quote by Hilary that he had used in his book *The Mind of Latin Christendom*,[6] published in 1937. In case there should be any doubt that these are the two quotations to which Whitehead was referring in his handwritten marginal note, it should be noted that Whitehead has the phrase "The mind of Latin Christendom" at the start of the second paragraph of the address. It seems evident that he had Pickman's book very much in mind when he wrote it.

As luck would have it, the occasion of Whitehead's delivering this paper is referenced by at least two scholars. The first is Victor Lowe, who briefly noted in his 1962 *Understanding Whitehead* that Whitehead had delivered an unpublished address to the Augustinian Society in Cambridge, Massachusetts, on March 30, 1939, characterizing it as Whitehead's explanation of "his excessive dislike of St. Paul."[7]

The other reference is meatier, a very extended footnote in a 1982 *Process Studies* article by Paul G. Kuntz entitled "Can Whitehead Be Made a Christian Philosopher?"[8] In the article, Kuntz dismisses Norman Pittenger's assertion that Whitehead regularly attended church services in Cambridge as "part of a legend. To make Whitehead a 'Christian' in this sense may require further pious fraud."[9] He followed this by noting that "the one encounter I witnessed between Whitehead and an orthodox Christian society was, to say the least, as cordial as the trial of a heretic by a court of the Inquisition."[10] It is in a more than thousand-word footnote to this statement that he describes Whitehead's encounter with the Augustinian Society in some detail.

Kuntz claimed to have been the only graduate student invited and that the majority of the people there were deeply devoted Christians, a great many of them priests. He described the members of the society as being "furious" at Whitehead's address,[11] and it is easy to see why. A part of one of his friend Pickman's two quotes reads: "The Church, who won believers by suffering exile and imprisonment, now commands faith by threatening exile and imprisonment."[12] This pretty well encapsulates the tone, if not all of the content, of Whitehead's RPWP address. Whitehead effectively marched into a religious society and told them that their most revered Church Fathers had steered Christianity as a whole in fundamentally the wrong direction, away from love and toward hatred. Kuntz's own take on Whitehead's anti-ecclesiastical message was that he was

> so jealous of his individual freedom of interpretation that he did not care to be enrolled as a member lest he become regarded as a "representative," and therefore compromised in thought and actions by a specific religious society . . . Whitehead was an articulate defender of sectarian vs. ecclesiastical Christianity.[13]

It is an opinion that seems to square with what Victor Lowe has said about Whitehead's religious commitments and opinions. Whitehead had at one time been much enraptured with Cardinal Newman, leading him to be "all but converted" to Catholicism.[14] The apparent stumbling block was submitting himself to the authority of a church on anything; he wanted to think for himself.[15] As a result, he would become an agnostic in the late 1800s, telling his children that they no longer needed to pray.[16] His eventual coming around to his own brand of theism was ascribed by Bertrand Russell and his children North and Jessie to Eric Whitehead's death in WWI,[17] but he apparently remained very conscious of not wanting to have himself identified with any religion. He even turned down a chance to speak at a Unitarian church in 1935—and if we are to believe Lucien Price, Unitarianism was at that time the Christian sect that he most preferred[18]—on the grounds that it would tend to identify him with Unitarianism and "impair the objectivity of his influence elsewhere."

WHITEHEAD AND WWII

Still, even all this does not seem to fully explain the combative nature of RPWP. And why would Whitehead speak to an Anglican society, if he had turned down an invitation to a Unitarian church? It seems unlikely that we will ever know all of Whitehead's reasons and motivations. But it seems virtually certain that the bleakness of the times had something to do with the bleakness of the address. Though WWII is usually reckoned to have begun in Europe with the German invasion of Poland in early September of 1939, Hitler and Germany had become a dangerous and destabilizing force long before this point. Most notably for the context of Whitehead's address, the Munich agreement had already been signed in September of 1938 in an attempt to appease Hitler by ceding Sudetenland—who then violated the agreement by invading Czechoslovakia only two weeks prior to Whitehead's delivery of RPWP in late March. It seemed evident that the world was headed toward another war, not unlike the one to which Whitehead had already lost a son.

If the tone of Whitehead's address was indeed influenced by the momentous events in Europe, it was hardly the only philosophical essay to be affected by the coming war. In writing an analysis of American Philosophical Association (APA) presidential addresses,[19] Brian G. Henning noted an obvious concern at Hitler's aggressiveness in the closing years of the decade. Even Joseph Alexander Leighton's address given on April 15, 1938—a year before Whitehead's RPWP—was already full of alarm.

> Democracy is emerging in one of the most momentous secular crises in the history of culture. On us teachers falls, I think, a heavy share of the burden

of democracy. If the confusion continues, and some rabble-rouser, greedy for power, arises, we may all be either shut up or shot. If you think this is unduly alarming, consider the case of Germany. . . . Civilization is poised on a razor edge over an abyss.[20]

But in point of fact, there is no need to survey other prominent philosophers writing at the time to get a sense of Whitehead's state of mind, for as luck would have it, Whitehead wrote a 7,000-word essay addressing the international situation for the *Atlantic Monthly* in early 1939 titled "An Appeal to Sanity."[21] It appeared in March 1939—the same month he delivered RPWP—though a $250 payment to Whitehead for the article provided in a letter from the *Atlantic Monthly* dated January 18, 1939, confirms that he finished writing it no later than mid-January.[22] A full analysis of this essay would be its own chapter—or perhaps several—but I will try here to summarize a few of the high points.

Whitehead states his main topic in the article thusly: "What is the justification of 'isolation' on the part of a powerful nation, when evil is turbulent in any part of the world?"[23] Due to the high costs of war, he advocates an isolationist policy unless the evils of the world threaten the supreme duty of a nation to foster its civilization.[24] Much of the early portion of the article is given over to a detailed analysis of the Czechoslovakia problem specifically. He observes that the creation of the Czech state had been clearly revealed as a failed experiment, for it "could be made adequately self-sufficient only by including alien groups, . . . [and] in fighting to maintain frontiers of the Czech State, we should be thwarting the keenest aspirations of the Poles and Hungarians."[25] He concludes that a war on behalf of Czechoslovakia's borders by England and France not only "would have the weakest moral justification" but would be tactically foolish.[26] In the end, he recommends appeasement, by "the release of the alien populations of Bohemia from inclusion in [the Czech] state,"[27] ending his article with the admonition that "war can protect; it cannot create. Indeed, war adds to the brutality that frustrates creation. The protection of war should be the last resort in the slow progress of mankind towards its far-off ideals."[28]

Importantly, though, Whitehead does not neglect an analysis of Hitler's character.

> Would Hitler have given way if England and France had threatened war? Hitler bears no analogy to the kings, presidents, and prime ministers who achieve their positions by the normal working of established constitutions. . . . For rulers such as Hitler and Mussolini . . . their cause depend[s] upon an atmosphere of inflamed emotion. In this way their power arose; in this way it maintains itself. The alternative for them is a dungeon and a firing squad. Hitler is an enraged mystic; that is to say, he belongs to one species of prophet. He is not

primarily thinking of personal safety. He is enjoying the hysteria which is the very lifeblood of his cause ... [W]hat is the sense of believing that Hitler, with these emotions and with this opportunity, would allow himself to be bluffed into inaction?[29]

The clear sense of this paragraph is that even though Whitehead recommended appeasement in the final equation, he feared that Hitler may not leave the world a choice. And for RPWP, his description of Hitler as an "enraged mystic" and "belong[ing] to one species of prophet" seems significant. As I move now to examine the text of RPWP, it will become apparent that Hitler can be seen in Whitehead's essay as the epitome of religion gone wrong, a world leader proselytizing hatred of the "other" made stronger by a framework of intellectual justification.

A final note here in this connection is warranted. On January 3, 1940, the Whiteheads would entertain none other than Charles Lindbergh and Anne Morrow Lindbergh for dinner. Both recall Whitehead speaking of the rise of "gentleness" over the centuries in a manner very similar to RPWP: "He spoke of the idea of gentleness. The failure of the Church in not emphasizing the essential message of Christianity—gentleness."[30] Moreover, Charles Lindbergh asked Whitehead a question: "I asked him if he thought it [gentleness] could exist without the protection of 'force.' He agreed with me that it could not. I was anxious to get his reaction to this, as I came to that conclusion long ago."[31] A more easily discernable subtext could hardly be imagined. It was eight months after the publication of Whitehead's "Appeal" and the delivery of his RPWP, and appeasement was no longer an option; the German invasion of Poland in September had necessitated a response.

In the context of such momentous events, it seems no great wonder that "Religious Psychology" would be the most emotionally forceful statement of Whitehead's career against a rigid and exclusionary religious orthodoxy which demands obedience over free thought. That it describes problems which remain as pervasive today as they were when Whitehead wrote it seems to assure its continued relevance. I can only hope that the following examination of the text will help convince readers that RPWP is one of the true gems in the trove of recently discovered Whitehead materials and seems destined to be of great interest to process theologians, as soon as they have become fully conscious of it.

REVELATION, CRITICISM, AND HATRED

In *Religion in the Making* (1926), Whitehead defined religion as "a system of general truths which have the effect of transforming character when they are sincerely held and vividly apprehended."[32] Something like this definition still holds for RPWP, written thirteen years later, but rather than a more positive sense of religion as a striving toward the truth, as we find in *Religion in the Making (RM)*, the emphasis here is on a more negatively connoted intellectual arrogance and inadequacy. He notes in RPWP that "thought . . . generalized itself and answered subconscious questions about the world. . . . The answers were clearer than the questions."[33] Primitive religion is then the "pre-existing," reflexive, emotional answer to humanity's unarticulated questions, the raw "revelation" which it is incumbent upon later civilization to criticize.

Whitehead then discusses the stage of criticism (of revelation), characterizing it as "contentious and unpopular."[34] Again the examples he provides and the arguments he makes highlight the arrogant self-righteousness of religion:

> In Hebrew legend Satan was the first critic, and in the Hellenic epic Thersites performs the same service. In both legends the critic creates the evils which he criticizes. So far as our direct experience is concerned, the maladjustments of nature precede the criticism. Socrates did not produce the evils of Athenian life.[35]

He is asserting, then, that the Hebrews had construed criticism of the religion itself as an evil. The critic who compares religion with fact, and finds it wanting, is liable to be seen to be creating problems rather than endeavoring to solve them, or to get at the truth. Even so, Whitehead sees religion as being (somewhat) purified by such criticism, which introduces "delicacies of moral judgment."[36]

But such criticism leading to a rational system of "general truths," as described in *RM*, produces something even worse than the dislike of the early critics: a hatred born from the surety of a system reinforced by intellectual justification. He cites Christianity in particular as popularizing the "lower forms of hatred," seeing God's own repulsion from evil as akin to "earthly tyrants,"[37] which recalls a more specific comparison he had made in *Process and Reality (PR)*: "The Church gave unto God the attributes which belonged exclusively to Caesar."[38] That Whitehead is even more appalled in RPWP about such hatred than he had been ten years earlier when delivering his Giffords is evident by what may be the most memorable line of the entire essay: "In reading ecclesiastical history one longs for the Athenian pagans who removed their finest moralist by the kindly device of a cup of hemlock."[39]

That Whitehead would deliver such a line to a room full of clergy is genuinely shocking. From all accounts of Whitehead I can find, he was genial and nonconfrontational,[40] albeit with a wry wit. He was not shy in his intellectual criticism, in having a spirited discussion of *ideas*, but rarely did he attack anyone, much less a whole group of people. And while Whitehead may not have been attacking the clergy before him directly, he was quite pointedly saying that the Church Fathers were *even worse* than those Athenian Greeks who had murdered Socrates for the crime of impiety. It is therefore no wonder at all that Kuntz describes Whitehead's audience as "furious."

The special peril of religious hatred, as opposed to other species of hatred, is that since it is a moral reaction against perceived evil, "precautions seem unnecessary" against possible excess: "It appears so obvious that our reaction against evil cannot be excessive."[41] The problem, of course, is that people do not always distinguish between a genuine evil and a doctrinal disagreement; morally neutral statements of belief in some contested historical fact (such as the life of Jesus) are endowed with moral significance by religious systems. Thus hatred is "a high-grade feeling, the product of civilization. In the origins of civilized life, it intensifies brutality by introducing an intellectual justification."[42] Whitehead then provides one of the better definitions of hatred—and particularly religious hatred—that I have seen, incorporating both intellectual arrogance and a fundamental stupidity:

> Hatred, in the vicious sense of the term, is the emotional reaction to the recognition of antagonistic forms of existence, when that recognition is unrestrained by adequate definition of the grounds of antagonism. In other words, hatred arises when limited intelligence perceives antagonism without recognition of its own limitations.[43]

In short, hatred presupposes a failure of both imagination and understanding. It perceives that something is against it, but cannot understand the opposing point of view, and/or makes no effort to understand. Certain of its own righteousness and indignant of criticism, it seeks simply to destroy the other.

Importantly, Whitehead goes on to note that when someone *is* aware of their own limitations, *hatred* becomes *repulsion*, that is, the "self-preservation of the excellencies of a form of life repels factors which are inconsistent with it," while recognizing that there can be other legitimate forms. "Thus hatred is the emotion of repulsion devoid of its proper qualifications. The difficulty is to preserve an adequate activity of repulsion, devoid of vicious hatred."[44]

If this sounds familiar, it should, because Whitehead's idea of "repulsion" here amounts to another way of describing the maintenance of a society of actual entities, which all share/inherit a similar character. The difference comes in the language used to describe it, and the context. In *PR*, Whitehead was talking in extremely abstract terms of the highest generality, and as such, it was hard to get emotionally worked up about the mechanics of a serially ordered society of actual entities. Repulsion from an antagonistic point of view in the context of religion, however, is something we can well understand. By choosing an emotional, non-technical word and an everyday context, Whitehead gives RPWP a rhetorical power that is practically unmatched in all his writings, even though the underlying ideas are mostly familiar.

The extended discussion of hatred—which is the major theme of the essay—can be seen in much the same way. Almost everything that Whitehead says about hatred in RPWP can be found elsewhere, particularly in *RM*, but under the heading of "evil." As discussed in the previous chapter, evil in *RM* is a good in itself, but also destructive—specifically, destructive of what it considers to be other evils.[45] The parallel to a religious hatred which seeks to destroy other religions or religious outlooks should be clear enough from this alone, but RM also provides the following extremely apt example:

> Good people of narrow sympathies are apt to be unfeeling and unprogressive, enjoying their egotistical goodness. Their case, on a higher level, is analogous to that of the man completely degraded to a hog. They have reached a state of stable goodness, so far as their own interior life is concerned. This type of moral correctitude is, on a larger view, so like evil that the distinction is trivial.[46]

We can see, then, that RPWP would not be the first time that Whitehead would harshly criticize narrow-minded, dogmatic people. But the word "evil," while certainly capable of arousing emotions in the right context, is again a much more abstract term than "hatred." It is a somewhat archaic word, little-used in everyday speech and thought; it is the stuff of political speeches and the occasional religious sermon, and the evil thing or person is almost always something distant, some remote "other."

"Hatred," by contrast, is a far more intimate and familiar concept. Yet before RPWP, it is simply not a word that Whitehead had used very often. A keyword search for "hate" and "hatred" in his philosophical books reveals only ten uses of the one and eleven of the other, most of them incidental—appearing in lists of emotions like "love, hatred, sorrow," and so on. Neither are any of the "real" uses of the word sustained discussions such as can be found in Whitehead's 1939 address.

A FORTUNATE BALANCE

After he is done excoriating Christian dogmatism in the early part of RPWP—something to which he returns at the end—Whitehead proceeds to the middle portion of the address, which aims to show the alternative to a narrow-minded and self-satisfied doctrinal orthodoxy. It is anchored by a number of different pairs of concepts which mutually require one another and yet have a certain amount of tension with each other as well. Whitehead seems to have been fond of such conceptual pairings; they recall the physical and mental poles, permanence and flux, God and the world, God's primordial and consequent nature, the maintenance of the symbolic code and the fearlessness of revision, and so on. In RPWP, there are at least three of these pairings, though two of the pairs seem to be synonyms.

In the first pairing, Whitehead tells us that "the importance of an idea is that it should purify emotion, and the importance of emotion is that it should vivify ideas."[47] He sees the power of the biblical narratives as emerging from the interplay of emotion and ideas; they are parables with a continuing relevance. The Pharisees can be seen as representing one end of this spectrum, the ideas—clarifying and codifying doctrinal questions, what Whitehead calls the "rationalistic development of experience."[48] But due to their one-sidedness, they are inferior to the "women of the town who have retained the delicacies of this interplay."[49]

Here we get our second pair of concepts: the women of the town who deal with the interplay of emotion and idea are seeking *value*, while the Pharisees with their coordination of concepts are seeking *truth*. "'Value' is enhanced by 'truth', and 'truth' is futile without 'value.'"[50] And finally, we get what appears to be a pair of synonyms for these: aesthetic and analytic experience.[51] Whitehead takes great pains to emphasize the importance of maintaining a balance between these types of experience. Both are good, and both are necessary, but if either one becomes too dominant, it leads to either the folly of dogmatic satisfaction or a needless aesthetic repetition: "The merit of religious or artistic ages is that they restrain the excessive emphasis on learning; and the merit of learned ages is that they undermine feeble repetitions of religion or art. In great ages there is a fortunate balance."[52]

It is interesting to note that while Whitehead usually regards such conceptual pairings as being on an equal footing, here he comes down squarely on one side over the other:

> It is obvious that the aesthetic mode of development of experience, involving fortunate interplay of emotion and idea, represents the dominant objective. The second mode of analytic coordination, which includes science and the pursuit of analytic understanding, is a secondary procedure with its justification in its services to the former mode.[53]

This is not the first time that Whitehead asserted the primacy of aesthetics.[54] And purely from a rhetorical perspective, Whitehead's assertion here in the context of his denouncement of religious dogmatism and hatred helps to drive the point home of how badly some of the Church Fathers failed by emphasizing the analytic side. The rest of the address is, in fact, a look at some of the "big names" in early Christianity who drove its development.

A RIGID ORTHODOXY

Lowe had described Whitehead's address as displaying his "excessive dislike of St. Paul,"[55] and Paul is indeed the first person who Whitehead takes to task, noting that due to his influence, "Unless your verbal doctrine is accurate, without doubt you will perish everlastingly."[56] He then describes a tension between the more exact formulae of Arius and Athanasius versus the more aesthetically focused Eusebius. He goes on to mention others, but the specifics are not particularly important. The point is that the analytic side eventually became the dominant one. As Whitehead had done many times before, he lamented the trust of these men in the adequacy of language: "The prose of thought lags behind the insight of aesthetic experience . . . Verbal learning, divorced from direct experience, is the perpetual danger of civilization."[57]

Finally, at the very end, Whitehead lays the blame for what he views as the unfortunate development of Christianity as a religion deeply tinged with hatred squarely at the feet of Augustine,[58] the namesake of the society to which he was speaking. The penultimate concluding paragraphs are powerful, and worth quoting at length:

> Christianity developed as the religion tainted with hatred derived from the self-confidence of analytic learning. Fanatics conceived the end of the Christian life to be adherence to the right formula. Many lapses of conduct could be condoned by adherence to a rigid orthodoxy.
>
> The truly religious use of formulae, as one subordinate means of stimulating delicacies of emotion inspiring purpose, was thrust into the background. If Augustine had taken the other side, the horrors of later Christian persecutions might have been restrained. Perhaps they were inevitable. And yet, to all appearance, Augustine had his chance and missed it. He bequeathed to the future a concept of the Deity as tinged with human hatred. . . . The Pharisaic spirit dominated over the Gospel message.[59]

The power in the address derives from a number of factors. The first, as already discussed, is Whitehead's use of more straightforward and yet emotionally charged language to adapt some of his pre-existing philosophical ideas to a more relatable context.

The second is that Whitehead is decidedly negative here, in a sustained way, which he had seldom done before. I am not saying that Whitehead was never harshly critical of particular ideas or concepts, or even religion itself. He said in *RM*, after all, that

> history, down to the present day, is a melancholy record of the horrors which can attend religion: human sacrifice, and in particular the slaughter of children, cannibalism, sensual orgies, abject superstition, hatred as between races, the

maintenance of degrading customs, hysteria, bigotry, can all be laid at its charge. Religion is the last refuge of human savagery. The uncritical association of religion with goodness is directly negatived by plain facts.[60]

Yet he tempers this by further saying that "religion can be, and has been, the main instrument for progress."[61] His philosophy also tended to deal with evil, with the darker sides of humanity and the world, in the abstract; here those dark aspects are the focus. And while RPWP does not preclude the future revival of religious feeling freed from the worst excesses of brutality and hatred, it is unflinching in its conclusion that such evil sentiments had become the dominant ones in the hour of its writing.

CONCLUSION: A SECOND "APPEAL"

I fear I may have to ask the reader's forgiveness, for I have cheated abominably and withheld some of the most relevant portions of Whitehead's "An Appeal to Sanity" until now, partly for dramatic effect. In my defense, the other reason I am returning to it now rather than having it all at the beginning is that "Appeal" and RPWP are practically companion pieces. Whitehead's rage in RPWP cannot be fully understood without the context of his consciousness of the international situation found in "Appeal," but neither can the dread and frustration of "Appeal" be fully appreciated without the discussion of religion as a driving force in the development of civilization found in RPWP.

The first half of "Appeal" is taken up with Czechoslovakia and Central Europe as I have already described. The second half addresses the problem of "the relation of the Jews to the various countries in which they dwell."[62] If anyone ever suspected Whitehead of anti-Semitism, this half of the article would disabuse them of the notion. A decade earlier, in *PR*, he had praised the "brief Galilean vision of humility [that] flickered throughout the ages, uncertainly."[63] His praise in "Appeal" of the Jews as a people is far more direct.

> The Greeks and the Jews, in the few centuries before and after the beginning of the Christian Era, intensified an element of progressive activity which was diffused throughout the many peoples in the broad belt from Mesopotamia to Spain. . . . So far as Greeks and Jews were active, progress was not in a rut, degenerating into conservation . . . . The Greeks have vanished. The Jews remain . . . . For two and a half thousand years, Semites have continuously provided suggestion, novelty, and achievement, whereby the life of Europe never lost the subconscious ideal of progress. Of course the Jews are not the only factor producing progress in Western life. But their services have been immense. . . . The Jews have been a priceless factor in the advance of European civilization. They belong to each

nation, and yet they impart a tinge of internationalism. They are eager in respect to concepts relevant to progress, just where we have forgotten them.[64]

It is a bit curious, given the above, that there is little mention of the Jewish influence on western religion in RPWP. Perhaps marching into an Anglican society and attributing everything good in Christianity to the Jews and everything bad to Augustine and the other Christian patriarchs was a bridge too far even for Whitehead. Nonetheless, he does spend a half-page in RPWP asserting that "the period of Jewish History with which the New Testament is concerned" exhibited a "fortunate balance" between overly learned and over religious/artistic ages.[65]

"Appeal" makes clear that Whitehead was all too aware of the danger of the international situation for the Jewish people. He noted that "An immediate war would probably lead to the massacre of hundreds of thousands of Jews, together with the slaughter of other millions throughout various nations," and advocated for their rescue from danger and resettlement.[66] The final section of his article is then devoted to Palestine and the notion of a Jewish state.[67]

All of this is background to passages in "Appeal" that directly address religion as a whole and connect it to RPWP about as closely as could be imagined:

To-day civilization is in danger by reason of a perversion of doctrine concerning the social character of humanity. The worth of any social system depends on the value experience it promotes among individual human beings.

It is true that there is a mystic sense of the coordination and eternity of realized value. But we here approach the basic doctrine of religion. To attach that coordination of value to a finite social group is a lapse into barbaric polytheism.

The tendency touches every country. But it is centered in Europe. And in Europe Germany is the main seat of the vicious explosion. The general character is overemphasis on the notion of nationality, producing the ideal of the totalitarian state. The activity, derivative from this debased notion, is the determination to exterminate international factors which exhibit human nature as greater than any state-system. The Jews are the first example of this refusal to worship the state. But religions, arts, and sciences will come next, until mankind are reduced to mean little creatures subservient to the god-state, embodied in some god-man. The worth of life is at stake.

Two problems of pressing importance are made urgent by the anti-Jewish explosion in Germany. How can the Jews in Germany be saved? How can the Jews from Germany and elsewhere be redistributed throughout the world?[68]

Whitehead's obvious concern for the Jewish people shown here, and his identification of Hitler as leading a "god-state, embodied in some god-man," should dispel any doubts about what was in Whitehead's mind when he wrote and delivered RPWP. Even aside from the connections in subject matter, it seems entirely likely that he wrote his March RPWP directly following his completion of "Appeal" in January. And if Whitehead's rage toward an Anglican society—and Christianity as a whole—seems misdirected, we need only note the rampant anti-Semitism that ran through the highest reaches of Harvard University at the time.

In fact, it was some of the very same people who were instrumental in Whitehead's recruitment to Harvard who were most strongly and explicitly anti-Semitic. Harvard's president from 1909 to 1933, A. Lawrence Lowell, did his utmost to impose a quota for Jewish students at Harvard. Lawrence J. Henderson introduced the motion for such a quota in June of 1922; it was voted down 64-41,[69] but Lowell would later find a way around the defeat in 1926, packing the Committee on Admissions with anti-Semites,[70] leading to a decrease from a 27.6% proportion of Jews in the class of 1925[71] to just 10% when he departed in 1933.[72]

Further, an article by Lewis Feuer, a student of Whitehead in the 1930s, recalled that "a well-modulated anti-Semitism combined with a judiciously considered pro-Nazi sympathy was not infrequent among the Harvard community and its philosophical scholars,"[73] citing specifically William Ernest Hocking,[74] Whitehead's assistants Otis Lee[75] and Hillis Kaiser,[76] and Henderson.[77] He even noted that "the instructor in my German class was a pro-Nazi enthusiast who declaimed against the Jewish department stores in Berlin."[78]

That Whitehead was aware that such views were widespread cannot be in any doubt. And indeed, Feuer wrote that "at the Whitehead household, an ill-defined tension prevailed as to the 'Jewish question.'"[79] Whitehead was always ready to talk, discuss, and genially argue about current events at his famous Sunday gatherings but seldom went in for heated in-person confrontations with his peers. I would argue that his "Appeal" constitutes a reveal of the fullness of his depth of feeling for an endangered religious and ethnic minority, a view that he refrained from loudly pronouncing at parties in mixed company. RPWP then became the culminating emotional outburst against the hatred and indifference which he found all around him in Cambridge and which in aggregate had helped lead to the international crisis that would become WWII.

In the end, RPWP directly addresses what remains a very live social issue in the twenty-first century: the scourge of religious hatred and religious extremism, coupled with an alarming emergent hypernationalism and political hyper-partisanship. In our modern context, these lines still haunt us: "Fanatics conceived the end of the Christian life to be adherence to the right formula. Many lapses of conduct could be condoned by adherence to a rigid orthodoxy." In this sense, nothing has changed, and RPWP's continued relevance only makes such problems all the more frustrating.

NOTES

1. Paul G. Kuntz, "Can Whitehead Be Made a Christian Philosopher?" *Process Studies* 12, no. 4 (Winter 1982): 241. Reprinted with permission.

2. Alfred North Whitehead, "Religious Psychology of the Western Peoples," March 30, 1939, ADD020 Whitehead Research Library, http://wrl.whiteheadresearch.org/items/show/1414.

3. The papers from George Whitehead included three typed versions of "Religious Psychology." Each of the three contains most of the same handwritten emendations. One has been re-titled as "I. The Individual Psychology" and followed by three handwritten pages titled "II. The Sociological Issue," which seems to indicate that Whitehead was in the process of editing the paper to serve as the first chapter of a larger (and ultimately unfinished) work.

4. Lewis Ford would interview Pickman's wife, Hester, in 1979 about the couple's friendship with the Whiteheads: Lewis Ford, "Interview with Mrs. Hester Pickman," July 17, 1979, DOC033, Whitehead Research Library, http://wrl.whiteheadresearch.org/items/show/539.

5. Edward Pickman, "Letter from Edward Pickman to Whitehead," n.d., LET1068, Whitehead Research Library, http://wrl.whiteheadresearch.org/items/show/2303.

6. Edward Pickman, *The Mind of Latin Christendom* (London: Oxford University Press, 1937), 17.

7. Victor Lowe, *Understanding Whitehead* (Baltimore: The Johns Hopkins Press, 1966), 94.

8. Kuntz, "Can Whitehead Be Made a Christian Philosopher?" 241.

9. Kuntz, "Can Whitehead Be Made a Christian Philosopher?" 233.

10. Kuntz, "Can Whitehead Be Made a Christian Philosopher?" 233.

11. Kuntz, "Can Whitehead Be Made a Christian Philosopher?" 241.

12. Pickman, *The Mind of Latin Christendom*, 17.

13. Kuntz, "Can Whitehead Be Made a Christian Philosopher?" 241.

14. Victor Lowe, "A. N. W.: A Biographical Perspective," *Process Studies* 12, no. 3 (Fall 1982): 140.

15. Lowe, *Alfred North Whitehead*, vol. 2, 187.

16. Lowe, "A. N. W.: A Biographical Perspective," 142.

17. Lowe, *Alfred North Whitehead*, vol. 2, 188.

18. Lucien Price, *Dialogues of Alfred North Whitehead* (New York: Mentor Books, 1954), 249.

19. Brian G. Henning, "Philosophy in the Age of Fascism: Reflections on the Presidential Addresses of the APA, 1931–1940," in *Historical Essays in 20th Century American Philosophy*, ed. John R. Shook (Charlottesville: Richard T. Hull, 2015): 69–95. Whitehead gave his own APA presidential address in 1931: Alfred North

Whitehead, "Objects and Subjects," *The Philosophical Review* 41, no. 2 (March 1932): 130–146.

20. J. A. Leighton, "History as the Struggle for Social Values," *The Philosophical Review* 48, no. 2 (March 1939): 153–154.

21. Alfred North Whitehead, "An Appeal to Sanity," *The Atlantic* 163 (March 1939): 309–320.

22. Atlantic Monthly Staff, "Letter from *Atlantic Monthly* to Whitehead," January 18, 1939, LET1349, Whitehead Research Library, http://wrl.whiteheadresearch.org/items/show/2574.

23. Whitehead, "An Appeal to Sanity," 309.

24. Whitehead, "An Appeal to Sanity," 309.

25. Whitehead, "An Appeal to Sanity," 311–312.

26. Whitehead, "An Appeal to Sanity," 312.

27. Whitehead, "An Appeal to Sanity," 313.

28. Whitehead, "An Appeal to Sanity," 320.

29. Whitehead, "An Appeal to Sanity," 312–313.

30. Anne Morrow Lindbergh, *War Within and Without, 1939–1944* (New York: Berkeley Books, 1981), 67.

31. Charles Lindbergh, *The Wartime Journals of Charles A. Lindbergh* (New York: Harcourt Brace Jovanovich, 1970), 303.

32. *RM*, 15.

33. RPWP, 1.

34. RPWP, 2.

35. RPWP, 2–3.

36. RPWP, 3.

37. RPWP, 3.

38. *PR*, 342. The same idea also appears in *RM*: "This worship of glory arising from power [in the Book of Psalms] is not only dangerous: it arises from a barbaric conception of God. I suppose that even the world itself could not contain the bones of those slaughtered because of men intoxicated by its attraction. This view of the universe, in the guise of an Eastern empire ruled by a glorious tyrant, may have served as purpose. In its historical setting, it marks a religious ascent. The psalm quoted gives us its noblest expression. The other side comes out in the psalms expressing hate, psalms now generally withdrawn from public worship. The glorification of power has broken more hearts that it has healed" (*RM*, 55).

39. RPWP, 3.

40. One story comes to mind in this regard—a 1913 Trinity College meeting in which the fellows were discussing whether to pressure students to attend church services. After an impassioned speech by James Ward in the affirmative, and as passions began to heat, Whitehead "rose to his feet and began a miniature filibuster with a series of unexceptionable remarks having no obvious connexion with the resolution under discussion which he continued until passions died down. The resolution was at once put to a vote resulting in an overwhelming defeat for the clerical party and the matter has never been raised again" (Joseph Gerard Brennan, "Alfred North Whitehead: Plato's Lost Dialogue," *The American Scholar* 47, no. 4 (1978): 517).

41. RPWP, 4.
42. RPWP, 6. Whitehead describes "brutality" here as "a survival from the primitive level of animal life. There is no reason to believe that the tiger hates the animal as he tears it to pieces" (6). Whitehead is, of course, neither the first nor the last to see hatred as an evil that is particular to humans, with other forms of life being innocent of it.
43. RPWP, 7.
44. RPWP, 7.
45. *RM*, 95–96.
46. *RM*, 98.
47. RPWP, 9.
48. RPWP, 10.
49. RPWP, 9.
50. RPWP, 10.
51. RPWP, 11.
52. RPWP, 13.
53. RPWP, 12.
54. See chapter 4, in which Whitehead argues for the derivative nature of ethics.
55. Lowe, *Understanding Whitehead*, 94.
56. RPWP, 15.
57. RPWP, 17.
58. It is an uncomfortable but legitimate question to ask whether Whitehead's criticism of Augustine was tinged with a degree of racism. He spent a paragraph discussing Augustine's racial extraction and social atmosphere:

> Augustine was primarily a North African, born in Numidia. His exact racial inheritance may be doubtful. But the social atmosphere surrounding him was beyond doubt African. However during a few critical years in his early thirties, he lived in North Italy. These few years included the crisis of his conversion, under the influence of St. Ambrose, and of his mother. Thus the impress of his Christianity was largely northern. But his subsequent life was again African. (RPWP, 17)

Why does Whitehead even mention any of this? Simply as a point of academic interest? Whitehead claims he does so because Augustine was such a key figure in the development of Christianity (RPWP, 17–18), but what exactly does he mean the information to illustrate? Is he denigrating Augustine's African heritage, or rather the North Italian influence of his middle years? Neither? Both? It is unclear.

Interestingly, though, Anne Morrow Lindbergh's account of a visit with the Whitehead on January 3, 1940 (mentioned above), recalls not only Whitehead discussing some of the issues of RPWP but also mentioning Africa: "He spoke of the idea of gentleness. The failure of the Church in not emphasizing the essential message of Christianity—gentleness. The North African and southern French culture was hard, ascetic" (Anne Morrow Lindbergh, *War Within and Without*, 67). This would seem to tip the scales toward Whitehead placing the blame on Augustine's African heritage, and yet Lindbergh's mention of France is curious; it is not mentioned in RPWP at all. It seems possible that she misremembered France in place of Italy.

59. RPWP, 18–19.
60. *RM*, 37. He also asked in *AI* (1933): "Must 'religion' always remain as a synonym for 'hatred'?" (*AI*, 172).
61. *RM*, 37–38.
62. Whitehead, "An Appeal to Sanity," 314.
63. *PR*, 342.
64. Whitehead, "An Appeal to Sanity," 315–316.
65. RPWP, 13.
66. Whitehead, "An Appeal to Sanity," 317.
67. Whitehead, "An Appeal to Sanity," 318–320.
68. Whitehead, "An Appeal to Sanity," 315–316.
69. Jerome Karabel, *The Chosen: The Hidden History of Admission and Exclusion at Harvard, Yale, and Princeton* (New York: Houghton Mifflin, 2005), 92.
70. Karabel, *The Chosen*, 109.
71. Karabel, *The Chosen*, 105.
72. Stephan Thernstrom, "Poor but Hopeful Scholars," in *Glimpses of Harvard Past*, ed. Bernard Bailyn et al. (Cambridge: Harvard University Press, 1986), 127–128.
73. Lewis S. Feuer, "Recollections of Alfred North Whitehead in the Harvard Setting (1931–1937)," *Yale Review* 76, no. 4 (1987), 542.
74. "Hocking was warmly appreciative of the organic idealism of the Nazi ideology" (Feuer, "Recollections," 542).
75. Lee wrote an article calling the Weimar Republic "simply intolerable" (Feuer, "Recollections," 542).
76. Kaiser "published a letter in the *Nation* defending the sixty million Germans against the disproportionate concern for Germany's six hundred thousand Jews" (Feuer, "Recollections," 542).
77. Feuer, "Recollections," 543.
78. Feuer, "Recollections," 543.
79. Feuer, "Recollections," 544. It is worth noting here that in addition to his anti-Semitic colleagues, Whitehead became fast friends with Felix Frankfurter, who was born into a Jewish family, had helped found the ACLU in 1920, and been given a chair at Harvard Law in 1921. Frankfurter helped defeat Lowell's first attempt at instituting a de facto Jewish quota at Harvard in 1922—despite the fact that Lowell pointedly excluded him from a committee tasked with evaluating the matter—by applying outside pressure (Karabel. *The Chosen*, 95–100). Frankfurter would become a Supreme Court Justice in 1939, much to Whitehead's delight. For more on the relationship between Whitehead and Frankfurter, see Joseph Petek, "Whitehead and Felix Frankfurter." Whitehead Research Project, November 13, 2019, http://whiteheadresearch.org/2019/11/13/whitehead-and-felix-frankfurter/.

Chapter 6

Redefining Wit and Humour

The essence of freedom is the practicability of purpose . . . The literary exposition of freedom deals mainly with the frills. The Greek myth was more to the point. Prometheus did not bring to mankind freedom of the press.

—Adventures of Ideas[1]

Whitehead's newly discovered address "Freedom and Order"[2] (FO) is a somewhat puzzling document in more ways than one.

The first reason that it is puzzling is that we have only the vaguest notions of the context in which it was delivered. We *can* be fairly certain that Whitehead delivered this address in America. The best indicator of this is probably on page 2, where he says that "another song brings in America in a complimentary fashion; so I will quote a verse."[3] He also talks of England in various places in a way suggesting that it is elsewhere, that is, not where he is speaking, and recalls the beginning of WWI.[4] So it seems safe to assume that he was delivering this address in the United States.

Further, the essay is not dated. One of the best clues to a date comes on page 2, where Whitehead writes that "as the generations pass in seventy years, behaviour patterns alter," but crossed out "seventy" and wrote "eighty." If Whitehead was talking about "generations of humanity" in general, then it seems like a strange thing to bother changing, since the average age of a generation does not often shift significantly. Given this, it may be possible that Whitehead was here referring to his own rough age at the time, which might in turn suggest that he was about seventy when he originally wrote it, and he was about eighty when he was revising it. But this is a very slender and uncertain basis for trying to date the address.

Another clue to a date is that Whitehead refers to Holland as "free,"[5] while Germany's "imaginative self-respect arising from a sense of freedom ... [has] been outweighed by inland sections with other traditions."[6] Taken together, these things suggest that the paper was written in the interwar years, not during WWII.[7] It is very unlikely to have been written after the war ended, as Whitehead did not publish anything after 1942.[8] But this still leaves a rather wide range of possible dates, from Whitehead's arrival in America in 1924 to the beginning of WWII in 1939. My own guess for a date of composition—based largely on a broad similarity with portions of *Science and the Modern World (SMW)*—is sometime after *SMW* but before Whitehead's delivery of his Gifford lectures in mid-1928. My reasons for this supposition will become clear later on in this chapter.

The second reason the essay is puzzling is the content itself, which sees Whitehead stressing two terms—"wit" and "humour"—that he does not use in a sustained, technical sense in any of his other works. In fact, the only other time he uses both words together is in the middle of *SMW*,[9] which makes similar arguments about the ultimate importance of aesthetic considerations while criticizing the current societal stress on economic considerations and instrumental morals. He pairs these two words with another two terms that are more familiar to readers of Whitehead—the titular "freedom" and "order"—but in a somewhat unexpected way.

To begin to understand this new dyad of Whitehead's, it seems best to start with his own definitions of the two terms within the essay. He begins by pointing out that both terms "have a close association with the notion of amusement" but that "a man's wits and his humours each stretch over regions removed from any taint of pleasure."[10] In the twenty-first century, we do not often think of "humour" in particular outside of a context of amusement, but of course the term has older roots—including the idea of the four cardinal humours of blood, phlegm, and yellow and black bile, or of humour as a mood or inclination. But as is often the case with Whitehead, he ends up re-appropriating these common terms for a technical usage that stretches them "towards a generality foreign to their ordinary usage," to borrow a phrase from *Process and Reality (PR)*.

"Humour" appears to be the more "primordial" term of the dyad. It is

> that functioning of the mind produced by the long unconscious association of emotion and habit that has persisted, during uncounted ages, in those continuous threads of existence from which we originate ... [It] is the first product of consciousness. It is the emotion produced by observation of the way that happenings are conditioned. It is not consciously effective. It results from the given "go" of the universe, as observed. It is awakened interest.[11]

"Wit," by contrast, is

> that functioning of mind produced by conscious discrimination and analysis. It is the synthesis, as seen in action or other expression, produced by a clear understanding of the details involved ... [It] is the later product of consciousness, when intelligence has disintegrated and re-combined the inherited factors. In this way, things are combined which have never met, and unions are dissolved which have the sanction of ages.[12]

It is tempting to immediately want to map these terms onto other, more familiar and established dyads of Whitehead's such "causal efficacy" and "presentational immediacy" from *Symbolism*. "Humour" does appear to bear some comparison to causal efficacy, as a sort of primordial feeling/emotion/understanding of the way things are. Identifying "wit" with presentational immediacy is more dubious, given that wit is defined as a synthetic phenomenon "produced by consciousness"; in this sense, it might be more accurately compared to Whitehead's "symbolic reference." But these comparisons are hardly exact, and it seems evident that Whitehead is trying to get at something a little different than is captured by any of his neologisms.

This conclusion is supported by the fact that Whitehead associates the two terms with "freedom" and "order" in a manner which at first blush seems unintuitive: "It is evident that 'Order' will be closely associated with the prevalent 'Humour' of the society concerned, and that 'Freedom' will be claimed for the prevalent scatter of its 'Wit.'"[13] When I first read this sentence, I at first wondered if Whitehead may not have accidentally reversed his terms. "Wit," with its "discrimination and analysis' and its conscious recombination of factors, seemed to me to be the element that would be more closely associated with "order." This interpretation appears somewhat reinforced by Whitehead's immediately preceding illustration that "it is humorous to want a summer holiday: it is witty to secure the berth."[14] Is it not true, then, that humour is the instinct toward freedom, while wit is the organizing principle, the *order*ing principle?

But as with many of Whitehead's dyads/antitheses/dualities, the two terms are used in such a way as to be mutually suggestive, mutually reinforcing, and ultimately inseparable. They are the "two extremes of the abstractive process of consciousness" which together form the synthetic "imagination."[15] In this sense, it is natural for the reader to spot cross-pollinations between the identification of wit with freedom and humour with order, all four of which are terms that Whitehead would have readily acknowledged as high abstractions. In fact, the essay's title recalls his 1923 address on "The Rhythmic Claims of

Freedom and *Discipline*" (emphasis added), in which the distinction between the two titular terms "is not so sharp as a logical analysis of the meanings of [them] might lead us to imagine."[16]

Still, there are a few keys that help to unlock Whitehead's meaning in drawing the comparison. The first is to recall that though we are used to thinking of "order" as something that is imposed by humans on their environment, for Whitehead it is also to be found in pre-existing and even primordial forms. For instance, when Whitehead talks about our "cosmic epoch" in *PR*, he is talking about a (very) broad sort of order: "For the *Timaeus*, the creation of the world is the incoming of a type of order establishing a cosmic epoch. It is not the beginning of matter of fact, but the incoming of a certain type of social order."[17]

The second is to realize that the confusion arises largely due to the fact that Whitehead's first identification of humour with order and wit with freedom on page 4 uses unhelpfully vague connective phrases ("associated with" and "claimed for"). His formulation on page 8 is more precise: "It is evident that humour is the product of order, and that wit is the spur towards freedom."[18] Notice that here the order *precedes* the humour; in this context his idea that humour is the "emotion produced by observation of the way that happenings are conditioned"[19] makes perfect sense. Humour is a sense of how things are, how the world works, and how it is all connected. By contrast, freedom does not *precede* wit (or not all freedom, at any rate), but just the opposite: wit is the *spur* toward freedom.

Here again, Whitehead has a more primordial notion of "freedom" than we are accustomed to thinking about. He laments in *Adventures of Ideas (AI)* that

> Unfortunately the notion of freedom has been eviscerated by the literary treatment devoted to it. . . . When we think of freedom, we are apt to confine ourselves to freedom of thought, freedom of the press, freedom for religious opinions. Then the limitations to freedom are conceived as wholly arising from the antagonisms of our fellow men. This is a thorough mistake.[20]

He tells us instead that

> The essence of freedom is the practicability of purpose. . . . The literary exposition of freedom deals mainly with the frills. The Greek myth was more to the point. Prometheus did not bring to mankind freedom of the press. He procured fire, which obediently to human purpose cooks and gives warmth. In fact, freedom of action is a primary human need.[21]

One can easily see that Prometheus's procurement of fire—or perhaps more accurately the taming of it—was the height of wit. He had "disintegrated and re-combined the inherited factors,"²² that is, discovered how to manipulate natural phenomena in order to create the *conditions* for a greater freedom. His wit was a spur toward freedom—not freedom *from* interference by other people, but freedom *for* a greater range of activity.

Yet it must be said that we would not be wrong to observe that this kind of wit is also creating a new, less primordial form of order, one which Whitehead discusses in the opening pages of *The Function of Reason* (*FR*). I refer to Whitehead's observation that "higher forms of life are actively engaged in modifying their environment."²³ Birds build nests, beavers build dams, humans build cars and interstate highways, and, well, *tame fire*, and so on. It is hard not to associate the type of wit that creates such structures with "order," which both illustrates the close relationship of all four terms and gives a clue as to why Whitehead did not carry through this set of dyads to his published work: these concepts and their stated relationships are just a little too fuzzy and confusing for the precision that Whitehead was ultimately aiming for in his metaphysics. In this sense, these terms appear to be a failed terminological experiment.

In any case, we do not necessarily need to go to *AI* to understand what Whitehead means by "freedom" here, since he gives a fairly robust example near the end of the address in pointing out that the Australian legal system in no way hinders the aboriginals from enjoying a performance of the Boston Symphony Orchestra.²⁴ The problem is that there are no orchestras near them, nor is it the kind of music that they have the cultural background to appreciate, and in this sense, "freedom must be *relevant*," or it means nothing.²⁵ So, too, must wit be relevant. It is "conscious discrimination and analysis" used for some purpose.

But now that we have gotten a better grasp of what Whitehead meant by the humour-order and wit-freedom comparisons, chiefly by examining what the more common Whiteheadian terms "freedom" and "order" have meant in other places in his corpus, what can we further say about the novel terms "wit" and "humour"? There are a number of intriguing connections we can make to other Whiteheadian concepts, though ultimately none of the most familiar ones can function as simple one-to-one correlations or substitutions.

Whitehead writes of wit that "it conceives of all possibilities in the materials provided . . . Wit is up in the clouds, unpractical, idealistic. But, when all is said, it does deal with fact: namely, the fact of what might have been."²⁶ This last phrase, "what might have been," is a pregnant one that recalls discussions of negative prehensions and feelings in *PR*,²⁷ his conviction that potentialities are not nonentity:

> A feeling . . . retains the impress of what it might have been, but is not. It is for this reason that what an actual entity has avoided as a datum for feeling may yet be an important part of its equipment. The actual cannot be reduced to mere matter of fact in divorce from the potential.²⁸

The talk of "all possibilities" also recalls his earlier discussion of what he called the "graded envisagement" in *SMW*:

> It is this realised extension of eternal relatedness beyond the mutual relatedness of the actual occasions, which prehends into each occasion the full sweep of eternal relatedness. I term this abrupt realisation the "graded envisagement" which each occasion prehends into its synthesis. This graded envisagement is how the actual includes what (in one sense) is not-being as a positive factor in its own achievement. It is the source of error, of truth, of art, of ethics, and of religion. By it, fact is confronted with alternatives.[29]

So, we can say that "wit" for Whitehead has something to do with negative prehensions, possibilities, potentials, eternal objects, and graded envisagements. Yet wit is not quite any of these. It is not itself a prehension, or possibility, or potential, or eternal object, but rather it perceives and judges these things. "Graded envisagement" seems closer, in the sense that it is a judgment, a product, a thing that describes the whole range of possible alternatives, and that defines the actual entity and holds it together. But wit is conceived in FO as a *faculty* that enacts these things, a capacity for judgment and synthesis one level removed/abstracted from the judgment itself. It is also, it must be said, a more colloquial and down-to-earth term than any of these others. Since the essay is not dated, we cannot be certain whether it represents a simplification and/or conflation of these other concepts, or rather a basis out of which the others may have grown.

Wit is also described as curiously lacking in feeling. Without humour—though the two can never be fully separated[30]—wit resembles an autistic individual, unable to comprehend the general feelings, habits, and instincts of the populace. Hence witty people "require looking after" and are "apt to upset things."[31] Whitehead's example is of a Londoner supporting the liberal candidate[32]—one who wished to "relieve agricultural labourers from complete economic dependence upon the farmers who employed them"[33]—proclaiming to the laborers of the Cambridgeshire fens that they were nothing but "slaves to their employers." This proclamation offended rather than convinced them. It was an instance of a witty person advocating for an unrealized ideal without adequately taking account of the established humour—or established *order*—of those around him. That sense of order fights to preserve itself, even through individuals who may be disadvantaged by it. It does so because wit is "critical, satirical,"[34] breaking down and *re*-ordering the *established* order, which is invested with an emotional sense of rightness. Indeed, without this "humour," we are told, "there is nothing tremendous," for "wit never understands the common goings-on of things."[35]

I have already related humour to another Whiteheadian term—causal efficacy—which is "the experience dominating the primitive living organisms, which have a sense for the fate from which they have emerged, and for the fate towards which they go,"* that is, a primitive understanding/sense/feeling of the order of things. Again, that there is some resemblance between the two terms seems fairly clear. However, a key difference is that "causal efficacy" is a highly technical term denoting what Whitehead calls a "pure perceptive mode" and carries with it a tautological infallibility.[37] Humour, by contrast, is not infallible. It cannot be, or the Londoner could not have misread his Cambridgeshire audience. Causal efficacy deals with the more metaphysically basic issue of the perception of a single actual entity, while humour carries a certain degree of inseparably communal feeling. True, humour as a collective feeling resides in individuals, but Whitehead's illustrations are all of groups of people, and the thrust of the essay is ethical rather than metaphysical, concerned with social interaction rather than the bare fact of perception. Aside from this important distinction, it seems to me that the two terms might be almost equated.

Together, Whitehead tells us in a hauntingly evocative passage, wit and humour produce imagination:

> The fusion of wit and humour produces the great imaginative feeling. It elicits pathos, tragedy, and the glory hidden in daily matter of fact. It is close to reality and yet tinges its heavy darkness with the glow of its light. The humour preserves the realization of the tremendousness of history, its fatefulness. The wit preserves the sense of its failure, its success, its ideal.[38]

In other words, wit and humour require one another. Without humour, wit could not sense the bone-deep importance of the existing order, while without wit, humour could never conceive of a new ideal. The balance is important. An excess of wit produces failed revolutions—idealized social changes that the general populace is not ready to take on. It can change social systems with its shrewd synthesis of ideals or destroy them with its autistic tactlessness. A *lack* of wit, on the other hand, leads to stagnation.[39]

Whitehead makes an interesting rhetorical split between "imagination" and his next topic, which also has the effect of more clearly splitting his two dyads. He says that imagination is his first topic, while the second topic is "a particular case of the former, at present urgent."[40] The second topic turns out to be "sociological. Hence the title of the paper, Freedom and Order."[41] He is therefore aligning wit and humour with imagination, and freedom and order with social systems, with the former grouping having broader applicability. Society/social systems can certainly be seen as a product or "particular case" of imagination (a *communal* kind of imagination), though I do not think that the four component terms can be placed in a similar hierarchy of abstraction or collectivism vs. individuality, nor is Whitehead himself careful to distinguish them in the ensuing discussion.

The rest of the essay, to which the first half had been building, is best described as an argument for the desirability of stressing aesthetic over economic ends in human societies, where the focus is currently reversed. This is not a new topic for Whitehead. It is broadly similar to arguments he made in both *SMW* and *AI*. He pithily wrote in *AI*, for instance, that "the teleology of the Universe is directed to the production of Beauty"[42] and also that "in the immediate present, economic organization constitutes the most massive problem of human relationships."[43] But the closest parallel of the second half of FO is surely to the last chapter of *SMW*. Though the terminology used is different, with some of it remaining unique to FO, the two are so broadly similar in their arguments and conclusions that I think it is reasonable to speculate that FO is a restatement of *SMW*.

For instance, after wrestling with the precise meanings of "wit" and "humour" in this essay—which as already mentioned were terms that Whitehead only ever used together (once) in *SMW*—the following paragraph becomes particularly striking:

> There are two principles inherent in the very nature of things, recurring in some particular embodiments whatever field we explore—the *spirit of change*, and the *spirit of conservation*. There can be nothing real without both. Mere change without conservation is a passage from nothing to nothing. Its final integration yields mere transient non-entity. Mere conservation without change cannot conserve. For after all, there is a flux of circumstance, and the freshness of being evaporates under mere repetition. The character of existent reality is composed of organisms enduring through the flux of things.[44]

I spent time above trying to relate "wit" and "humour" to other, more established and recurring technical Whiteheadian terms. Yet here, I would say, is the closest parallel that can be found: wit as the "spirit of change," and humour as the "spirit of conservation." The problem is that these are not phrases that Whitehead ever repeats; they are one-offs even in *SMW*, and he never returns to them in future work. In this sense, they were hiding in plain sight. The fairly exact nature of this match can be seen in relating them to the examples Whitehead gives in FO: the liberal candidate who imagines a new ideal and the agricultural laborers who resist the change. These "spirits of change and conservation" are in some ways more apt terms for such examples, since they better emphasize the social and communal nature with which Whitehead's usage of both "wit" and "humour" seem incurably tinged, despite a surface-level application to individuals rather than social orders.

This paragraph from *SMW* in turn suggests another parallel: the later formulation of "permanence" and "flux" found in *PR* three to four years later.[45] Readers who do not immediately connect "humour and wit" with "permanence and flux" would have to be forgiven, for this similarity is not at all clear. The relation only becomes obvious when the connective tissue is pointed out.

Nor, still, are the ideas exact matches. "Permanence/flux" is a more developed, more precise, less vague, and more metaphysically basic formulation than either "wit/humour" or the "spirits of change and conservation." Describing phenomena as the "spirit of" *anything* tends to be a little hazy and vague—nor does the phrase "spirit of conservation," in particular, have much rhetorical bite ("spirit of change" is a little better). And "wit/humour," as technical terms, are too colloquial and too likely to be misconstrued, in a way that "permanence/flux" are unlikely to be. Permanence/flux have also shed most of the communal connotation suggested by the other pairs of terms.

Here I would like to briefly revisit the idea of the possible chronology of these works, and why I believe FO is most likely located between *SMW* and *PR*. "Wit" and "humour" appear to be a terminological experiment/expansion following *SMW*; the two terms first appeared together there and seem to be substituted for the "spirits of change and conservation," terms which Whitehead clearly (and rightly, I think) did not like much, but he had not come up with anything better at the time. Yet the fact that "wit and humour" do not later recur but are seemingly replaced with the more familiar "permanence and flux" in *PR* suggests a further development. I do not think that Whitehead would have talked of "wit and humour" if he had already come to "permanence and flux"—not without at least *mentioning* the latter comparison. Perhaps I am wrong in this, but I feel comfortable enough to propose the notion.

It may be worth noting here that Whitehead spent the spring of 1926 guest lecturing at a number of universities, including McGill University and the University of Michigan. Victor Lowe mentions that he read a paper to the Philosophical Society at both places, that neither was ever published and that they might have been one and the same paper.[46] It seems entirely possible that FO could have been this paper—the timing would be a nice fit with what I have argued above. But there will likely never be enough evidence to say for sure.

In any case, it is time to return to the second half of FO to draw out a few more of the promised parallels to *SMW*.

Aside from freedom, Whitehead identifies feudalism and religion as the other factors influencing "England's reaction to violent change."[47] For Whitehead, England's feudalism helped explain its retention of distinct social "grades" or classes along the transition to a mildly socialist government, in which "free hospital treatment for the labouring classes provided by the more fortunate grades has been a matter of course ever since I can remember."⁴⁸ That this process was being taken over by the government was a change in method but not in attitude, not in humour. "The fact is that the difference between mild socialism and mild feudalism is very slight,"⁴⁹ Whitehead observes. But aside from the fact that this discussion of feudalism throws a little doubt upon my guess for the date of the document,⁵⁰ it is incidental to the main thrust of Whitehead's argument.

Religion, Whitehead tells us, is "the sense of perfection, the glimpse of the ideal and the aim at it. The essence of this motive is its sense of the unattainable, which shapes our routes of approximation."⁵¹ This is remarkably similar to his formulation of religion in *SMW* as "something which is the ultimate ideal, and the hopeless quest."⁵² His basic argument in FO is that we have lost religion as the ideal, using a striking term that he would never use anywhere else: "propaganda."⁵³ "All expression of ideal aim is termed propaganda. The Psalms of David would today be termed 'propaganda'; a mother's love is propaganda with its aim to keep the children quiet."⁵⁴ Propaganda is undoubtedly a derogatory term here, one indicating that an intrinsic good is being confused for an instrumental one. Specifically, the intrinsic good of beauty has been replaced with the instrumental good of right conduct, and with economic motives. ⁵⁵

> The emphasis on moral imperatives has had the effect of putting the problem of the aesthetic training of the general population into the background. The slogan of the last two centuries in many lands has been—Be good, sweet maid, and let aesthetic development take its chance. Adam Smith has added to this severance of the Good and the Beautiful . . . In fact economic motives usurped the position that in Greek thought belonged to the Beautiful. The modern world has replaced "The Good and the Beautiful," by "The Good and Economic Success."⁵⁶

Here again, the parallels to passages in the final chapter of *SMW* are striking. Just as in FO, Whitehead singles out Adam Smith for criticism, saying that "it is very arguable that the science of political economy, as studied in its first period after the death of Adam Smith (1790), did more harm than good."⁵⁷ He speaks of the importance of art and aesthetics even more emphatically than in FO; it is necessary for "fertilisation of the soul" and "is more than a transient refreshment," but "is something which adds to the permanent richness of the soul's self-attainment."⁵⁸ The main difference between the two documents lies in the fact that in *SMW* Whitehead has not blamed institutional religion for the failure to properly emphasize the ultimacy of aesthetic value. The blame is left more squarely on the shoulders of Adam Smith and "political economy" while maintaining a place for religions as keepers of ideals:

The abstractions of political economy . . . are in fact the abstractions in terms of which commercial affairs are carried on. Thus all thought concerned with social organisation expressed itself in terms of material things and of capital. Ultimate values were excluded. They were politely bowed to, and then handed over to the clergy to be kept for Sundays. A creed of competitive business morality was evolved, in some respects curiously high; but entirely devoid of consideration for the value of human life. The workmen were conceived as mere hands, drawn from the pool of labour.[59]

In short, FO retains the same basic arguments of the final chapter of *SMW* about the evils of economic motives displacing aesthetic ones, but additionally distinguishes *true* religion as the keeper of ideals and ultimate values, versus actual institutional Christianity[60] which expresses "the *imperatives* of God as distinct from his *purposes*,"[61] producing a similar loss of appreciation for the ultimacy of aesthetics, a kind of Pascal's wager in the sense that we have lost our sense of the intrinsic worth of "the good and the beautiful."[62] The essay as a whole is yet another reminder that the primacy of beauty as an intrinsic good in Whitehead's philosophy and metaphysics can hardly be overstressed.

Overall, however, if I were to try here at the end to give a general characterization of the significance of FO in Whitehead's philosophy (as a new essay in Whitehead's corpus), I would have to say that it mostly appears to represent a failed terminological experiment. As I noted early on, the core dyads used in FO are downright perplexing at times in their relationship to one another.[63] If my guess at the timing of the composition and delivery is correct—and it may not be—then Whitehead was endeavoring to re-formulate and clarify concepts that appeared in *SMW* a year before and that *would* appear in his Gifford lectures two years hence. The dyads he came up with had the advantage of being readily recognizable common words but stretched to a usage that was as likely to confuse as illuminate. This being the case, it seems to be no great wonder that he never repeated them in any of his published writings.

NOTES

1. *AI*, 66. Reprinted with permission from the Alfred North Whitehead literary estate.
2. Alfred North Whitehead, "Freedom and Order," n.d., ADD019, Whitehead Research Library, http://wrl.whiteheadresearch.org/items/show/1413.
3. FO, 2.
4. FO, 9.
5. FO, 11, 13.
6. FO, 13.
7. This was pointed out to me by Eric Elder during a discussion of the Whitehead Reading Group: Whitehead Research Project, "Whitehead Reading Group: 12 March

2021, 'Freedom and Order,'" YouTube Video, March 12, 2021, https://www.youtube.com/watch?v=u3YrugJiegA&t=4381s.

8. With the exception of *Essays in Science and Philosophy*, which was composed of essays written pre-1942.

9. "This fertilisation of the soul is the reason for the necessity of art. A static value, however serious and important, becomes unendurable by its appalling monotony of endurance. The soul cries aloud for release into change. It suffers the agonies of claustrophobia. The transitions of humour, wit, irreverence, play, sleep, and—above all—of art are necessary for it" (*SMW*, 202).

10. FO, 3.
11. FO, 3–4.
12. FO, 3, 5.
13. FO, 4.
14. FO, 4.
15. FO, 6.
16. Alfred North Whitehead, "The Rhythmic Claims of Freedom and Discipline," *Hibbert Journal* 21 (1923): 658.
17. *PR*, 96.
18. FO, 8.
19. FO, 4.
20. *AI*, 65–66.
21. *AI*, 66.
22. FO, 5.
23. Alfred North Whitehead, *The Function of Reason* (Boston: Beacon Press, 1958), 8.
24. FO, 18.
25. FO, 18, emphasis added.
26. FO, 6.
27. The term "negative prehensions" is not used in either *HL1* or *HL2* and seems to appear first in *PR* (at least until and unless the upcoming *HL3* proves differently).
28. *PR*, 226–227.
29. *SMW*, 176–177.
30. FO, 11–12.
31. FO, 8.
32. Whitehead's politics are not often discussed, but he was a supporter of the Liberal Party until the ascension of the Labour Party, which became the main opposition to the Conservatives (Tories) in the early 1920s, at which point Whitehead began backing Labour candidates. Another unpublished address of Whitehead's that was delivered in 1923—"Science and Economic Liberty"—was delivered at an unspecified Labour Party gathering in support of their ideals: Alfred North Whitehead, "Science and Economic Liberty: A Comparison of England and America," 1923, Alfred North Whitehead Collection, MS-0282, Special Collections, Johns Hopkins University.
33. FO, 10.
34. FO, 6.

35. FO, 7.
36. S, 44.
37. "Direct experience is infallible. What you have experienced, you have experienced" (S, 6).
38. FO, 6–7.
39. FO, 12.
40. FO, 6.
41. FO, 8.
42. *AI*, 265.
43. *AI*, 62.
44. *SMW*, 201. Emphasis added.
45. Depending on whether one goes by the delivery of the Gifford lectures in mid-1928 or by the publication of the actual book in late 1929.
46. Lowe, *Alfred North Whitehead*, vol. 2, 206.
47. FO, 13.
48. FO, 14.
49. FO, 14.
50. Whitehead's only sustained use of the word "feudal" or "feudalism" is in *AI* (1933), though the parallels, I hold, remain closer to *SMW*.
51. FO, 15.
52. *SMW*, 192.
53. The term certainly brings WWI immediately to mind, though this observation is not especially illuminating since it is already obvious that the essay was written post-WWI.
54. FO, 16–17.
55. FO, 20.
56. FO, 20.
57. *SMW*, 200.
58. *SMW*, 202.
59. *SMW*, 202–203.
60. He calls out the Methodism of the British Labour Party specifically (FO, 16).
61. FO, 19, emphasis added.
62. FO, 19–20.
63. It is perhaps worth noting that the Whitehead Reading Group met to discuss this essay on March 12, 2021, and the recording of the discussion reveals that almost all participants found the two dyads ambiguous: Whitehead Research Project, "Whitehead Reading Group: 12 March 2021."

Chapter 7

Whitehead's Other Dialogues

> *This further question lands us in the ocean of metaphysic, onto which my profound ignorance of that science forbids me to enter.*
>
> —Whitehead to Russell, February 13, 1895

It is a well-known anecdote among Whiteheadians that the first philosophy class he attended was the one that he himself taught at Harvard in the fall of 1924. I know of no record of the classes that Whitehead attended at Sherborne and Trinity, and so cannot verify the truth of the saying. But even if it is true, it does not tell the whole story, for the philosophy that he began delivering to his new American audience could hardly have sprung up out of nothing. Whether or not Whitehead ever attended formal philosophy classes, he did a lot more thinking about philosophy at Trinity, and the period shortly afterward, than is often appreciated.

The problem is that there has been—and remains—a dearth of documents which could tell us something about how Whitehead's interest in philosophy first arose, how his thinking developed, and how and when he decided to leave his old field of mathematics behind him—which he had worked in and taught for more than thirty years—to begin a new career in philosophy. Nonetheless, such documentation is not *completely* absent, and through the Critical Edition of Whitehead, some mostly forgotten documents have recently been rediscovered. The object of this chapter is to explore the earliest influences on Whitehead's philosophical thinking, establish how some of his thinking may have evolved, and examine when and how his transition into a professional career in philosophy occurred.

The single most important and substantive document in this endeavor is a 1911 letter of Whitehead's to Russell in which he gave fourteen pages of critique on the latter's manuscript for *The Problems of Philosophy*, which would be published the following year. It is a unique look at an unguarded Whitehead wading into broad philosophical topics just after his departure from Trinity, and by all appearances before a philosophical career was even a thought for him. But even before looking at that, it will be well to begin even earlier, with his participation in the debates of the Cambridge Apostles as chronicled by Victor Lowe.

THE CAMBRIDGE APOSTLES

Supporting the idea that Whitehead never attended a philosophy course before his own at Harvard is his assertion in his "Autobiographical Notes" that *all* of his classes as an undergraduate at Trinity were in mathematics. However,

> the lectures were only one side of the education. The missing portions were supplied by incessant conversation, with our friends, undergraduates, or members of the staff. This started with dinner at about six or seven, and went on till about ten o'clock in the evening, stopping sometimes earlier and sometimes later.[1]

Whitehead recalled that by the time he got his Trinity fellowship in 1885, he "nearly knew by heart parts of Kant's *Critique of Pure Reason*."[2]

Most of this informal education of Whitehead can never be fully known, of course. Rarely are any records of such conversations kept outside of the odd diary entry. Happily, however, there is *some* record of the discussions that took place between Whitehead and his fellow members of the Cambridge Apostles—an elite, secretive, and highly selective discussion society to which he was elected in May of 1884. Whitehead wrote that his conversations with fellow students had "the appearance of a daily Platonic dialogue . . . [and] the 'Apostles' who met on Saturdays in each other's rooms, from 10 P.M. to any time next morning, were the concentration of this experience."[3]

Although it had not been unusual for the Apostles to elect mathematicians as members, it so happened that Whitehead was the last one elected for about eight years—until the election of C. P. Sanger and Bertrand Russell in 1892. Its members at the time were composed largely of classicists and philosophers, including J. M. E. McTaggart, who Whitehead himself nominated in 1886.[4] The topics discussed were broad and philosophical in nature. A society secretary recorded the dates of discussions, the subject of presenters' papers, and the question on which its members voted at the end—with votes occasionally accompanied by a short comment. R. B. Braithwaite allowed Victor Lowe to peruse these records, from which we have some sparse but nonetheless important clues to his early philosophical thinking.

He attended meetings for four years, from his election in May 1884 to May 1888.[5]

One of the most arresting records is one in which Whitehead did, in fact, leave an additional comment. The question for the meeting of February 14, 1885, was "Does the devil exist, or is he merely loathsome?" Less significant than the fact that Whitehead was one of two members who voted "yes" is his comment that "He [the devil] is the Homogenous."[6] Here, then, one day shy of Whitehead's twenty-fourth birthday, we see that his firm philosophical conviction about the evil of sameness—and, by extension, the importance of diversity, especially *aesthetic* diversity—was already established. His conviction here is wholly consistent with his statement in *Science and the Modern World (SMW)*, forty years later, about the necessity of art: "A static value, however serious and important, becomes unendurable by its appalling monotony of endurance. The soul cries aloud for release into change."[7]

The record of a meeting three weeks later illustrates a similar sort of conviction when Whitehead voted that it was Heraclitus, rather than Democritus, who came closest to describing the true nature of the universe.[8] He did not discuss either man often in his published work, at least not directly. In Whitehead's entire corpus, Heraclitus is only mentioned three times, all in *Process and Reality*. Democritus is only mentioned eight times across a few different books, usually in connection with atomism. But Heraclitus's idea of a world that was defined by change, by flux, by process is Whitehead all over. "The world was to be pictured as an ever-living fire, destructive and creative, with perpetual tensions between opposites that arise and perish."[9] And so Whitehead's own penchant for stressing becoming over being and for setting up philosophical dyads which are opposed and yet require one another appears to also be identifiable in this early period.[10]

Another trait entirely familiar to Whitehead scholars that displayed itself in these early Apostles' discussions was his fascination with language, and poetry in particular. A question in March 1886 was, "Is a poet a prophet or a piano?" Predictably, Whitehead responded "prophet."[11] For Whitehead, poets were never merely making rhymes or writing lyrics. The great ones were doing something that was more than just aesthetically pleasing (though saying that something had "only" aesthetic value for Whitehead is of course a dangerous statement, since aesthetics was itself the highest value for him). One could not read his extended discussion of Wordsworth and Shelley in *SMW* and think otherwise. After citing a part of a Wordsworth poem, he writes:

> In thus citing Wordsworth, the point which I wish to make is that we forget how strained and paradoxical is the view of nature which modern science imposes on our thoughts. Wordsworth, to the height of genius, expresses the concrete facts

of our apprehension, facts which are distorted in the scientific analysis. Is it not possible that the standardised concepts of science are only valid within narrow limitations, perhaps too narrow for science itself?[12]

For Whitehead, poetry was an endeavor to describe experiences and meanings that ordinary language was unable to convey. He often talked in his philosophical writings, and in his Harvard classroom, of a naive trust in grammar and language among philosophers, a grammar which by its very structure suggested a simplicity to reality that was belied by our everyday experiences. Great poetry, for Whitehead, never started with the words, as so much of philosophy seemed to do, but the other way around:

> Why do we say that the word "tree"—spoken or written—is a symbol to us for trees? . . . It would be just as sensible, viewing the question abstractedly, for trees to symbolize the word "tree" as for the word to symbolize the trees.[13]

This passage, along with his discussion of the artist, the puppy dog, and the chair,[14] illustrates that for Whitehead, it is poets and artists, rather than scientists, who see the world the most clearly.

I am not saying that for Whitehead all of this later philosophy was as developed in his head in that March 1886 meeting of the Apostles as it was forty years later. But the general outlook seems to have already been there, a notion reinforced by his answer to another question put to the Apostles in autumn 1886, "Facts or feelings?" Whitehead of course responded, "Feelings."[15] It was another aspect that the dry scientific facts overlooked but that Whitehead believed was completely metaphysically central, and not to be written off as an epiphenomenon unique to human beings.

Lowe discusses dozens more of Whitehead's responses to various prompts from his Apostles discussions, but the ones I have cited are the most important and revealing of his early philosophical opinions, and though they can provide only the broadest of sketches, they are sufficient to show that the seeds of Whitehead's mature philosophy were already present in his twenties, many decades before he would enter professional philosophical circles.

LETTERS TO RUSSELL

As far as Whitehead's philosophical opinions and inclinations go, between these records of his discussions with the Apostles in the 1880s and his departure from Trinity College in 1910, there is a great gap. Even if his thinking evolved or developed significantly during this time, we will probably never know it. He toiled away in his Trinity lectureship in mathematics for a solid twenty-five years, and all his publications were mathematical in nature.¹⁶ In fact, somewhat ironically, given that he turned out to be one of the twentieth century's most important metaphysicians, in an 1895 letter to Russell discussing the meaning of the word "absolute" and whether science is merely descriptive or is explanatory, Whitehead exclaimed that "this further question lands us in the ocean of metaphysic, onto which my profound ignorance of that science forbids me to enter."[17]

Then came his departure from Trinity in 1910. His colleague and friend in the math department, Andrew Forsyth, had fallen in love and eloped with a married woman. Forsyth resigned both his chair and his fellowship at Trinity, yet Whitehead hoped that the Trinity Council would allow Forsyth to keep the fellowship, since he was a friend and had served the school well for decades. But a motion to ask Forsyth to reconsider his fellowship resignation got nowhere, and in the end his resignation was accepted by a vote of 8-to-4. Whitehead was not alone in being angry at the decision, as twenty-seven fellows would subsequently protest the acceptance of Forsyth's resignation. Whitehead responded by resigning his own lectureship about two months later, then moved from Cambridge to London without first lining up a new job.[18] The Forsyth affair was apparently not the only reason for Whitehead's departure; he told Victor Lowe that he had been "in a groove in Cambridge" and needed a change of scenery.[19] Interestingly enough, Forsyth would gain a new chair in mathematics at Imperial College in 1913, and he ended up hiring Whitehead for a position under him a year later.

But Whitehead was unemployed for the 1910–1911 academic year. He used the time to write *An Introduction to Mathematics* and continue finalizing the proofs for the latter two volumes of the *Principia Mathematica* with his former student and long-time collaborator, Bertrand Russell. He would accept a position to be lecturer in Applied Mathematics and Mechanics at the University of London in July 1911. It was only a month after accepting this position that Whitehead wrote some philosophically significant letters to Russell, most notably a critique of Russell's manuscript for his book *The Problems of Philosophy*, which was his first book on philosophy generally, though he had written books and articles on specific philosophical topics previously.[20] In any case, when Whitehead wrote his criticisms, he was still teaching and focusing solely on the mathematics that had been his entire career up to that point.

The existence and survival of these 1911 letters to Russell is an unexpected boon for Whitehead's scholarship, a boon bordering on the miraculous, because as a rule Whitehead did not write about philosophy in his letters. He mostly used letter-writing for the maintenance of his personal relationships, and even then he was notoriously bad about sending responses to time-critical business inquiries, such as those of his publishers.[21] He seemed to regard letters as an inherently private medium of communication and likely would have been horrified at the idea of any portion of his correspondence being published. This point is driven home by a 1942 letter to Victor Lowe in which Whitehead told him, "Please do not quote my letters."[22]

But it seems that Whitehead had got used to sharing thoughts and ideas with Russell through letters during the period of their collaboration. Though by the mid-1910s his correspondence with his former pupil had become more cagey,[23] at the time the two men were still busy with the laborious task of correcting the proofs of the *Principia*, and their decade-long collaboration led Whitehead to respond with a critique of Russell's manuscript that was frank and unguarded.

These letters to Russell are the only record we have of Whitehead's philosophical views from this period. Their importance in the study of the development of his philosophy is, thus, very great, and yet today they are largely unknown and forgotten. Victor Lowe published an article about the letters in the *Russell* journal in 1974,[24] but I have never heard a Whitehead scholar discussing them, and I did not even know of the existence of Lowe's article until staff of the Russell archives at McMaster University told me about it.

Whitehead begins his letter to Russell by saying that

> What I recognize as distinctively yours, seems to me to be excellent. But where (in my ignorance) I guess that you are repeating received ideas, I cannot follow. You seem to me to lack self-confidence (or rather, time) to systematize philosophy afresh, in accordance with your own views.[25]

I would argue that the idea of "systematizing philosophy afresh" reflected Whitehead's own latent desires in this direction rather than any need or ambition on Russell's part. The book was aimed at a popular audience for the newly created Home University Library series and was centered on the theory of knowledge; it was not the appropriate venue for "systematizing philosophy afresh," even if Russell had been so inclined at the time.

I would also argue that a core part of their disagreement can be traced to differing attitudes toward language and logic. Both men were world-class mathematical logicians who were, after all, busy finalizing the *Principia*, but while Whitehead regarded a foundation of mathematical knowledge as important for philosophy,[26] he saw it as necessary but not sufficient and always stressed the deceptive simplicity of grammar and language.[27] Russell did not harbor the same deep distrust. He wrote of the book to a friend in 1912 that "I achieved a simplicity beyond what I thought possible,"[28] and his 1905 "On Denoting"[29] underscored his view that language, while problematic, could ultimately be made clear and unambiguous. This difference in outlook is nicely summed up by Whitehead's famous observation that Russell thought he was muddle-headed, while he thought Russell was simple-minded.[30]

Whitehead would write in *The Concept of Nature* that "We are apt to fall into the error of thinking that the facts are simple because simplicity is the goal of our quest" and that we should "seek simplicity and distrust it";[31] Russell was simply not as distrustful as Whitehead was. This is echoed in a criticism Whitehead made of Russell at Harvard, many years later, recalled by George Conger:

> We used to try slyly to get Whitehead to comment on Bertrand Russell, who in those middle years had diverged from him and was not above making snippy remarks about him ("he comes from a long line of bishops."). Usually every trap we laid for Whitehead failed to spring, but one night it worked. "The trouble with Bertie is" he said, "all you have to do is to show him a wild idea and he will take it for the fun of running it."[32]

In short, in Whitehead's view, Russell simply was not careful enough. He got excited and carried away by clever new ideas that were ultimately unsupported by common sense.

A key paragraph of Whitehead's criticism comes from the second page of his critique:

> Here in pages 5, 6 and 10 you seem by a sleight of hand to take away the table which I (= the plain man) perceive. I see a "yellow table' and I feel a "hard table" and I infer that I feel what I see. You (rather obscurely) tell me that I see yellowness and feel hardness, and <u>infer</u> a real table. Such inferences are quite beyond plain people like myself. I perceive <u>objects,</u> and want to know about the reality of the objects I perceive. You ignore this object (or rather smuggle it away) and proceed to talk about sensations of yellowness and hardness and of an <u>inferred</u> object which causes them.[33]

It is hard to read this passage and not again think immediately of Whitehead's artist and puppy dog in *Symbolism*. His mature theories of perception argue, as he does here, for a sort of uncognitive, pre-epistemic perception of objects. Some fifteen years later, he would discuss "causal efficacy" as a "vague, haunting, unmanageable"[34] sort of primitive perception, which nonetheless holds a "vulgar obviousness": "When we hate, it is a man that we hate and not a collection of sense-data—a causal, efficacious man."[35]

Of course, his response to Russell here is not nearly so developed and sophisticated as his later ideas of prehension, causal efficacy, and presentational immediacy. Indeed, Whitehead's use of the rhetorical device of referring to himself as "the plain man" here is something which Lowe regards as "much too rough to fit the real Whitehead," who was more likely to talk of "common sense" or "appealing to naive experience."[36] But once again we see that Whitehead's early philosophical/metaphysical convictions match up neatly with his later work. He was always experimenting with neologisms and alternative ways of expressing himself, but these evolutions in the methods of his expression do not appear to reveal any large shifts in his metaphysical opinions. Whitehead seems always to have been a realist about perception as far back as we can see, and that did not change.

Whitehead also spent a significant portion of his critique arguing that Russell misunderstood and mischaracterized Kant, particularly in identifying the "physical object" with the "thing-in-itself."[37] Besides "muddling" the two, he again asserts that Russell had already "smuggled away" the phenomenal object with which Kant had started.[38] Interestingly, Whitehead's defense of Kant appears to be the only thing that elicited a change in Russell's book. Lowe notes that from Russell's correspondence with his publisher, it seems very likely that he submitted his final typescript before even receiving Whitehead's critique, but he *did* add a footnote clarifying the relation between "physical object" and "thing-in-itself" for the second printing of the book in 1913.[39]

But despite the fact that Russell appears to have taken at least a small portion of Whitehead's criticism seriously, it is not clear that Whitehead's defense of Kant has any bearing on his own philosophy. He merely sought to clarify Kant's position without arguing for its correctness. In fact, at the beginning of the letter, he noted that Russell's philosophy was "in the same state of transition as that in which Kant unfortunately wrote his *Critique*."[40] He would later say to his Harvard class that Kant was "never vague, but not consistent"[41] and that while Kant's "conceptual machinery becomes particularly relevant" in a discussion of perceptual objects,[42] Whitehead himself was in some senses "anti-Kantian"[43] and "trying to stand Kant on his head,"[44] for "Kant's Excessive Subjectivism lands him in hopeless difficulties."[45]

There is a paragraph near the end of his letter to Russell in which Whitehead says that "You have entirely failed to convince me that there is such an universal as 'whiteness.'"[46] This would, of course, be hugely important if Whitehead was actually asserting that he himself did not believe in universals. But it would appear to be a great stretch to interpret this sentence in that way. He once again notes that Russell's argument is very unconvincing to "the plain man" and that "I am in such doubt as to the status of . . . the physical world as left by you, that your argument doesn't carry much weight."[47] So his objection would appear to be on behalf of the general readership to which Russell's book was to be targeted.

But perhaps the most interesting thing of all that seems to have arisen from this letter of Whitehead's was what came after. Whitehead wrote another letter to Russell eight days later. Like the first letter, he prefaced it with shop talk about the *Principia* proofs, but what followed was a giddy Whitehead describing a philosophical epiphany:

Last night when I should have finished them,[48] the idea suddenly flashed on me that <u>time</u> could be treated in exactly the same way as I have now got space [which is a picture of beauty, by the bye]. So till the small hours of the morning, I was employed in making notes of the various ramifications. The result is a relational theory of time, exactly on four legs with that of space. As far as I can see, it gets over all the old difficulties, and above all abolishes the instant in time. . . . According to the theory, the time-relation as we generally think of it [sophisticated by philosophers] is a great cook up. Simultaneity does not belong to it. . . . Also each object runs its own time. . . . My root idea is that an object has essential extension in time as well as in space, and that there are time-parts of an object just as there are space-parts. In fact the time and space extensions are the object. . . . The general result seems to me to help a naive realism.[49]

It is readily apparent that Whitehead is describing not just a theory of physics, but metaphysics—a metaphysics which is a protean form of his later work. Consider that he describes his "root idea" as being that "an object has essential extension in time as well as in space, and that there are time-parts of an object just as there are space-parts." This is essentially Whitehead's idea of the primacy of becoming over being, his epochal theory of time, and his rejection of the specious present. He has either not yet decided or is not yet able to articulate here that the "time-parts" are more basic than the "objects" themselves; that is, actual occasions (time-parts) in a serially ordered society of occasions ("the object"). The letter also lays out other metaphysical convictions which would carry through to his mature philosophy, such as the idea that "each object runs its own time," and "the time and space extensions *are* the object"—time is not a great river in which persistent physical objects are swept along, but rather the objects *generate* the time. One of his clearest statements of this is in his chapter on time in *The Concept of Nature* (1920), nine years later:

> The dissociation of time from events discloses to our immediate inspection that the attempt to set up time as an independent terminus for knowledge is like the effort to find substance in a shadow. There is time because there are happenings, and apart from happenings there is nothing.[50]

Is it possible that this letter represents a key moment when Whitehead's career trajectory began to shift toward philosophy and metaphysics? It seems plausible.

For one, it does not seem to be anything like a reach to believe that in the week after sending his critique of the *Problems*, Whitehead either consciously or unconsciously continued to chew on these ideas and criticisms during the week that followed, including one of the core problems of the book—the perception of physical objects—culminating in a philosophical epiphany which contained recognizable seeds of his later metaphysics and that he believed "help[ed] a naive realism,"[51] contra Russell, who was busy smuggling away tables and inferring them from hardness and yellowness (or in the later language of Whitehead, "bifurcating nature").

Then there is the fact that Whitehead had just recently departed Trinity, where he had been "in a groove," and seems likely to have wanted to expand his horizons, or at least to make some kind of change, even if he did not exactly know what form the change might take. Finally, his very first philosophical paper, delivered to the Aristotelian Society in 1915, was on "Space, Time, and Relativity," which gestured at some of the same ideas that Whitehead excitedly discussed in his letter, though with a timidity before a society of learned philosophers that was entirely absent in his private communication with a collaborator and former student.

If this moment of inspiration of Whitehead did represent a turning point, it was not precisely a sharp one, though this very possibly can be attributed to the onerous academic post that he had just accepted in July 1911. After being out of work for a year following the resignation of his lectureship at Trinity, he had agreed to teach *all* classes in the Department of Applied Mathematics and Mechanics at University College, London (including astronomy), which had suddenly been left without a single lecturer, for an unusually low salary of 300 pounds.[52] He was thus too busy for a number of years to attempt to shift his thinking in a different direction. In another letter to Russell around this time, he apologized for keeping some *Principia* proofs overlong, complaining that "this wretched astronomy (interesting enough in itself) has taken all my time."[53] It was only in mid-1914 that Whitehead was able to attain a less burdensome (and better paying) academic post,[54] and it was shortly afterward (in 1915) that he joined the Aristotelian Society.

THE ARISTOTELIAN SOCIETY

Interestingly, Victor Lowe writes of his earliest philosophical work that "although tempting, it would be a fundamental error to view these works as epistemological preparation undertaken for the construction of Whitehead's later metaphysical system."[55] As justification, he cites a conversation with Whitehead in 1941 in which he said that his philosophical interest grew out of a desire to provide a logical analysis of space for the fourth volume of the *Principia*, which was never completed, though he had apparently intended to do so even after migrating to Harvard.[56] A letter to Russell confirms that he was still actively writing this fourth volume on geometry as late as October 1913,[57] and at one point intended his "La Théorie Relationniste de L'Espace" to be included within it.[58] But despite Whitehead's specifically recalled conscious motivations, I do not think that any of this precludes the idea that his interests were shifting into a new realm, toward the philosophy of science and metaphysics more generally and that he may have simply been fooling himself in believing that a return to the *Principia* would ever be in the cards, especially after his move to America. Lowe himself acknowledged that "his thought was always pushing on to new ground; he would have had little patience with what would have amounted to backtracking."[59]

Even for a man who tended to habitually sell short his own expertise, some of the language found in Whitehead's early papers on philosophy is unusually timid. He must have been acutely conscious that when he joined the Aristotelian Society in 1915, it was full of younger men like Russell and G. E. Moore—both more than ten years Whitehead's junior—who had been active members for decades.[60] Thus we get Whitehead saying things like "the ideas are mostly philosophical, and the summary has been made by an amateur in that science; so there is no reason to ascribe to it any importance except that of a modest reminder," and "If I understand Kant rightly—which I admit to be very problematical," and "I would suggest—rather timidly—that this doctrine should be given a different twist."[61]

Nonetheless, we *do* see Whitehead making (timid) gestures toward "epistemological preparation" for his later metaphysics, as Lowe puts it. For instance:

> It needs very little reflection to convince us that a point in time is no direct deliverance of experience. We live in durations, and not in points. But what community, beyond the mere name, is there between extension in time and extension in space? In view of the intimate connection between time and space revealed by the modern theory of relativity, this question has taken on a new importance. I have not thought out an answer to this question.[62]

But he *had* thought out an answer—or at least the beginnings of one—years earlier, in his letter to Russell: "an object has essential extension in time as well as in space, and that there are time-parts of an object just as there are space-parts. In fact the time and space extensions are the object."[63]

He elaborates in what are labeled as "Supplementary Notes on the Above Paper." This addition is curious, and it is not clear to me when exactly it was added. He had first read the paper to the British Association for the Advancement of Science before reading it to the Aristotelian Society;[64] were these remarks added for the second presentation, or as a supplement to the version that appeared in print in 1916? (Overall, the "supplement" certainly seems to make bolder assertions.) Regardless, he explains that

> Kant . . . holds that in the act of experience we are aware of space and time as ingredients necessary for the occurrence of experience. I would suggest . . . that this doctrine should be given a different twist, which in fact turns it in the

opposite direction—namely, that in the act of experience we perceive a whole formed of related differentiated parts. The relations between these parts possess certain characteristics, and time and space are the expressions of some of the characteristics of these relations. Then the generality and uniformity which are ascribed to time and space express what may be termed the uniformity of the texture of experience.

[But] I am quite ready to believe that [this uniformity] is a mere illusion. . . . The uniformity which must be ascribed to experience is of a much more abstract attenuated character than is usually allowed. . . . It is not true that we are directly aware of a smooth running world, which in our speculations we are to conceive as given. In my view the creation of the world is the first unconscious act of speculative thought; and the first task of a self-conscious philosophy is to explain how it has been done.[65]

He is here unpacking and expanding on the idea that he had proposed to Russell as one that "help[s] a naive realism."[66] He notes that space and time are usually taken as baseline assumptions, brute facts of experience, when in fact they arise in the relations between objects, with the "uniformity" and "smoothness" of experiential space and time derived therefrom actually being an abstraction, a "mere illusion." We do not start with *the world*, but with the fragmentary time-extended, space-extended individual experiences that are the fundamental units of reality, and we must explain how "the world" arises out of them. He goes on to sketch some ideas toward answering this problem, but it would take years for Whitehead to begin answering it more robustly, and a decade before he would famously coin the phrase "fallacy of misplaced concreteness," first in his classroom,[67] and then in print in *SMW* as a shorthand for the sort of problems he was gesturing toward here. Nonetheless, the broad strokes of the solution were already present.

CONCLUSIONS

What are we to conclude from all this? By the admittedly scant evidence at our disposal, it appears that many of Whitehead's core philosophical/metaphysical convictions were present from at least his mid-twenties with the Apostles. His college education, which could be described as composed of two parallel components—the *formal* mathematical training, and the *informal* discussions in the humanities—had the effect of leaving him relatively free of what might be termed strong or "coercive" influence toward adopting any particular "received" philosophical opinions. That is, he was never enrolled in a class on philosophy at a formative age with a venerable professor who told him which pieces of the western philosophical canon were "correct." His celebrated philosophical originality emerged from a total immersion in mathematical methods by which he could approach that canon from a fresh perspective and have the temerity to do such things as "turn Kant on his head." As he said in his first paper to the Aristotelian Society, "By a healthy independence of thought perhaps we sometimes avoid adding other people's errors to our own."[68]

His career shift from mathematics to philosophy may have been driven in some sense by individual philosophical epiphanies such as the one on display in his 1911 letter to Russell which convinced him that he had something truly original to contribute, but as a whole the transition was a gradual one that grew organically from the same kind of desire that led Whitehead to rail against the teaching of "inert ideas": to find a yet broader and more practical application for his insights into the workings of reality than pure math. For while metaphysics might be considered the most abstract of all disciplines, it is simultaneously the most practical: "Every scientific man in order to preserve his reputation has to say he dislikes metaphysics. What he means is he dislikes having his metaphysics criticized."[69] Whitehead was the very broadest of thinkers, and it is only natural that he ended up working in the academic discipline which had the very broadest of applications and had implications to every aspect of our daily lives.

NOTES

1. Alfred North Whitehead, "Autobiographical Notes," in *The Philosophy of Alfred North Whitehead*, ed. Paul Schilpp (New York: Tudor Publishing, 1941), 7.
2. Whitehead, "Autobiographical Notes," 7.
3. Whitehead, "Autobiographical Notes," 7.
4. Lowe, *Alfred North Whitehead*, vol. 1, 129.
5. Lowe, *Alfred North Whitehead*, vol. 1, 136.
6. Lowe, *Alfred North Whitehead*, vol. 1, 136.
7. *SMW*, 202.
8. Lowe, *Alfred North Whitehead*, vol. 1, 137.
9. Lowe, *Alfred North Whitehead*, vol. 1, 137.
10. Lowe himself points out that scholars have sometimes tended to attribute certain aspects of Whitehead's early philosophy to readings of Bergson, but in 1885 Bergson had published nothing but *The Philosophy of Poetry* (1884). Thus, even though the two men would come to think highly of one another's work—with Bergson saying prior to Whitehead's Harvard appointment that he was "the best philosopher writing in English" (Lowe, *Alfred North Whitehead*, vol. 2, 133) and Whitehead acknowledging that he was "greatly indebted to Bergson" in *PR* (xii)—there could not have been any linkage between them in the mid-1880s.
11. Lowe, *Alfred North Whitehead*, vol. 1, 138.
12. *SMW*, 84.
13. *S*, 11–12.

14. *S*, 2–4.
15. Lowe, *Alfred North Whitehead*, vol. 1, 138.
16. Aside from a few fanciful pieces of short fiction—"Davy Jones" and "A Celebrity at Home. The Clerk of the Weather"—and a few pieces on Cambridge life—"A Visitation" and "The Fens as Seen from Skates": Alfred North Whitehead, "Davy Jones," *The Cambridge Review* (May 12, 1886): 311–312; Alfred North Whitehead, "A Celebrity at Home. The Clerk of the Weather," *The Cambridge Review* (February 10, 1886): 202–203; Alfred North Whitehead, "A Visitation," *The Cambridge Fortnightly* 1, no. 4 (March 6, 1888): 81–83; Alfred North Whitehead, "The Fens as Seen from Skates," *The Cambridge Review* (February 20, 1891): 212–213.
17. Whitehead to Russell, February 13, 1895, 4.
18. Lowe, *Alfred North Whitehead*, vol. 1, 316.
19. Lowe, *Alfred North Whitehead*, vol. 1, 317.
20. E.g., Bertrand Russell, *A Critical Exposition of the Philosophy of Leibniz* (Cambridge: Cambridge University Press, 1900).
21. Macmillan's records of correspondence with Whitehead reveal an amusing degree of exasperation on their part about his frequent lack of interest and understanding when it came to dealing with the business side of his publications.
22. Whitehead to Lowe, August 21, 1942.
23. In a January 1917 letter, Whitehead sternly refused to send some philosophical notes of his to Russell (Alfred North Whitehead, "Letter from Alfred North Whitehead to Bertrand Russell, January 8, 1917," LET1014, Whitehead Research Library, http://wrl.whiteheadresearch.org/items/show/1425). At this point, he had begun his own philosophical writing and had become understandably protective of his own ideas. Their relationship was also not helped by their differing views on WWI; Whitehead was unimpressed by Russell's denunciation of the war while all three of his children participated in it (Lowe, *Alfred North Whitehead*, vol. 2, 35).
24. Victor Lowe, "Whitehead's 1911 Criticism of *The Problems of Philosophy*," *Russell*, Old Series 13 (Spring 1974): 3–10.
25. Alfred North Whitehead, "Letter from Alfred North Whitehead to Bertrand Russell, August 26, 1911," Box 5.54, Bertrand Russell Archives, 81679, McMaster University.
26. In a diary entry of George Conger, he recalls Whitehead lamenting of Samuel Alexander's *Space, Time, and Deity* that "I'm afraid the dear man doesn't know enough mathematics" (*HL2*, 436).
27. "It is obvious that philosophy started from language and a rather naive trust in grammar. It was a great calamity that Aristotle didn't know Chinese. I have no doubt that it is an equal calamity in China that the Chinese don't know Greek" (*HL2*, 114).
28. Lowe, "Whitehead's 1911 Criticism," 5.
29. Bertrand Russell, "On Denoting," *Mind* 14, no. 4: 479–493.
30. Lucas, "'Muddleheadedness' vs. 'simplemindedness.'"
31. *CN*, 163.
32. *HL2*, 436.

33. Alfred North Whitehead, "Letter from Alfred North Whitehead to Bertrand Russell, August 26, 1911," Box 5.54, Bertrand Russell Archives, 81679, McMaster University.

34. *S,* 43.

35. *R,* 45. Whitehead's discussion of the boy and the cricket ball in his first Harvard lecture also leaps to mind in this connection: "If you are a school-boy with an important catch coming your way, it is not the colour you ever think of: it is the object exhibiting the colour. These objects are the most insistent things in our experience. They are vague in definition, but insistent for apprehension. You may forget the colour of the ball, but the ball imprints itself on your memory" (Whitehead, "First Lecture," 22).

36. Lowe, "Whitehead's 1911 Criticism," 9.

37. Whitehead to Russell, August 26, 1911, 7.

38. Whitehead to Russell, August 26, 1911, 10.

39. Lowe, "Whitehead's 1911 Criticism," 8. The added footnote is as follows: "Kant's 'thing in itself' is identical *in definition* with the physical object, namely, it is the cause of sensations. In the properties deduced from the definition it is not identical, since Kant held (in spite of some inconsistency as regards cause) that we can know that none of the categories are applicable to the 'thing in itself.'" Bertrand Russell, *The Problems of Philosophy* (London: Williams & Norgate, 1912).

40. Whitehead to Russell, August 26, 1911, 1.

41. *HL2,* 172.

42. *HL1,* 30.

43. *HL1,* 39.

44. *HL1,* 113.

45. *HL1,* 311.

46. Whitehead to Russell, August 26, 1911, 14.

47. Whitehead to Russell, August 26, 1911, 14–15.

48. That is, the *Principia* proofs.

49. Alfred North Whitehead, "Letter from Alfred North Whitehead to Bertrand Russell, September 3, 1911," Box 5.54, Bertrand Russell Archives, 81680, McMaster University.

50. *CN,* 66.

51. Whitehead to Russell, September 3, 1911.

52. Lowe, "Whitehead's 1911 Criticism," 4; Lowe, *Alfred North Whitehead,* vol. 2, 7.

53. Whitehead to Russell, September 20, 1911.

54. Lowe, *Alfred North Whitehead,* vol. 2, 26–27.

55. Lowe, *Alfred North Whitehead,* vol. 2, 92.

56. Lowe, *Alfred North Whitehead,* vol. 2, 92–93.

57. Lowe, *Alfred North Whitehead,* vol. 2, 15.

58. Lowe, *Alfred North Whitehead,* vol. 2, 94.

59. Lowe, *Alfred North Whitehead,* vol. 2, 95.

60. Lowe, *Alfred North Whitehead,* vol. 2, 90.

61. Alfred North Whitehead, "Space, Time, and Relativity,' *Proceedings of the Aristotelian Society,* New Series 16 (1915–16): 121.

62. Whitehead, "Space, Time, and Relativity," 107–108.
63. Whitehead to Russell, September 3, 1911.
64. Lowe, *Alfred North Whitehead*, vol. 2, 90.
65. Whitehead, "Space, Time, and Relativity," 121–122.
66. Whitehead to Russell, September 3, 1911.
67. *HL1*, 26.
68. Whitehead, "Space, Time, and Relativity," 104.
69. *HL2*, 375.

Chapter 8

Conclusion

Footnotes to Whitehead

> Science and the Modern World, *regarded as the exposition of a metaphysic, is a disappointment. I was the more disappointed in that I am a sincere admirer of Dr. Whitehead's philosophy of nature, and am convinced that the truth about the natural world lies somewhere along its lines. For the philosophy expounded in this book Dr. Whitehead gives hardly any reasons, nor for the connexion of his* Metaphysik *with his* Naturphilosophie, *so that the reader is continually asking plaintively "Why?" "Why?" "Why?" The "philosophy of organic mechanism" appears here as an intuition of Dr. Whitehead's, which may, of course, be as correct as is his reasoning about the Method of Extensive Abstraction. But the reasoning is lacking: we are given the answer to the sum, we want the working out. Will not Dr. Whitehead give us this in a still "more complete metaphysical study"?*
>
> —R. B. Braithwaite[1]

This book has endeavored to examine the significance of Whitehead materials that have been newly discovered and/or newly published by the Critical Edition project—from his Harvard lectures to unpublished public addresses and private letters—and ask how they impact our views of Whitehead and his philosophy. If the preceding chapters have been at all successful, then they have already provided some conclusions about how each of these individual pieces shifts our understanding. Yet the reader may also reasonably wish here, at the end, for some broader takeaways, as well as vectors for further development. Where has the Critical Edition already taken us, and where is it going?

THE NATURE OF THE HARVARD LECTURES

The largest portion of new material is the notes from Whitehead's lectures—a thousand pages for the first two books alone (not counting front or back matter), with four more to come. Outside of the first two chapters that provided general assessments on the accuracy of the notes and their relationship to Whitehead's books, I have only examined selected portions of them in detail here—namely the social ethics seminar presentation and the bits that discuss C. D. Broad—and the full impact of these volumes will probably not be felt for quite some time, until a critical mass of scholars has had the time to dissect them in more granular detail. But I think we may conclude here, based on both the nature and sheer volume of the material, that these notes are bound to have a more lasting and significant impact on Whitehead scholarship than any of the other materials that have been examined in this book.

But what exactly *is* the nature of these notes? When I began to write chapter 2 on "Whitehead's Lectures as Book Drafts," I had believed there would be clear correspondences between the lectures and Whitehead's books in a way that demonstrated that he developed material in his classroom which he later sharpened and honed and delivered as public lectures and published books. I even wrote a blog for Edinburgh University Press which had this idea as its central claim.[2] On closer examination, of course, as I ended up concluding in that second chapter, this notion does not really hold up. While there are similarities and parallels, Whitehead's Harvard lectures and his monographs appear to be fairly separate things. With the major exception of *Process and Reality*, Whitehead was more likely to bring an already-published work into his classroom than he was to go the other direction and develop classroom material into books, at least in an obviously traceable way.

As coeditors of the second volume of lectures, this conclusion was surprising to both Brian Henning and myself. In editing the volume, we had seen so much material that seemed familiar that the idea of "Lectures as Book Drafts" was an entirely natural theory. When I told Dr. Henning what I had found—that the parallels were much less distinct and more hazy than we had imagined—he asked me the next obvious question: how exactly would one characterize the volumes if not as an earlier stage of published material? What *are* the Harvard lectures?

At first, I could not say. It seemed like a large question. There is a lot of material, after all, and Whitehead covers a wide range of subjects in his lectures, sometimes spending a week re-presenting recently published work or recently delivered public lectures, like his "Time" paper[3] and his Barbour-Page lectures,[4] and sometimes spending an extra session reversing some of the material he had presented in a previous class.[5] A definitive characterization of

Whitehead's Harvard lectures would thus seem to require a detailed analysis of the whole, a daunting task for a thousand pages of very dense material (in practice, more than a thousand, since the form factor of notes means there is very little "filler" or "fluff," as students were trying to record/summarize the high points).

But in writing the rest of this book and meditating on the issue for some time, I have come to appreciate that a general characterization of the nature of Whitehead's Harvard lectures is indeed possible, without the need to analyze every portion; I had been so caught up in editing the individual pieces for *HL2* that I had somewhat missed the forest for the trees. It actually seems obvious when framed correctly.

This characterization arises from a few key observations and comparisons. The first has to do with the mundane necessities of teaching a class to a different set of students every semester versus Whitehead's stated intention of teaching what he was currently thinking about. The second actually has more to do with our own unconscious tendencies in the reception of the lectures (of which I am guilty as much as anyone), namely the problem of order of authorship versus order of discovery.

WAVES ON A BEACH

Speaking to the first point, I have already taken some pains to argue that we cannot simply write off the lectures as wholly repetitive from year to year and semester to semester in the way that one might expect for a course that he taught at the same institution with the same course number (Philosophy 3b) for thirteen years. It would have been easy for Whitehead to develop a syllabus and a set of lectures that he simply kept repeating for each new set of students, and yet it is very clear that he did not do this. My favorite piece of evidence for this remains Heath's first line at the top of her notes for Whitehead's second year: "Theoretically same course as 1924, but I credited it because actually it was quite different."[6] Whitehead did cover many of the same concepts and ideas, of course, and assigned a lot of the same texts across multiple years. But as his thinking and interests changed, Whitehead's lectures changed with them.

The key point is that there was a useful tension between Whitehead's desire to simply teach whatever he was currently thinking about—that is, "expressing in lectures and in less formal manner the philosophical ideas which have accumulated in my mind"[7]—and the fact that he had a new crop of students every term, which necessitated a certain degree of repetition and a certain degree of returning to the beginning, of reiterating some of the basic concepts and distinctions in his philosophy. The result is that Whitehead was sketching a broad overview of his philosophy and metaphysics anew every year.[8] It was repetition of a kind, yes, but can perhaps best be thought of as waves on a beach, with each one getting a little further along, and high water marks rising, before retreating to the beginning.

Take, for instance, the first lecture of the fall term in 1925 versus the first lecture in fall 1926. Both focus on the emergence of philosophy of science and of scientific thought generally. Both emphasize the particular importance of the seventeenth century in this regard, and acknowledge an indebtedness to the ancient Greek outlook. But the 1925 lecture is rougher, less defined, and less organized; for example, Heath's 1925 notes say that the scientific state of mind "appeared in Europe in 16th century, and fully active in 17th century," with "Sporadic occurrences before," including Aristotle and Archimedes—the ancient Greeks.[9] He then went back and traced a general line of development in Europe, from Greek drama, to Roman law, to the Catholic Church, to the Roman Empire, and to the rise of Aristotelian logic.[10] There is no great detail to any of this; they are simply bullet points in the notes of Heath and Roethlisberger.

By the time the first lecture of fall 1926 first rolls around, we get a lot of the same material, but put in a more logical and digestible order, along with more of what could properly be called Whitehead's original philosophy, as opposed to mere historical context and background. He straightaway identifies three distinct epochs in the development of the scientific outlook: the ancient Greeks, the seventeenth century, and the modern period.[11] After going into some detail on the importance of each, he discusses the misleading nature of propositions that can only be "true" or "false" when considered in their proper context ("Descartes is wrong only if we take him out of his background"),[12] and ends with a clear contrast between his own philosophy and that of the great Enlightenment masters:

> Whitehead's objection to Descartes, Leibniz, Kant, and to a less extent, Locke, is that they tacitly or explicitly presuppose that the final reality is an enduring subject with adventures . . . The world is a system of occasions whose nature is that they are continually superseded.[13]

In the final analysis of the two, there is both repetitious material and material exclusive to each lecture, but the 1926 lecture is more developed, more organized, and has more of Whitehead's original thought in it. Both cover the rise of the scientific mentality, but with different emphases, different orders of presentation, and different conclusions. The improvement in clarity of expression brings to mind part of a letter that Whitehead wrote to his son, North, about how he felt about his first year of lectures: "It might have been done much better, but it was done . . . I now know what I ought to have said as distinct from what I did say."[14]

Of course, it becomes harder to directly compare individual lectures in one year to those of another as the academic term and academic year move on, as Whitehead understandably tended to start with a lot of these same basics before heading off in different directions.[15] But the larger point is that each year Whitehead was presenting the core of his philosophy anew to the latest crop of students, with whatever evolutions and clarifications had since come to his mind. As a result, the Harvard lectures can be characterized as broad statements of his current thinking, in contrast to his books, which were more focused, unified efforts on specific topics. Put another way, the lectures could be considered a sort of baseline or starting point which *framed and circumscribed the questions* Whitehead was interested in addressing, while the books are the considered *answers* to some portion of those questions.

Such a characterization might at first strike the reader as a back door attempt at again claiming that Whitehead's lectures are something like an early draft of his books after I have already concluded that this is not the case. But there is a difference between saying that Whitehead took his Harvard class lecture notes and *turned them into* books and saying that the Harvard lectures *set the stage* for the books.

Probably the clearest example I can give to support this characterization is the line that can be drawn from Whitehead's discussion in his classroom of Broad's "critical" vs. "speculative" philosophy distinction in the opening pages of *Process and Reality (PR)*. To summarize an argument that is made more fully near the end of chapter 3, Broad had elevated critical philosophy—"the analysis and definition of our fundamental concepts, and the clear statement and resolute criticism of our fundamental beliefs"[16]—as a scientific endeavor that is mostly objective and exempt from the kind of error so common in philosophy of the speculative type. This latter he defined as

> tak[ing] over the results-of the various sciences, to add to them the results of the religious and ethical experiences of mankind, and then to reflect upon the whole . . . to reach some general conclusions as to the nature of the Universe.[17]

He denigrates it as producing

> elaborate systems which may quite fairly be described as moonshine . . . consist[ing] of more or less happy guesses, made on a very slender basis . . . [and] peculiarly liable to be biased by [the philosopher's] hopes and fears, his likes and dislikes, and his judgments of value.[18]

Whitehead seems to have assigned Broad's *Scientific Thought* to his Philosophy 3b students largely to criticize Broad's disparagement of "speculative philosophy." He tells his students that Broad has not properly appreciated the crucial place of speculation in philosophy—and, indeed, in science, which is driven by speculative hypotheses. He says that Broad's refusal to speculate is "cowardice" and "the great refusal," that "the way to correct [errors] is to speculate more."[19] Four years later, Whitehead begins his Gifford lectures by framing them as an essay in speculative philosophy. This is literally the first sentence of *PR*: "This course of lectures is designed as an essay in Speculative Philosophy. Its first task must be to define 'speculative philosophy,' and to defend it as a method productive of important knowledge."[20]

In this sense, the whole of *PR* can be seen as an (very thorough) answer to the question Whitehead had raised with his students about the viability of speculative philosophy, of which Broad had been so dismissive. The lectures provided the starting point, and *PR* the enlargement. Yet as I pointed out in chapter 3, Broad is never mentioned in *PR* at all. In a sense Whitehead erased his tracks behind him, or, more charitably, he simply did not consider those tracks to be especially important things to present to his public audience. After all, he had told his students quite explicitly that the critical-speculative distinction had come from Broad, then questioned the bifurcation, and explained the crucial task of speculation.

But though Broad's distinction represented a starting point for Whitehead in developing his metaphysics, in *PR* "critical philosophy" is mentioned only once—on page 50 in relation to Kant—and is not compared with "speculative philosophy" at all. As late as fall 1926, he had agreed with Broad that speculative philosophy presupposed critical philosophy,[21] but by the time he was giving his Gifford lectures, he seems to have reversed this order, or else decided that Broad's distinction was too much of a faulty bifurcation to be carried forward to a public audience. Evidence for the reversal can be found in a spring 1927 seminar, when Whitehead opined that "If you don't go into metaphysics, you assume an uncritical metaphysics . . . Every scientific man in order to preserve his reputation has to say he dislikes metaphysics. What he means is he dislikes having his metaphysics criticized."[22] In short, metaphysics encompasses all our unstated working hypotheses about the nature of the universe, and these must be clearly explicated before anything else can be done. Thus readers of *PR* are left with many of the same results that Whitehead's Harvard students got—that is, the crucial importance of speculation in philosophy and speculative hypotheses in science—but cannot trace the line of development through which Whitehead got to what he was presenting.

This shrouding of the development of Whitehead's philosophy is why I began this final chapter with a quote from R. B. Braithwaite's review of *SMW*, which concluded that "the reasoning is lacking: we are given the answer to the sum, we want the working out."[23] Now, one can certainly see *PR* as the "more complete metaphysical study" that Braithwaite was pleading for, which would not be a faulty characterization. But even in *PR* Whitehead has a tendency to pontificate, and I would argue that Whitehead's Harvard lectures provide another part of the "working out" that Braithwaite wanted. In them, he is freer in the attribution of influences and open to changing his mind, sometimes from one class session to the next, as he continually re-imagined and evolved the scope of his philosophy, so that we can clearly see how he got from A to B to C. Many of his convictions remain largely the same, and yet we see the actual, technical formulation evolving, the clarity of expression improving, and superfluous distinctions falling away, as the waves move further and further up the shore.

THE OCEAN OF METAPHYSIC

The other point I want to address with regard to how the Harvard lectures might best be characterized, and what their relationship is to Whitehead's published books, is the idea of order of authorship versus order of discovery. It seems quite natural, since the material in the Harvard lectures is newly published, for readers to orient themselves to it based on established Whitehead canon, and to interpret the newly discovered lectures through the lens of Whitehead's published works.[24] It is natural, and also not wrong, in one sense.

But such an approach also self-evidently distorts the true relationship of the one to the other. For as much as it might be convenient for us to view the Harvard lectures as a sort of supplement to Whitehead's published works, they simply cannot be defined this way; they are not a supplement to anything. Rather, they constitute a record of the philosophical ocean in which Whitehead was swimming from day to day, one which he was revising and renewing from year to year. His most famous philosophical books—*SMW*, *RM*, *S*, *PR*, *FR*, *AI*, *MT*—were all based on individual invited series of public lectures, that is, specific topics, snapshots in time. But he delivered all of them in the midst of the daily task of his Harvard lectures,[25] and when each was finished, it was the Harvard lectures to which he returned. It is thus the Harvard lectures that contain the truest record of the development of Whitehead's philosophy—including the false starts and dead ends that the published works obscure—a development which previously could only be inferred as taking place in the gaps between books.

This is all to say that a more fruitful endeavor than starting with Whitehead's books and interpreting the Harvard lectures through them would be to do it the other way around: start with the Harvard lectures, and interpret the books through the lens of Whitehead's baseline, everyday philosophy, the one that he spent thirteen years repeating and polishing on a daily basis. This approach is, to put it mildly, rather *inconvenient* for Whitehead scholars who have spent decades delving into the intricacies of Whitehead's philosophy as revealed in his published works, and who understandably do not wish to return, in a certain sense, to the beginning, and learn a new baseline through which to approach Whitehead's thought. But the inconvenience does not make the point less valid; it simply makes adopting it more difficult and also potentially that much more worthwhile.

The reader may well be thinking at this stage that this is all a little overstated. For one, both the books and the Harvard lectures must at times be interpreted in terms of each other. This is both obvious and unavoidable, particularly given the sometimes summary nature of notes that leave more scope for ambiguity. But this clarification of ambiguities arising from the imperfect records of student notes is just that: vulgar clarification of meaning. For example, "It is unclear what Whitehead is saying here, let us look at his books to see if we can find a similar passage that is more robust/transparent." There can be nothing new and original discovered by doing this; we simply end up reading the "old," well-known Whitehead of the published books into his lectures. Not much to be seen there aside from the order of (Whitehead's) discovery. But in the other direction, we find transitional material that the books, as snapshots in time, miss (providing examples of this is the main objective of the following section).

Then again there is the fact that Whitehead's books are what he self-consciously intended for wide public distribution. Surely this must have some bearing on the discussion. Indeed, the fact that Whitehead appears to have taken no care at all to preserve his original manuscripts and that he seems to have requested the destruction of at least a portion of his papers makes this point more acute. Victor Lowe wrote that

> He held an almost fanatical belief in the right to privacy, and thought that the only subject of rightful public interest in him was the work he had published . . . [also] He idealized youth and wanted young thinkers to develop their own ideas, not spend their best years on a Nachlass.[26]

He even wrote to Lowe in 1942 that "I am not prepared to sit down and comment on my past work. Please do not quote my letters."[27]

It must be said that Whitehead was a little naive on this point. A philosopher of his caliber was never going to simply be left alone. The lack of a *Nachlass* likely delayed a Critical Edition of his works by decades, but it was never going to stop it; it simply made the exercise more difficult, forcing scholars to track down student notes in the absence of a carefully preserved collection of his own lecture notes and book manuscripts. Nor do I think it is a particularly strong argument to say that the Harvard lectures should be relegated to second-class status in his corpus merely because he did not explicitly intend their publication. These lectures, after all, were not *private* things—he was not lecturing to an empty room. He was teaching his own philosophical views to a room full of interested students. And though he may have written to Lowe that he was not prepared to comment on his past work, this is exactly what he did in his classroom, frequently commenting on how his own thought had evolved since some past book,[28] and even sitting down with Allison Heartz Johnson once a week for an entire semester while the latter peppered him with questions about Whitehead's philosophy as he wrote his thesis on "Whitehead's theory of relativity."[29]

It is notable that Whitehead remarked to Johnson at the outset: "Don't hesitate to criticize. There are contradictions. Mine is not a final and complete system."[30] Johnson also agreed with Paul Weiss on one point regarding Whitehead—when they agreed on little else[31]—that Whitehead would have been "amazed by the fact that *Process and Reality* is regarded as *the* book to be read in order to understand Whitehead—the rest can be safely neglected."[32] If Johnson exaggerates the sentiment among some sets of Whitehead's present-day admirers, it is not by much; there is still a tendency to regard *PR* as the definitive Whitehead, and everything else as a mere supplement. But the truth is that Whitehead's philosophy never stopped evolving and that his books were buoys in a continuing journey, snapshots of his thought at that time, and not definitive or inviolable. Indeed, Whitehead "admitted serious defects [in *PR*] with cheerful candor."[33] After all, the ocean of metaphysic which Whitehead spent his life in America exploring—both in his books and his classroom—is the widest possible ocean of thought, and he knew better than anyone that he was bound to get many things wrong as he swam through it. That the lectures delivered in his Harvard lectures more clearly display his hesitations and changes of mind make them all the more valuable.

TRANSITIONS

But perhaps I am belaboring these points overmuch, or else simply engaging in too much poetry about oceans in lieu of robust examples. The reader will want some concrete illustrations of what I mean. Why is it better to start with the Harvard lectures and then interpret Whitehead's books by means of them, rather than the reverse?

For the following example, much of the hard work has already been done for me by Ronny Desmet, in one of his contributions[34] to *Whitehead at Harvard, 1924–1925*, an anthology of essays exploring the significance of *HL1*. It remains for me only to summarize the high points of his rather detailed and highly technical argument and apply it to the matter at hand.

The issue surrounds Whitehead's (supposed) shift from an understanding of becoming as continuous to one of becoming as atomic, an issue that has been a bone of contention among Whiteheadians since the publication of Lewis Ford's *The Emergence of Whitehead's Metaphysics* in 1985.[35] It remains a live issue. Paul Bogaard, in his introduction to *HL1*, argues that the first year of Harvard lectures disproves Ford's theory that Whitehead's understanding shifted during his first year of teaching:

> We can only assume that without any Hocking notes before the beginning of November, Ford missed Whitehead's setting up of the challenge of finding an adequate way to interweave atomism with the continuity also required for any process philosophy . . . Ford seems to have missed Whitehead's building up to an insight he had already anticipated.[36]

Moreover, Gary Herstein argues that Ford's method of "compositional analysis" was "profoundly questionable" and that "there is no trace of such a notion to be found *anywhere* in the Harvard lectures; indeed, throughout the lectures Whitehead unqualifiedly rejects any discontinuity of *either* space *or* time."[37]

But Desmet *does* find evidence for Ford's theory, and in my estimation, his explanation is the one that holds the most water. Bogaard's observation that Whitehead had been "building up to an insight he had already anticipated" probably referred to this passage from Whitehead's second Harvard lecture: "Consideration of process throws light on two contrasting ideas: continuity [and atomicity]. Process exhibits atomic character imposed upon a continuous field."[38] But Desmet points out that our anticipation of *PR* causes us to read more into this passage than is actually there, because it ignores Whitehead's prior distinction (in *CN*, and held through this stage) between the passage of nature and the time of the field of extension.

In August 1924—the very month that he set sail for America—Whitehead had added some notes to the second edition of *PNK*, one of which read:

> In §15.8 [of this book] it is pointed out that continuity is derived from events, and atomicity from objects. This . . . requires development. It must suffice for the moment to suggest that a scientific object is an atomic structure imposed upon the continuity of events.[39]

The key word here is "imposes," for Whitehead was attempting to heal the bifurcation between psychological time and the mathematical time of physicists like Einstein. So this "atomic structure" is "imposed" upon the "continuity of events." But what does Whitehead mean by "continuity of events"? He tells us quite clearly in *CN*:

The continuity of nature arises from extension. Every event extends over other events, and every event is extended over by other events. Thus in the special case of durations which are now the only events under consideration, every duration is part of other durations; and every duration has other durations which are parts of it. Accordingly there are no maximum and no minimum durations. Thus there is no atomic structure of durations.[40]

So the "atomic structure" only applies to scientific objects, which are abstractions, while psychological time, which Whitehead is trying to rescue from the physicists, is a continuity of events. In short, he is still arguing for the continuity of process. But from the first to the second semester of the Harvard lectures, a change occurs. Desmet sums it up this way:

> In *The Concept of Nature*, Whitehead makes a distinction between the passage of nature and the time of the field of extension, but—as the passage of nature is the passage of events and the extensive relatedness of events accounts for continuity—he holds that both are continuous . . . In the [first semester of Harvard lectures] Whitehead holds that the distinction is one between the *continuous* process of becoming and the *continuous* time of the field of extension, whereas in the latter [semester] he holds that the distinction is one between the *atomic* process of becoming and the *continuous* time of the extensive continuum.[41]

Whitehead thus adopted the idea that was later to be found in *PR*, that the processes of becoming were atomic, but located within the extensive continuum. At first he had said in his October 2, 1924, lecture at Radcliffe that "reality is . . . a continuity of becoming,"[42] in *PR* he specifically denies this ("There can be no continuity of becoming. There is a becoming of continuity, but no continuity of becoming"),[43] and in the second semester we see him saying things like

> Whitehead going on line that <u>atomic</u> side of things is what finds its home in <u>generation</u>. Generation, process, must be atomic (Zeno) . . . Under influence of <u>quantum</u> theory, atomic view growing. Jeans:—you've got to take your Time in chunks[44]

and

> As being real the Subject has to be taken atomically[45]

and

> That atomic independence of what is immediately present, is absolutely necessary if you are to have any Freedom or any Error. And these <u>are</u> in the Universe.[46]

142   *Chapter 8*

He has decided that becoming is atomic.

This insight also appears clearly, at times, in *SMW*. The problem is that it really had been a recent transition for Whitehead. Price's *Dialogues* have Whitehead saying that he wrote each of his eight Lowell lectures—which took place on Mondays and Thursdays in February of 1925, starting on February 2[47]—no more than a week in advance of their delivery,[48] while Whitehead's own letter to his son North gives an only slightly rosier picture when he says that the Lowell lectures "amounted to writing a book in about two months."[49] And in the compressed time frame, he sometimes confused the issue. Here Desmet is very helpful, and I quote him at length, since his explanation of some of the confusions in *SMW* cannot be shortened without losing the plot:

> [In *SMW*] Whitehead holds that "temporalisation is realisation," that "realisation is the becoming of time in the field of extension," and that consequently "temporalisation is not another continuous process" but "an atomic succession" (*SMW*, 126)—so far, so good. However, Whitehead's next sentence reads: "Thus time is atomic, (i.e. epochal)" (*SMW*, 126). This comes as a surprise and seems to lead to a *reductio ad absurdum*. If time is atomic, then time is an atomic succession (in fact, Whitehead writes: "Time is sheer succession of epochal durations" (*SMW*, 125)). Hence there is no difference between time and temporalisation and, consequently, time is the becoming of time. The last phrase seems absurd indeed. However, if we are careful and observe the distinction between $time_1$ = the time of the becoming of time in the field of extension, and $time_2$ = time in the field of extension, then the seemingly absurd phrase still makes sense. It then means: the time of becoming is the atomic becoming of the continuous time of extension. And indeed, Whitehead warns the readers of *Science and the Modern World*: "In this account 'time' has been separated from 'extension'" (*SMW*, 125). So when he says that time is atomic or epochal, he is actually saying that the time of becoming is epochal, without implying that the time of extension is.[50]

With material like this, it is no wonder that Whitehead scholars are confused about Ford's temporal atomism thesis: Whitehead himself is confused, at least in his prose, at this moment. And consider that this is the text as it appeared *after* Whitehead had revised it for publication in the summer of 1925, after his Harvard classes had ended; who knows what Whitehead's audience to his first series of Lowell lectures actually heard, and how much more muddled it may have been?

And now we finally return to the point at hand. Now, clearly Desmet has rightly used Whitehead's books in places to clarify his uses of the term "atomism" in the fall 1924 Harvard lectures, for example, via the notes added to the second edition of *PNK*. Desmet's careful and detailed clarifications are very much necessary, for they are not easy to digest even when they have been laid out in full. But the real interest lies in the other direction. The Harvard lectures show us a Whitehead who is in the midst of finding his philosophical feet, and admits his confusion with what Johnson aptly labeled "cheerful candor." Desmet focused on the clear distinction between Whitehead's lectures of September and October versus March and April with respect to the atomism-continuity problem. But let us look at what was happening in February.

It was February 10, Whitehead's first lecture of the spring term, a Tuesday. He had begun delivering his Lowell lectures that would become *SMW* on February 2 and had just finished his third lecture on February 9, the day prior, with another to come two days hence. His subject was not "Time" but a related topic: "extensive abstraction." He began by talking about an event as the most concrete thing, saying that we "must start from the psychological field," as opposed to "what it is that Physicist assumes re ultimate entities with which he starts."[51] This sounds rather suspiciously like Whitehead's attempt to rescue psychological time from the abstract time of the physicists.

And then, in the very next paragraph, we abruptly get a hefty dose of Whitehead's "cheerful candor":

Details of what lecturing on worked out somewhat clumsily in 3rd Part of *Principles of Natural Knowledge* and throughout *Concept of Nature* and 1st Part of *Principle of Relativity*. Not so concerned now in following systematic details as in pointing out confusion etc. in those books[,] as in pointing out what lies behind ideas there . . . Also:—Whitehead only knows three ways of getting up a subject: (1) to be "taught" it; (2) to write a book on it; (3) to lecture on it. Advantage of lecturing is that your pupils teach you as much as you them.[52]

If there is any more perfect distillation than this one of why the Harvard lectures are so valuable, I do not know it. *He comes right out and says* that he is aiming to explicate his own past (and perhaps current) confusions and get behind the technicalities of the underlying ideas. And points (2) and (3) about how to learn a subject have a special significance here, because Whitehead was literally right in the middle of "writing a book," as he had described writing the Lowell lectures to his son, North, as well as giving lectures to his Harvard students at the same time. That he was in such an intense period of both writing and lecturing at this moment also strongly implies to me that he was very conscious of "getting up" on his subject(s), that is, he knew that he was making breakthroughs.

And this is hardly the only place where something like this occurs. It is all over the Harvard lectures. Another prominent example that happens to

Philosophy 20h: Seminar in Metaphysics, fall semester 1926

dipolar occasion. Contrast of importance between the two poles. Mental pole may be negligible.

Each occasion supersedes others, is superseded by others, is internally a ~~part of~~ process of supersession.

|2| Paper

Potential and actual.

Potential – to Descartes

        Bergson, *durée*

Mental supersedes physical. Physical must be explained first.

Linkage between physical and mental poles illustrates truth that category of supersession transcends time – Linkage is extratemporal, yet supersession.

{Event as physical pole, mentality as functioning as a mental pole}
V(Working toward)V[1]

⟨**II. Prehension**⟩ **Time: Supersession, prehension, incompleteness.**[2]
Trying to describe same thing as Dewey.

Prehension. How world is a system of organisms.

Occasion is a concretion of diverse elements.

Elements as organized fall into two classes.

(1) The other occasions {Dewey really takes each occasion on its own}.
Otherwise *deus ex machina*

(2) Universals. Eternal objects.

World can't be a system unless get ----[3]

Definite way in which *a* includes other occasions is here called prehension. Blind physical perceptivity.

Kant: intuitions without concepts are blind. Suggest Kant – missed way.

Physical world includes eternal objects as its defining elements, but only intuitively.

Trick of organization of world into a system and of ⟨?⟩ physical world each physical occasion as organization of whole world from one point of view implementing concrete individuality upon organization as done by this blind perceptivity.[4]

Pure perception is the fundamental relationship of physical occasions in physical world.

Occasion *a* prehends *b* under limitation of objectification (an object for something else) – Same as Leibnizian perspectives.

Subject is prehending occasion.

Objectification is provided by eternal objects – *b* is prehended into *a* as example of these objects.

Universals are functioning.

---

1. Parentheses supplied.
2. Cf. Whitehead: 'The concept of time is complex, and arises from the interplay of three fundamental categories, namely, *Supersession, Prehension,* and *Incompleteness*' (Whitehead, 'Time', p. 60).
3. Conger seems to have misheard here. Cf. Whitehead: 'Because the other occasions are each in a definite way required for the organization of any one occasion A, the world is called a system' (Whitehead, 'Time', p. 60).
4. This entire paragraph appears as a kind of marginal note on the right of the preceding paragraph.

Figure 8.1   Page 343 from *HL2*. *Source*: Edinburgh University Press, 2021.

follow the concept of time in Whitehead's philosophy has to do with his paper "Time," presented at the Sixth International Congress of Philosophy in mid-September 1926.[53] Two weeks later, Whitehead would re-present the paper to his seminar students in the first session of the year,[54] *but with additional commentary*. Here I believe sharing a page from the lectures will help illustrate the extent of that commentary (see figure 8.1).

The bolding on the page was an editorial device that we introduced to the volume to indicate when Whitehead was reading something aloud, verbatim. Hence the bold portions indicate him delivering his "Time" paper as written, while the non-bolded portions indicate additions and commentary. As can be seen by only a quick glance at this page, Whitehead is hardly simply reading. Already he is drawing many more connections than he made at the Congress.

Then, two months later, in December, Whitehead would spend no less than *four class sessions* of his Philosophy 3b lecturing on the subject of time, using his recent paper as a skeleton, but expanding upon it significantly.[55] The lectures make all kinds of references to people and things that appear nowhere in the "Time" paper, like William James, Hegelians, and God. Whitehead is unpacking and expanding upon his original paper to such a degree that it is practically unrecognizable apart from a shared set of major headings.

The larger point here is that Whitehead's books and papers came into his classroom all the time, but not as settled matters. At times, as can be seen from the earlier extended example, he would disparage his past work as confused while attempting to chart a new course. At other times, he would bring in recent work and provide additional commentary and context that may not have shifted the core argument but did provide further insights not to be found in the original. That is, Whitehead's Harvard lectures not only set the stage for the monographs by circumscribing the philosophical questions that Whitehead was most keen to tackle in a robust way, but those monographs were then immediately brought back into his classroom for further consideration and development. Thus the books presuppose the lectures but do not fully contain them, whereas the lectures are a vaster sea in which the books are floating, each one surrounded by the tides of developmental lines behind them and tides of criticism and refinement ahead.

THE FUTURE

I have titled this final chapter "Footnotes to Whitehead" for a number of reasons. It is firstly an obvious reference to Whitehead's most famous quotation, "The safest general characterization of the European philosophical tradition is that it consists of a series of footnotes to Plato."[56] Another reason is that, though I have been arguing for a kind of primacy of Whitehead's

Harvard lectures as the baseline of his philosophical canon and the truest record of his philosophical development, another valid reading is to see the Harvard lectures as a series of footnotes to Whitehead, by Whitehead. They are not *only* this, but they are this also. His frequent commentary on past published works in his classroom makes this luminously obvious, that he did not sit on his philosophical laurels and consider his most recent publications to be endings, definitive and inviolable. Not two weeks would go by before he was back in his classroom giving his students footnotes, additions, and alterations to what he had just recently presented to a wider public.

Whitehead's books will always be enormously important. They are not going anywhere. But the Harvard lectures are alive in a way that the books are not. An obituary written by a number of Whitehead's teaching assistants and other grad students said that

> In the lecture room he gave the appearance of complete spontaneity. He did not deliver a set piece; his lecture was thought in action. Those who know him only from his books have missed something of his mind; for he was happier, easier, freer in speech than in writing. The listener had the experience of being taken behind the scenes and witnessing the very process of creative thinking, with its doubts and queries, its problems genuinely felt, in an unfinished but living form.[57]

This concluding chapter has endeavored to provide some substance to this characterization by examining the relationship between *HL1* and *HL2* and Whitehead's published writings, in order to show that there is more in the Harvard lectures than we had dared hope. Maybe in one sense they are just a series of footnotes to Whitehead, but the footnotes are the philosophy in action. It is now incumbent upon us to engage with Whitehead in an entirely new way, to return to the beginning and see his mind anew, for the Harvard lectures are likely to shift and enlarge our understanding of every portion of Whitehead's philosophy. It will not be easy or comfortable to venture beyond the familiar confines of his well-established books, but worthwhile endeavors rarely are.

Nor, of course, is the Critical Edition of Whitehead anywhere close to finished. For one, there are four more volumes of Harvard lecture notes planned, and though it will be some time before they are edited and published, I am in the fortunate position of having overseen the initial transcription of all materials for *HL3*, *HL4*, and *HL5* (as of this writing, transcription of materials for *HL6* has only just begun). This allows me here at the end to at least gesture toward a few of the more obvious impacts that these future volumes are likely to have on Whitehead scholarship.

As already discussed somewhat in chapter 2, *HL3* will cover the year leading up to Whitehead's Gifford lectures which would become his most famous book, *Process and Reality*. An examination of notes by Sinclair Kerby-Miller, Edwin Marvin, and Susanne Langer[58] reveals that Whitehead was presenting drafts of his Gifford lectures to his Harvard students before he delivered them in Edinburgh. Though Victor Lowe did not believe these lecture notes showed a genetic development from the lectures to the book, in my own estimation and that of Lewis Ford, they very much do, showing, for example, an early list of eight "principles" that would later be part of a larger list of Whitehead's twenty-seven "categories of explanation" in *PR*, even given in a different order than would appear in the finished book. It would be hard to overstate the significance of getting a look at what appears to be, in effect, an early draft of *PR*, when all of Whitehead's own book drafts have been lost. I cannot predict what an analysis of the differences will show, but I feel quite safe in asserting that we will discover much about *PR*'s composition that we never could have hoped to discover before now.

HL4 will cover 1930–1933, the years leading up to the publication of *Adventures of Ideas*. It is unclear to me if these notes will throw much light upon that book in particular, especially since *AI* is not a unified series of lectures delivered all at once in the style of *SMW*, *RM*, *S*, and *PR*. What *is* clear to me is that Whitehead's lectures here contain a great deal of formidable and rhetorically powerful material. This was brought home to me especially when I finished transcribing the last of these notes shortly after a Whitehead Research Project conference that I helped to organize on Whiteheadian propositions.[59] Whitehead's Harvard lectures provided a passage that I would have dearly liked to have as guiding thought for that conference:

> Essence of proposition: clothing a nexus' appearance with some qualitative reaction. Mother towards her child, we towards a picture—beautiful, ugly. Marriage of qualitative enjoyment with physical origination. Thus propositions should not be handed over to logicians to study; logicians are dry, hard people. "Propositions fall properly within the province of artists, lovers and lunatics."[60]

If there is a passage like this in any of Whitehead's books, I do not know it. A keyword search for "lunatic" in all of Whitehead's philosophical books turns up only one result[61] that bears no relation to what we see here. It goes to show that even though student notes are almost necessarily truncated from the lecturer's original delivery (stenographic accounts excepted), this does not always preclude rhetorical elegance or the presence of passages that seem bound to be repeatedly quoted and discussed for many years to come.

As for *HL5*, it covers 1933–1935, the last few years in which Whitehead would conduct his Friday seminars; he would drop these and only teach his lecture course for his final two years (1935–1937). Importantly, two of these final seminars were co-taught with William Ernest Hocking—one of Whitehead's great admirers in Harvard's Philosophy Department—who kept extensive notes and records of lesson plans and ensuing discussions in these sessions, the best accounts of these seminars that we have.[62] This is rather significant since the seminars were much more discussion-based than Whitehead's lectures, and so we will get to see Whitehead thinking on his feet and responding to direct critiques and questions more often than anywhere else in any of the Harvard lectures volumes. Hocking's recollections seem to confirm this:

> The success of this joint enterprise obviously depended on complete frankness on both sides, and on the part of the students as well. Whitehead was most insistent on this point: in the nature of any new point of view there is required "a certain measure of ferocity." When a student modestly suggested that his point of criticism "may be superficial," Whitehead's swift word was, "Don't be polite to me." After accusing me on one occasion of having spoken from a Hegelian standpoint, he added, "Don't be afraid of exposing my ignorance before the class—say anything you like—I speak in complete ignorance of Hegel."[63]

Beyond the Harvard lectures volumes, there will also be two volumes of correspondence, one with Russell and one covering correspondence with everyone else. I have already examined a few of the letters to Russell in the previous chapter that I deemed to have special significance in showing us Whitehead's initial turn away from mathematics and toward philosophy. But this is, of course, only a beginning. Whitehead wrote many letters to other philosophers which may yet reveal previously unsuspected interests and influences.

As one small example, in 1931, Whitehead wrote a letter to G. E. Moore indicating an interest in Wilhelm Dilthey:

> [George Morgan's] thesis and [his] article have interested me considerably . . . His work convinced me that it is important to know about Dilthey as an important figure in a big German school, of which Nietsche [sic] and later men form another (and more brilliant) section.[64]

But despite this letter to Moore, Dilthey is never mentioned anywhere in Whitehead's books. Moreover, beyond the philosophical implications, there are all the letters to and from friends and family that provide so much of the missing context of Whitehead's life, from wartime letters from his children, to correspondence with close friend Felix Frankfurter (a US Supreme Court justice),[65] and a bundle of correspondence with Paul Schilpp concerning the publication of Whitehead's *Library of Living Philosophers* volume—including the scholars whose participation he invited but did not receive.

Finally, there are the two forthcoming volumes of Whitehead's Collected Papers, transcriptions of which we are in the process of verifying as I write this.[66] The publication of these two volumes stands to accomplish a great deal. For one, there are often numerous errors in Whitehead's original published articles. Lest the reader think I am exaggerating, a careful review of the twenty-seven-page first part of Whitehead's "Memoir on the Algebra of Symbolic Logic"[67] has revealed no less than fifteen substantive errors in the mathematical/symbolic expressions of the original.

Beyond all the errors to be corrected, many of Whitehead's previously published articles are hard to find and/or largely forgotten, such as Whitehead's literary efforts for the *Cambridge Review* in the late 1880s which have never been published anywhere else,[68] or his "La Théorie Relationniste de L'Espace"[69] in *Revue de Métaphysique et de Morale* that appeared originally in French and was never translated in Whitehead's lifetime, or the numerous essays that have only otherwise appeared in little-known collections edited by A. H. Johnson.[70] I suspect that the editing and publication of all these essays together in chronological order will do much to help illuminate connections and developments in Whitehead's thought that are currently difficult to spot. This will be aided further by the "splitting up" of some of Whitehead's books that were always looser, "Frankenstein's monster" collections of essays written at very different times. It is often forgotten, for instance, that *Aims of Education* and *Organisation of Thought* are virtually the same book, sharing six chapters in common.[71]

Then, of course, there is the material set to appear in these volumes that was never published at all. I have undertaken in this book to do a first analysis of two of the more crucial pieces: "Religious Psychology of the Western Peoples" (chapter 5) and "Freedom and Order" (chapter 6). If I have argued my cases well, then RPWP, together with the often forgotten yet epic 7,000-word "An Appeal to Sanity," reveals a Whitehead who was becoming more concerned and preoccupied with the negative influence of rigid religious orthodoxy toward the end of his life than has previously been realized, providing us with a new and powerful denunciation of religious hatred and the dangers of religious extremism and creeping authoritarianism; these are subjects only lightly touched on in his books, but given sustained attention in RPWP. FO, meanwhile, shows us a Whitehead experimenting with previously unseen technical terminology in a piece that is likely transitional between *SMW* and *PR*. Though it repeats many of the arguments found in *SMW*, the terminological experiment itself is instructive and much resembles similar lines of development that have popped up all over the Harvard lectures. I have not had the space here to examine other previously unknown pieces of Whitehead's such as his "Science and Economic Liberty: A Comparison of England and America,"[72] his toast of the Democratic Presidential candidate Al Smith,[73] and tributes to friends and colleagues A. Lawrence Lowell[74] and Philip Cabot.[75]

Suffice it to say that the Critical Edition of Whitehead project is still near the beginning of a very long journey. I have endeavored here to make a first attempt at exploring the significance of only a relatively small portion of it. I can only hope that this effort has demonstrated the importance of this new material to Whitehead scholarship, for I truly believe that it has the potential to revolutionize the field. It remains only for the project to continue and complete its work, and for scholars to fully come to grips with the fruits of it.

NOTES

1. From his review of *SMW* in *Mind*: R. B. Braithwaite, review of *Science and the Modern World*, by Alfred North Whitehead, *Mind*, New Series 35, no. 140 (October 1926): 500. Whitehead commended the review to his students (*HL2*, 233).

2. Joseph Petek, "The Missing Drafts of Whitehead's Books," Edinburgh University Press Blog, January 15, 2021, https://euppublishingblog.com/2021/01/15/the-missing-drafts-of-whiteheads-books/.

3. *HL2*, 342–347.

4. *HL2*, 336–337.

5. *HL2*, 179.

6. *HL2*, 3.

7. Lowe, *Alfred North Whitehead*, vol. 2, 134.

8. I say "year," though technically Whitehead's class was separate per term and could be taken individually. In practice, many students attended both terms of the course, and he tended to focus on slightly different things in the fall and the spring. In later years this would be formalized when the catalog number for Whitehead's class was changed from being "Philosophy 3b" in both terms to being "Philosophy 3" in one term and "Philosophy 3b" in the other.

9. *HL2*, 4.

10. *HL2*, 5.

11. *HL2*, 170.

12. *HL2*, 171.

13. *HL2*, 172.

14. Alfred North Whitehead, "Letter from Alfred North Whitehead to T. North Whitehead, 31 May 1925," Alfred North Whitehead Collection, MS-0282, Box 2, Folder 19, Special Collections, Johns Hopkins University.

15. E.g., the final lecture of the fall 1925 term focused on causality (*HL2*, 110), while the final lecture of the fall 1926 term focused on motion (*HL2*, 285).

16. Broad, *Scientific Thought*, 18.

17. Broad, *Scientific Thought*, 20.

18. Broad, *Scientific Thought*, 20–21.

19. *HL1*, 248.

20. *PR*, 3.
21. *HL2*, 189.
22. *HL2*, 375.
23. See opening citation.
24. In this connection, there has even been the suggestion—due to the nature of the material as notes taken by Whitehead's audience—that we should be suspicious of novel material in the lectures (i.e., material that is not exactly reflected in Whitehead's books). This is certainly a clear example of the idea of interpreting the Harvard lectures by means of the published works, but it is also a different can of worms than what I am discussing now. See chapter 1 for a detailed discussion of the authorship problem.
25. With the exception of *MT*, which was delivered the year after his retirement.
26. Lowe, *Alfred North Whitehead*, vol. 1, 7.
27. Whitehead to Lowe, August 21, 1942.
28. Chapters 6 and 7 of *An Enquiry Concerning the Principles of Natural Knowledge* (*PNK*) are "frightfully confused chapters," while chapter 3 of *The Concept of Nature* (*CN*) is "better, but one gets out of a confused state by dropping the difficulty [of change, motion, time], so in some sense this is not so good" (*HL1*, 69); "*Principle of Relativity* (*R*) doesn't make distinction between physical concrescence and conceptual analyses" (*HL2*, 236); "Obviously left out something [of *PNK*]—then wanted to define what we should mean by a point. Couldn't define it properly—without bringing in further question of how measured time, idea of a duration. . . . Fairly obvious that that was because I left out some element" (*HL2*, 304); "Epochal physical occasion—becomes as one divisible but not divided in its becoming. In *The Concept of Nature*, no epochal view, nor of relationship of physical and mental" (*HL2*, 351).
29. Johnson, *Whitehead and His Philosophy*, 21.
30. Johnson, *Whitehead and His Philosophy*, 22.
31. Johnson, *Whitehead and His Philosophy*, 69.
32. Johnson, *Whitehead and His Philosophy*, 72.
33. Johnson, *Whitehead and His Philosophy*, 71.
34. Ronny Desmet, "From Physics to Philosophy, and from Continuity to Atomicity," in *Whitehead at Harvard, 1924–1925*, ed. Brian G. Henning and Joseph Petek (Edinburgh: Edinburgh University Press, 2020), 132–153.
35. Lewis Ford, *The Emergence of Whitehead's Metaphysics: 1925–1929* (Albany: State University of New York Press, 1985), chapter 3.
36. *HL1*, xlvi.
37. Gary Herstein, "Quanta and Corpuscles: The Influence of Quantum Mechanical Ideas on Whitehead's Transitional Philosophy in Light of *The Harvard Lectures*," in *Whitehead at Harvard, 1924–1925*, ed. Brian G. Henning and Joseph Petek (Edinburgh: Edinburgh University Press, 2020), 128.
38. *HL1*, 6.
39. *PNK*, 203.
40. *CN*, 59.
41. Desmet, "From Physics to Philosophy," 146.

42. *HL1*, 417.
43. *PR*, 35.
44. *HL1*, 309.
45. *HL1*, 321.
46. *HL1*, 353.
47. Lowell Institute, "Public Lectures in the City of Boston under The Lowell Institute: Program for 1924–1925," 1924, DOC034, Whitehead Research Library.
48. Price, *Dialogues of Alfred North Whitehead*, 149.
49. Lowe, *Alfred North Whitehead*, vol. 2, 303.
50. Desmet, "From Physics to Philosophy," 147.
51. *HL1*, 195.
52. *HL1*, 195.
53. Alfred North Whitehead, "Time," in *Proceedings of the Sixth International Congress of Philosophy*, ed. Edgar Sheffield Brightman (New York: Longmans, Green and Co., 1927), 59–64.
54. *HL2*, 342–347.
55. *HL2*, 245–258.
56. *PR*, 39.
57. Demos, "Proceedings," 469.
58. See chapter 2.
59. Eighth International Whitehead Research Project Conference, "A Whiteheadian Laboratory: Featuring Erin Manning, Brian Massumi, and the SenseLab," December 1–3, 2016, Claremont, California.
60. Charles Habib Malik, "Philosophy 3: Philosophy of Science," May 4, 1933, Charles Habib Malik Papers, Box 251, Folder 5, Manuscript Division, Library of Congress, Washington, D.C. Thomas G. Henderson recorded it a little differently: "Associate particular facts with ideas—associate a table as a thing of beauty—association of abstract notions, of qualitative types of things, with objects is the basis of our mentality—association of quality with the particular thing is the proposition. Proposition has been handed over to Logicians—shouldn't have been—Logicians are last people in the world who should handle the proposition—should be handled by poets, lovers and lunatics" (Thomas G. Henderson, "Whitehead lecture notes: Philosophy and the Methods of Science," May 4, 1933, Alfred North Whitehead Collection, MS-0282, Box 6, Folder 7, Special Collections, Johns Hopkins University).
61. *R*, 50.
62. The only other account of Whitehead's seminars that we possess that are anywhere close to as good as Hocking's are Conger's record of Whitehead's seminars for 1926–27, which appear in *HL2*.
63. Hocking, "Whitehead as I Knew Him," 512.
64. Alfred North Whitehead, "Letter from Alfred North Whitehead to G. E. Moore, June 15, 1931," George Edward Moore: Personal Papers and Correspondence, Add.8330 8W/20/6, Cambridge University Library.
65. See Petek, "Whitehead and Felix Frankfurter."
66. That is, Brian G. Henning, Robert J. Valenza, and myself.

67. Alfred North Whitehead, "Memoir on the Algebra of Symbolic Logic," *American Journal of Mathematics* 23, no. 2 (April 1901): 139–165.

68. Whitehead, "A Celebrity At Home," and Whitehead, "Davy Jones."

69. Alfred North Whitehead, "La Théorie Relationniste de L'Espace," *Revue de Métaphysique et de Morale* 23, no. 3 (May 1916): 423–454.

70. Alfred North Whitehead, "The Importance of Friendly Relations Between England and the United States," *Phillips Bulletin* 19, no. 3 (1925): 15–18; Whitehead, "Time"; Alfred North Whitehead, "The Problem of Reconstruction," *The Atlantic Monthly* 169 (February 1942): 172–175.

71. And *OT* only has eight chapters! *AE* has ten.

72. Whitehead, "Science and Economic Liberty."

73. Alfred North Whitehead, "Governor Alfred Smith," May 14, 1929. ADD017, Whitehead Research Library, http://wrl.whiteheadresearch.org/items/show/1412.

74. Alfred North Whitehead, "Abbott Lawrence Lowell," February 1943. DOC184, Whitehead Research Library, http://wrl.whiteheadresearch.org/items/show/1417.

75. Alfred North Whitehead, "Philip Cabot," 1941. DOC177, Whitehead Research Library, http://wrl.whiteheadresearch.org/items/show/1416.

References

Allan, George. "Diagrams and Myths." In *Whitehead at Harvard, 1924–1925*, edited by Brian G. Henning and Joseph Petek, 283–306. Edinburgh: Edinburgh University Press, 2020.

Aristotelian Society. "Abstract of the Minutes of the Proceedings of the Aristotelian Society for the Forty-Fourth Session." *Proceedings of the Aristotelian Society*, New Series 23, (October 1922–1923): 273–277.

———. "Back Matter." *Proceedings of the Aristotelian Society*, New Series 15 (1914–1915): 437–441.

Atlantic Monthly Staff. "Letter from *Atlantic Monthly* to Whitehead." January 18, 1939. LET1349, Whitehead Research Library. http://wrl.whiteheadresearch.org/items/show/2574.

Barr, Mark. "Letter from Mark Barr to Whitehead." January 2, 1924. LET1052, Whitehead Research Library. http://wrl.whiteheadresearch.org/items/show/1418.

Bogaard, Paul A. "Examining Whitehead's 'First Lecture: September, 1924'." In *Whitehead at Harvard, 1924–1925*, edited by Brian G. Henning and Joseph Petek, 56–72. Edinburgh: Edinburgh University Press, 2020.

Bogaard, Paul A., and Jason Bell, eds. *The Harvard Lectures of Alfred North Whitehead, 1924–1925: Philosophical Presuppositions of Science*. Edinburgh: Edinburgh University Press, 2017.

Braithwaite, R. B. "Review of *Science and the Modern World*, by Alfred North Whitehead." *Mind*, New Series 35, no. 140 (October 1926): 489–500.

Brennan, Joseph Gerard. "Alfred North Whitehead: Plato's Lost Dialogue." *The American Scholar* 47, no. 4 (1978): 515–524.

Broad, C. D. "A General Notation for the Logic of Relations." *Mind* 27, no. 107 (July 1918): 284–303.

———. "Alfred North Whitehead (1861–1947)." *Mind* 57, no. 2 (April 1948): 139–145.

———. "Critical and Speculative Philosophy." In *Contemporary British Philosophy: Personal Statements*, edited by J. H. Muirhead, 75–100. London: George Allen & Unwin, 1924.

———. "Hume's Theory of the Credibility of Miracles." *Proceedings of the Aristotelian Society*, New Series 17 (1916–1917): 77–94.

———. "Mechanical Explanation and Its Alternatives." *Proceedings of the Aristotelian Society*, New Series 19 (1918–1919): 86–124.

———. *Perception, Physics, and Reality; an Enquiry into the Information That Physical Science Can Supply About the Real*. Cambridge: Cambridge University Press, 1914.———. "Review of *An Enquiry Concerning the Principles of Natural Knowledge*, by Alfred North Whitehead." *Mind*, New Series 29, no. 114 (April 1920): 216–231.

———. "Review of *The Principle of Relativity, with Applications to Physical Science*, by Alfred North Whitehead." *Mind*, New Series 32, no. 126 (April 1923): 211–219.

———. *Scientific Thought*. London: Kegan Paul, Trench, Trubner & Co., 1923.

———. "The External World." *Mind* 30, no. 120 (October 1921): 385–408.

———. *The Mind and Its Place in Nature*. London: Kegan Paul, Trench, Trubner & Co., 1925.

———. "Time." In *Encyclopedia of Religion and Ethics*, edited by James Hastings, 334–345. Edinburgh: T. & T. Clark, 1921.

———. "Whitehead Notes: Principles of Natural Knowledge." 1919–20. Papers of C. D. Broad, C1/17–18, Trinity College Cambridge Archives.

Cabot, Richard Clarke. "The Fundamentals of Social Science, 1926–1927." Papers of Richard Clarke Cabot, HUG 4255, Box 90, Harvard University Archives.

Cope, J. Raymond. "Philosophy 3b: Philosophy of Science." 1929–1930. MS Am 2079, Houghton Library, Harvard University.

Demos, Raphael, and Thomas G. Henderson, Otis Lee, Victor Lowe, Arthur E. Murphy, F.S.C. Northrop, Paul Weiss, and Ralph Barton Perry. "Proceedings of the American Philosophical Association 1948–1949." *The Philosophical Review* 58, no. 5 (September 1949): 468–469.

Desmet, Ronny. "From Physics to Philosophy, and From Continuity to Atomicity." In *Whitehead at Harvard, 1924–1925*, edited by Brian G. Henning and Joseph Petek, 132–153. Edinburgh: Edinburgh University Press, 2020.

Eddington, A. S., W. D. Ross, C. D. Broad, and F. A. Lindemann. "The Philosophical Aspect of the Theory of Relativity: A Symposium." *Mind*, New Series 29, no. 116 (October 1920): 415–445.

Emmet, Dorothy. *Philosophers and Friends: Reminiscences of Seventy Years in Philosophy*. Houndmills: Macmillan, 1996.

Feuer, Lewis S. "Recollections of Alfred North Whitehead in the Harvard Setting (1931–1937)." *Yale Review* 76, no. 4 (1987): 530–550.

Ford, Lewis. "Interview With Mrs. Hester Pickman." July 17, 1979. DOC033, Whitehead Research Library. http://wrl.whiteheadresearch.org/items/show/539.

———. *The Emergence of Whitehead's Metaphysics: 1925–1929*. Albany: State University of New York Press, 1984.

Goheen, John D. "Essays on Whitehead." 1933–1935. John D. Goheen Papers, SC0267, Additional Papers, ARCH-1994-080, Subseries 3, Box 10, Folder 15, Yale University Archives.

Harvard Alumni Bulletin Staff. "Social Ethics." *Harvard Alumni Bulletin* 23, no. 30 (May 5, 1921): 688–689.

Henderson, Thomas G. "Whitehead Lecture Notes: Philosophy and the Methods of Science." 1933. Alfred North Whitehead Collection, MS-0282, Box 6, Folder 7, Special Collections, Johns Hopkins University.Henning, Brian G. "On the Recently Discovered Whitehead Papers." *Whitehead Research Project*, January 14, 2019. http://whiteheadresearch.org/2019/01/14/on-the-recently-discovered-whitehead-papers/.

———. "Philosophy in the Age of Fascism: Reflections on the Presidential Addresses of the APA, 1931–1940." In *Historical Essays in 20th Century American Philosophy*, edited by John R. Shook, 69–95. Charlottesville: Richard T. Hull, 2015.

———. "Preface: A Brief History of the Critical Edition of Whitehead." In *Whitehead at Harvard, 1924–1925*, edited by Brian G. Henning and Joseph Petek, ix–xxi. Edinburgh: Edinburgh University Press, 2020.

———. "Whitehead in Class: Do the Harvard-Radcliffe Course Notes Change How We Understand Whitehead's Thought?" In *Whitehead at Harvard, 1924–1925*, edited by Brian G. Henning and Joseph Petek, 337–356. Edinburgh: Edinburgh University Press, 2020.

———. "Whitehead's Daughter, Jessie." *Whitehead Research Project*, January 15, 2020. http://whiteheadresearch.org/2020/01/15/jessie-marie-whitehead/.

Henning, Brian G., Joseph Petek, and George Lucas, eds. *The Harvard Lectures of Alfred North Whitehead, 1925–1927: General Metaphysical Problems of Science*. Edinburgh: Edinburgh University Press, 2021.

Herstein, Gary. "Quanta and Corpuscles: The Influence of Quantum Mechanical Ideas on Whitehead's Transitional Philosophy in Light of *The Harvard Lectures*." In *Whitehead at Harvard, 1924–1925*, edited by Brian G. Henning and Joseph Petek, 119–131. Edinburgh: Edinburgh University Press, 2020.

Hocking, William Ernest. "Whitehead as I Knew Him." *The Journal of Philosophy* 58, no. 19 (September 14, 1961): 505–516.

Johnson, A. H. *Whitehead and His Philosophy*. Lanham: University Press of America, 1963.

Karabel, Jerome. *The Chosen: The Hidden History of Admission and Exclusion at Harvard, Yale, and Princeton*. New York: Houghton Mifflin, 2005.

Kerby-Miller, Sinclair. "Notes on Whitehead's 1928 Philosophy of Science Course in Metaphysics (Non-Mathematical Part)." 1928. STU059, Whitehead Research Library.

———. "Notes on Whitehead's Fall 1927 Philosophy 3b Course and Other Related Materials." 1927. STU060, Whitehead Research Library.

———. "Notes on Whitehead's Spring 1928 Course on Mathematics—Extension." 1928. STU061, Whitehead Research Library.

King, Lester S. "Letter From Lester S. King to Lewis S. Ford." May 3, 1978. LET322, Whitehead Research Library. http://wrl.whiteheadresearch.org/items/show/565.

Krupsaw, David Loeb. "Philosophy 3 Notes and Exams." 1932–1933. David Loeb Krupsaw personal archive, HUD 930.46, Folder 10, Box 2, Harvard University Archives.

Kuntz, Paul G. "Can Whitehead Be Made a Christian Philosopher?" *Process Studies* 12, no. 4 (Winter 1982): 232–242.

Laird, John. "Synthesis and Discovery in Knowledge." *Proceedings of the Aristotelian Society*, New Series 19 (1918–1919): 46–85.

Langer, Susanne K. "Notes on Whitehead's Course on Philosophy of Nature." 1927. Susanne Langer papers, MS Am 3110, Box 5, Houghton Library, Harvard University.

Leighton, J. A. "History as the Struggle for Social Values." *The Philosophical Review* 48, no. 2 (March 1939): 118–154.

Lindbergh, Anne Morrow. *War Within and Without, 1939–1944*. New York: Berkeley Books, 1981.

Lindbergh, Charles. *The Wartime Journals of Charles A. Lindbergh*. New York: Harcourt Brace Jovanovich, 1970.

Loewenberg, J., C. D. Broad, and C. J. Shebbeare. "Symposium: Critical Realism: Can the Difficulty of Affirming a Nature Independent of Mind Be Overcome by the Distinction Between Essence and Existence?" *Proceedings of the Aristotelian Society, Supplementary Volumes* 4 (1924): 86–129.

Lowe, Victor. *Alfred North Whitehead: The Man and His Work, Vol. 1, 1861–1910*. Baltimore: Johns Hopkins University Press, 1985.

———. *Alfred North Whitehead: The Man and His Work, Vol. 2, 1910–1947*. Edited by J. B. Schneewind. Baltimore: Johns Hopkins University Press, 1990.

———. "A. N. W.: A Biographical Perspective." *Process Studies* 12, no. 3 (Fall 1982): 137–147.

———. *Understanding Whitehead*. Baltimore: The Johns Hopkins Press, 1966.

———. "Whitehead's 1911 Criticism of *The Problems of Philosophy*." *Russell*, Old Series 13 (Spring 1974): 3–10.

———. "Whitehead's Gifford Lectures." *Southern Journal of Philosophy* 7, no. 4 (Winter 1969): 332.

Lowell Institute. "Public Lectures in the City of Boston Under the Lowell Institute: Program for 1924–1925." 1924. DOC034. Whitehead Research Library.

Lucas, George. "'Muddleheadedness' vs. 'Simplemindedness' – Comparisons of Whitehead and Russell." *Process Studies* 17, no. 1 (spring 1988): 26–39.

Macmurray, J., R. B. Braithwaite, and C. D. Broad. "Symposium: Time and Change." *Proceedings of the Aristotelian Society, Supplementary Volumes* 8 (1928): 143–188.

Malik, Charles Habib. "Philosophy 3: Philosophy of Science." 1933. Charles Habib Malik Papers, Box 251, Folder 5, Manuscript Division, Library of Congress, Washington, D.C.

Marvin, Edwin L. "Whitehead Lecture Notes." 1927–1928. Victor Lowe Papers, MS-0284, Series 2, Box 2.9, Special Collections, Johns Hopkins University.

Petek, Joseph. "Introduction: Tales from the Whitehead Mines – On Whitehead, His Students and the Challenges of Editing the Critical Edition." In *Whitehead at Harvard, 1924–1925*, edited by Brian G. Henning and Joseph Petek, 1–37. Edinburgh: Edinburgh University Press, 2020.

———. "The Missing Drafts of Whitehead's Books." *Edinburgh University Press Blog*, January 15, 2021. https://euppublishingblog.com/2021/01/15/the-missing-drafts-of-whiteheads-books/.

———. "The Whitehead Book that Never Was." *Whitehead Research Project*, April 16, 2020. http://whiteheadresearch.org/2020/04/16/the-whitehead-book-that-never-was/.

———. "Whitehead and Felix Frankfurter." *Whitehead Research Project*, November 13, 2019. http://whiteheadresearch.org/2019/11/13/whitehead-and-felix-frankfurter/.

———. "Whitehead and James Haughton Woods." *Whitehead Research Project*, October 8, 2018. http://whiteheadresearch.org/2018/10/08/whitehead-and-james-haughton-woods/.

———. "Whitehead Papers Now Available Online." *Whitehead Research Project*, April 9, 2020. http://whiteheadresearch.org/2020/04/09/whitehead-papers-now-available-online/.

Pickman, Edward. "Letter From Edward Pickman to Whitehead." n.d. LET1068, Whitehead Research Library. http://wrl.whiteheadresearch.org/items/show/2303.

———. *The Mind of Latin Christendom*. London: Oxford University Press, 1937.

Price, Lucien. *Dialogues of Alfred North Whitehead*. New York: Mentor Books, 1954.

Quine, W. V. O. "Whitehead Lecture Notes: Philosophy and the Sciences." Victor Lowe Papers, MS-0284, Series 2, Box 2.9, Folder 52, Special Collections, Johns Hopkins University.

Russell, Bertrand. *A Critical Exposition of the Philosophy of Leibniz*. Cambridge: Cambridge University Press, 1900.

———. "On Denoting." *Mind* 14, no. 4 (1905): 479–493.

———. *The Problems of Philosophy*. London: Williams & Norgate, 1912.

Scarfe, Adam C. "Review of *The Harvard Lectures of Alfred North Whitehead, 1924–1925: Philosophical Presuppositions of Science*, edited by Paul A. Bogaard and Jason Bell." *Process Studies* 48, no. 1 (Spring–Summer 2019): 141–147.

Schilpp, Paul. "Letter From Paul Schilpp to Alfred North Whitehead, April 5, 1941." Library of Living Philosophers Records, 1938–1981, Series 3, Box 5, Folder 1, Southern Illinois University, Carbondale.

Stedman, R. E. "A Defence of Speculative Philosophy." *Proceedings of the Aristotelian Society*, New Series 38 (1937–1938): 113–142.

Thernstrom, Stephen. "Poor But Hopeful Scholars." In *Glimpses of Harvard Past*, edited by Bernard Bailyn, Donald Fleming, Oscar Handlin, and Stephan Thernstrom, 115–128. Cambridge: Harvard University Press, 1986.

Weiss, Paul. *Philosophy in Process, Volume 10*. Carbondale: Southern Illinois University Press, 1966.

———. "Recollections of Alfred North Whitehead." *Process Studies* 10, nos. 1–2 (1980): 44–56.

———. "Whitehead Lecture Notes: Seminary in Metaphysics." 1927. STU063, Whitehead Research Library. http://wrl.whiteheadresearch.org/items/show/590.

Whitehead, Alfred North. "A Celebrity at Home: The Clerk of the Weather." *The Cambridge Review* (February 10, 1886): 202–203.

———. "A Visitation." *The Cambridge Fortnightly* 1, no. 4 (March 6, 1888): 81–83.
———. "Abbott Lawrence Lowell." February 1943. DOC184. Whitehead Research Library. http://wrl.whiteheadresearch.org/items/show/1417.
———. *Adventures of Ideas*. New York: The Free Press, 1967.
———. Alfred North Whitehead Collection, MS-0282, Special Collections, Johns Hopkins University.
———. "An Appeal to Sanity." *The Atlantic* 163 (March 1939): 309–320.
———. "Autobiographical Notes." In *The Philosophy of Alfred North Whitehead*, edited Paul Schilpp. New York: Tudor Publishing, 1941.——— . "Davy Jones." *The Cambridge Review* (May 12, 1886): 311–312.
———. "First Lecture." September 25, 1924. ADD020, Whitehead Research Library. http://wrl.whiteheadresearch.org/items/show/2093.
———. "Freedom and Order." n.d. ADD019, Whitehead Research Library. http://wrl.whiteheadresearch.org/items/show/1413.
———. "Governor Alfred Smith." May 14, 1929. ADD017. Whitehead Research Library. http://wrl.whiteheadresearch.org/items/show/1412.
———. "La Théorie Relationniste de L'Espace." *Revue de Métaphysique et de Morale* 23, no. 3 (May 1916): 423–454.
———. "Letter From Alfred North Whitehead to G. E. Moore, June 15, 1931." George Edward Moore: Personal Papers and Correspondence, Add. 8330 8W/20/6, Cambridge University Library.
———. "Letters From Whitehead to Schilpp." Library of Living Philosophers Records, 1938–1981, Series 3, Box 5, Folder 1, Southern Illinois University, Carbondale.
———. "Letters to Bertrand Russell." Bertrand Russell Archives, McMaster University.
———. "Memoir on the Algebra of Symbolic Logic." *American Journal of Mathematics* 23, no. 2 (April 1901): 139–165.
———. *Modes of Thought*. New York: Free Press, 1966.
———. "Objects and Subjects." *The Philosophical Review* 41, no. 2 (March 1932): 130–146.
———. "Philip Cabot." 1941. DOC177. Whitehead Research Library. http://wrl.whiteheadresearch.org/items/show/1416.
———. *Process and Reality*. New York: The Free Press, 1978.
———. *Religion in the Making*. New York: Fordham University Press, 1996.
———. "Religious Psychology of the Western Peoples." March 30, 1939. ADD020, Whitehead Research Library. http://wrl.whiteheadresearch.org/items/show/1414.
———. "Science and Economic Liberty: A Comparison of England and America." 1923. Alfred North Whitehead Collection, MS-0282. Special Collections, Johns Hopkins University.
———. *Science and the Modern World*. New York: The Free Press, 1967.
———. "Space, Time, and Relativity." *Proceedings of the Aristotelian Society*, New Series 16 (1915–1916): 104–129.
———. *Symbolism: Its Meaning and Effect*. New York: Fordham University Press, 1985.

———. "The Aims of Education—A Plea for Reform." *Mathematical Gazette* 8, no. 121 (January 1916): 191–203.

———. *The Concept of Nature*. Cambridge: Cambridge University Press, 2000.

———. "The Fens as Seen From Skates." *The Cambridge Review* (February 20, 1891): 212–213.

———. *The Function of Reason*. Boston: Beacon Press, 1958.

———. "The Importance of Friendly Relations Between England and the United States." *Phillips Bulletin* 19, no. 3 (1925): 15–18.

———. *The Interpretation of Science: Selected Essays*. Edited by A. H. Johnson. Indianapolis: Bobbs-Merrill, 1961.

———. *The Organisation of Thought, Educational and Scientific*. London: Williams & Norgate, 1917.

———. *The Principle of Relativity, with Applications to Physical Science*. Cambridge: Cambridge University Press, 1922.

———. "The Problem of Reconstruction." *The Atlantic Monthly* 169 (February 1942): 172–175.

———. "The Rhythmic Claims of Freedom and Discipline." *Hibbert Journal* 21 (1923): 657–668.

———. "Time." In *Proceedings of the Sixth International Congress of Philosophy*, edited by Edgar Sheffield Brightman, 59–64. New York: Longmans, Green & Co., 1927.

———. "Whitehead's Grading Notebook." 1924–1937. Papers of Alfred North Whitehead, HUG 4877.10, Harvard University Archives.

———. "Whitehead's Will." March 27, 1891. DOC332, Whitehead Research Library. http://wrl.whiteheadresearch.org/items/show/2739.

Index

Adventures of Ideas (*AI*), 10, 69, 101, 104–5, 108; composition of, 147
aesthetic experience, 91
aesthetics, 37, 68–71, 78, 81n59, 91, 108, 110–11, 117; ethics as subservient to. *See* ethics, as subservient to aesthetics
The Aims of Education (AE), 80n28, 149
Alexander, Samuel, 23, 59, 60, 128n26
Allan, George, 59
analytic experience, 91
"An Appeal to Sanity," 86–87, 93–95
anti-Semitism. *See* Jewish people
Aristotelian Society, 44–45, 47, 51, 52, 55, 124–27
art. *See* aesthetics
atomism, 117, 140–43
Augustine, 10–11, 92, 94, 98n58
Augustinian Society, 84, 88–89, 92 94–95

Barbour-Page lectures of Whitehead. *See Symbolism: Its Meaning and Effect* (*S*)
Barr, Mark, 9, 28
beauty. *See* aesthetics
becoming:; atomic *vs.* continuous, 140–43
Bell, Winthrop Pickard, 15–21, 38, 51
Bergson, Henri, 127n10
Berkeley, George, 52

Blackwell, Kenneth, 9
Bogaard, Paul, 15, 140
Braithwaite, R. B., 116, 131, 136–37
Broad, C. D., 15, 43, 67, 74, 135–36; Aristotelian Society participation of, 44–45, 47, 51, 52; "critical" *vs.* "speculative" philosophy distinction, 49–51, 53–54, 57–58, 61, 64n39, 65n55, 135; dissertation of, 44; influence on Whitehead, 43, 45, 56–62; interactions with Whitehead, 44–46; *The Mind and Its Place in Nature*, 43, 46, 48–49, 51–52, 55, 60; relationship with Whitehead, 46; review of Whitehead's *PNK*, 45, 47, 48; review of Whitehead's *PrR*, 45, 48–49, 61–62; *Scientific Thought*, 19–20, 48–54, 57, 59, 61–62; Whitehead assigning and lecturing on books of, 19–20, 23, 43, 50–56; Whitehead's influence on, 46–51
brutality, 89, 98n42
Buddhism. *See* religion, Buddhism
Burch, George Bosworth, 14

Cabot, Philip, 150
Cabot, Richard Clarke, 68, 71–73, 76, 79n24, 80n27
Cambridge Apostles, 116–18
Carr, H. Wildon, 45

categories of explanation, 29–31
Catholicism. *See* religion, Catholicism
causal efficacy, 33–35, 103, 107, 121
Christianity. *See* religion, Christianity
The Concept of Nature (CN), 45–46, 48, 52, 60, 121, 123, 140–41, 143
Conger, George Perrigo, 14, 19–21, 35, 51, 121, 128n26
contemporaneousness. *See* simultaneity
continuity, 140–43
Cornford, F. M., 44
creativity, 31, 40n20
critical philosophy, 19–20, 49, 50, 53–54, 57–58, 64n39, 74, 135–36

Democritus, 10, 117
Demos, Raphael, 13
Descartes, René, 74–77, 134
Desmet, Ronny, 139–43
devil. *See* Satan
Dilthey, Wilhelm, 148

economics, 108–11
education, 72–73, 80n28
Einstein, Albert, 140
Emmet, Dorothy, 32, 33
emotions, 91
An Enquiry Concerning the Principles of Natural Knowledge (PNK), 39, 45, 47, 48, 52, 56, 61, 140, 142–43
ethics, 36–37, 54, 67–71, 74–78, 81n59, 91; as subservient to aesthetics, 37, 69–71, 78, 81n59, 91. *See also* aesthetics; Harvard lectures of Whitehead, social ethics seminar in
evil, 36–37, 41n44, 69–70, 76, 89–90, 92–93. *See also* hatred
extension, 57, 123, 125, 140–43

fallacy of misplaced concreteness, 126
fallacy of simple location, 54
feelings, 35, 89, 103, 105–7, 118
feudalism, 109–10
Feuer, Lewis, 95
flux, 109, 117

Ford, Lewis S., 13, 29, 140, 147; temporal atomism thesis of, 140–43
Forsyth, Andrew, 44, 119
Frankfurter, Felix, 99n79, 148
freedom, 69, 75–76, 78, 101–5, 107, 109, 141
"Freedom and Order," 101–11, 149
The Function of Reason (FR), 105
future. *See* time, future

Gifford lectures of Whitehead. *See Process and Reality (PR)*
God, 37, 68–71, 76–78, 88, 97n38, 111, 145
Goheen, John, 67, 73
graded envisagement, 68–69, 75, 106

Haldane, J. S., 60
Hartshorne, Charles, 20, 21, 37, 70, 79n14
Harvard lectures of Whitehead:; accuracy of notes, 5–7, 9–23; attribution of influences in, 61, 137; comparing competing accounts, 10–12, 14–20; difficulty of Whitehead's students understanding, 13–14; editing of, 18–20; errors in, 10, 13–14, 19; first lecture, 15–17; future volumes of, 146–48; incoherence of, 6, 18, 21–22; length of, 10; number of note-takers, 10; reception of, 6; relationship to Whitehead's published writings, 7, 10, 27–39, 132–46; repetition in, 133–37; social ethics seminar in, 10, 25n16, 25n18, 67–78, 80–81n31; time of delivery, 25n17; value of, 7, 23, 136–39, 143, 145–46; Whitehead's confusion while delivering, 18, 21–22, 25n29; Whitehead's goals for, 22, 28, 133
hatred, 83, 87–90, 92–96, 98n42, 149; definition of, 89. *See also* evil
Heath, Louise R., 15–18, 20–22, 28, 51, 133–34

Index

Hegel, Georg Wilhelm Friedrich, 22, 145, 148
Henderson, Lawrence J., 95
Henning, Brian G., 13, 52, 53, 85, 132
Heraclitus, 117
Herstein, Gary, 140
Hicks, Dawes, 52
Hilary of Poitiers, 83–84
Hitler, Adolf, 85–87, 94
Hocking, Agnes, 80n27
Hocking, William Ernest, 17–18, 21, 22, 51, 95, 99n74, 148
humour, 102–11

ideas, 91
imagination, 103, 107
ingression, 52
An Introduction to Mathematics, 119

Jackson, Gardner, 19
James, William, 15, 145
Jeans, James, 141
Jewish people, 93–95, 99n79
Johnson, A. H., 22, 139, 149

Kaiser, Hillis, 95, 99n76
Kant, Immanuel, 64n39, 70, 116, 122, 125–27, 129n39, 134, 136
Kerby-Miller, Sinclair, 29–31
King, Lester S., 13, 19
Kropotkin, Peter, 81n49
Kuntz, Paul G., 83–84, 88

Lagrange, Joseph-Louis, 59–60
Laird, John, 45
Langer, Susanne, 29
language, 35, 92, 117–18, 120, 125n27
lecture notes. *See* Harvard lectures of Whitehead
Lee, Otis, 95, 99n75
Leibniz, Gottfried, 134
Leighton, Joseph Alexander, 85–85
Lindbergh, Anne Morrow, 87, 98n58
Lindbergh, Charles, 87

Locke, John, 134
Lowe, Victor, 5, 8, 15, 27–29, 31, 46, 84–85, 92, 109, 116, 118, 120–21, 124–25, 127n10, 138–39, 147; papers of, 24n12; relationship with Whitehead family, 8–9
Lowell, A. Lawrence, 95, 150
Lowell lectures of Whitehead. *See Religion in the Making* (*RM*); *Science and the Modern World* (*SMW*)
Lucas, Jr., George R., 5, 8

Marvin, Edward, 29–31
Maupertuis, Pierre Louis, 60
McLarty, Furman G., 11–12
McTaggart, J. M. E., 44, 116
mechanism, 60–61
metaphysics, 43, 50, 53, 58, 67–70, 74–78, 89, 123–27, 131, 134–36. *See also* speculative philosophy
method of extensive abstraction, 56–57, 131
Michelson-Morley experiment, 38
Miller, James Wilkinson, 15
Modes of Thought (*MT*), 57–58, 78, 81n59
Moore, G. E., 52, 125, 148
morality. *See* ethics
Morgan, C. Lloyd, 23, 39, 60
Munsterberg, Hugo, 15
mutual aid/intensification, 76

National Endowment for the Humanities (NEH), 6, 23n3
Nelson, Everett John, 19
Newman, John Henry, 85
Newton, Isaac, 59–60
Nietzsche, Friedrich, 148

order, 102–7
The Organisation of Thought (*OT*), 68, 149
original sin/virtue, 74–75, 77
Osborn, Andrew D., 9

past. *See* time, past
Paul the Apostle, 84, 92
perception. *See* sense perception
perceptual objects, 52, 54
permanence, 109
Philo, 11
Pickman, Edward, 83–84, 96n4
Pittenger, Norman, 84
Plato, 59, 104, 145
poetry, 117–18
prehension, 33–34, 105–6, 112n27, 121
presentational immediacy, 33–36, 103, 121
Price, Lucien, 85, 142
Principia Mathematica (*PM*), 13, 44, 47, 119–20, 122, 124
principle of extensive abstraction, 48
The Principle of Relativity (*PrR*), 19, 39, 45, 48–49, 52, 56, 61–62, 62n3, 68, 143
privacy, 75–76, 78
Process and Reality (*PR*), 54–58, 62, 67–69, 71, 74, 76, 78, 88, 93, 102, 104–5, 109, 111, 117, 132, 135–37, 139–41, 149; composition of, 27–33, 36, 39, 146–47
Prometheus, 101, 104–5
propaganda, 110
propositions, 147

Quine, Willard Van Orman, 11–12

relatedness, 68, 75–76, 78, 106, 141
religion, 32, 37, 68, 87–88, 91–94, 109–11, 149; Buddhism, 37, 41n53; Catholicism, 85; Christianity, 37, 83–84, 87–92, 94–96, 98n58; criticism of, 88; definition of, 87–88, 110; religious experience, 50–51, 53–54; religious hatred/extremism. *See* hatred; Unitarianism, 85
Religion in the Making (*RM*), 28, 70–71, 76–78, 87–88, 90, 92–93, 97n38; composition of, 36–37, 39

"Religious Psychology of the Western Peoples" (RPWP), 83–96, 96n3, 149
repulsion, 89
robbery, 74–76
Robinson, Edward S., 20, 21
Roethlisberger, Fritz Jules, 20, 21, 51, 79n14, 134
Royce, Josiah, 15
Russell, Bertrand, 44, 48, 62, 67, 85, 116, 119–21, 125–27, 128n23, 129n39, 148; Whitehead's criticism of *The Problems of Philosophy*, 115–16, 119–24

Sanger, C. P., 116
Satan, 88, 117
Scarfe, Adam, 6, 7, 10, 15, 18, 21
Schilpp, Paul Arthur, 43, 46, 148
Science and the Modern World (*SMW*), 23, 28, 59–61, 68, 70, 75, 102, 106, 108–11, 117, 126, 131, 136, 142–43, 149; composition of, 36–39, 41n60
sense data. *See* sense perception
sense perception, 34, 35
Shelley, Percy Bysshe, 37–38, 41n56, 117
simple location. *See* fallacy of simple location
simultaneity, 34, 123
Smith, Adam, 110
Smith, Al, 150
social ethics. *See* ethics
Social Ethics Department, 72, 79–80n24
socialism, 75–76, 78, 109–10
Socrates, 88–89
space, 123–26. *See also* space-time
space-time, 49, 54, 123, 140–43
speculative philosophy, 43, 49–51, 53–54, 57–58, 64n39, 74, 135–36. *See also* metaphysics
Spinoza, 17
spirits of change and conservation, 108–9
symbolic reference, 34, 103

Symbolism: Its Meaning and Effect
  (*S*), 14, 28, 77, 103, 121, 132;
  composition of, 32–36, 39

Tarner lectures of Whitehead. *See The Concept of Nature* (*CN*)
Taylor, A. E., 46
temporal extension. *See* time
Tenney, Charles Dewey, 11–12
Thersites, 88
time, 56–57, 123, 125–26, 140–43;
  future, 55, 60; past, 57. *See also* space-time
"Time" (Whitehead essay), 15, 19, 22, 33, 34, 132, 144–45
Trinity College, Cambridge, 44, 45
truth, 91

Unitarianism. *See* religion, Unitarianism
universals, 122

value, 91
vitalism, 60

Weiss, Paul, 13–14, 21, 33
Whitehead, Alfred North:; Aristotelian Society participation of, 44–45, 47, 51, 52, 124–26; education of, 115–18, 126–27; errors in publications of, 149; first lecture. *See* Harvard lectures of Whitehead. first lecture; Harvard lectures. *See* Harvard lectures of Whitehead; inconsistencies in philosophy of, 22; lecturing style of, 27–28, 132; letter-writing of, 119–20, 128n21; non-confrontation nature of, 97n40; papers of, 8–10, 24n12, 27; politics of, 112n32, 149–50; religious views of, 84–85; transition from mathematics to philosophy, 47, 115–16, 123–25, 127; will and testament of, 9, 24n12
Whitehead, Eric, 85
Whitehead, Evelyn, 9, 24n12, 80n27
Whitehead, George, 8, 15, 83
Whitehead, Jessie, 9, 24n14, 85
Whitehead, Thomas North, 8, 29, 41n60, 80n27, 85, 134, 142–43
wit, 102–9
Woods, James Haughton, 15, 41n53, 59
Wordsworth, William, 37–38, 41n56, 117–18
World War I, 44, 85, 101, 128n23
World War II, 46, 63n9, 85–87, 93–95, 102

Yale Philosophy Club, 20

Zeno, 30, 141

About the Author

Joseph Petek received his PhD in Religion / Process Studies from Claremont School of Theology in 2022. He is the chief archivist of the Whitehead Research Project and associate series editor for the Critical Edition of Whitehead. He has coedited three books on Whitehead: *Rethinking Whitehead's Symbolism* (2017), *Whitehead at Harvard, 1924–1925* (2020), and *The Harvard Lectures of Alfred North Whitehead, 1925–1927: General Metaphysical Problems of Science* (2021).

www.ingramcontent.com/pod-product-compliance
Lightning Source LLC
Chambersburg PA
CBHW020123010526
44115CB00008B/954